RELEASED

SOCIAL SCIENCE
AND PSYCHOTHERAPY
FOR CHILDREN

CONTRIBUTIONS OF THE BEHAVIOR SCIENCES
TO PRACTICE IN A PSYCHOANALYTICALLY
ORIENTED CHILD GUIDANCE CLINIC : : :

By OTTO POLLAK *and Collaborators*

RUSSELL SAGE FOUNDATION
New York   ~   ~   *1952*

Copyright, 1952, by
RUSSELL SAGE FOUNDATION
Printed in the United States
of America

*Library of Congress
Catalog Card Number: 52-5925*

WM. F. FELL CO., PRINTERS
PHILADELPHIA, PA.

Collaborators

BERTRAM J. BLACK, Assistant Executive Director, Jewish Board
of Guardians

DOROTHY DUNAEFF, Borough Supervisor, Brooklyn Office, Child
Guidance Institute

YONATA FELDMAN, Borough Supervisor, Bronx Office, Child
Guidance Institute

BERNICE WOLF FRECHTMAN, Director, Volunteer Department,
Jewish Board of Guardians*

MAURICE R. FRIEND, M.D., Clinical Director, Child Guidance
Institute

LIA KNOEPFMACHER, Senior Supervisor, Bronx Office, Child
Guidance Institute

BETTINA LEHNERT, Supervisor-in-Charge, Brownsville Office,
Child Guidance Institute

FREDERIKA NEUMANN, Director, Casework Services, Jewish Board
of Guardians

S. R. SLAVSON, Director, Group Therapy, Jewish Board of
Guardians

* Currently Executive Director, New York Section, National Council of Jewish
Women.

Contents

Foreword

In 1948 Russell Sage Foundation announced its intention to give main emphasis in its program to the improvement of the relation of research to practice in the disciplines and professions concerned with social behavior. When the Foundation was established by Margaret Olivia Sage in 1907, its purpose was defined as "the improvement of social and living conditions in the United States" by such means as the Trustees might from time to time deem best. Over the succeeding years great advances have been made both in the methods and practices of the professions working to improve the lot of mankind and in the underlying disciplines devoted to promoting the understanding of the facts and principles governing man's behavior. Unfortunately, too often these advances in research and in practice have been not only parallel in time but parallel also in the sense that they did not meet. *Social Science and Psychotherapy for Children* is the report of a successful two-year venture by the Foundation in collaboration with the Jewish Board of Guardians in the development of mutually beneficial liaison between the behavior sciences and a specialty in social practice, child guidance.

The Foundation is gratified that the report of this venture by Dr. Otto Pollak and his associates at the Jewish Board of Guardians gives evidence of significant benefits derived from the integration of pertinent data and principles selected from the fields of sociology, cultural anthropology, and social and learning psychology into the psychoanalytically oriented child guidance practice of that agency. While the work covered by the report was an initial two-year experiment within a single agency, it has nevertheless demonstrated that such interdisciplinary rapport can be rewarding in terms of practice, and that further explorations in similar agencies may be undertaken with confidence in their potential fruitfulness.

7

The present report should be of greatest interest to specialists in child guidance concerned with the particular therapeutic approach adopted by the Jewish Board of Guardians, but it is the hope of the Foundation that it also may be of value to a much wider audience. Psychiatrists and others in the health services concerned with social factors in diagnosis, therapy, and preventive medicine during recent years have been making progress through various approaches in utilizing the results of social research. Social workers in general have been making advances in the same direction. Social scientists at the same time are showing increasing interest in the application of their findings, and the number of studies designed to be of utility in the health services is growing rapidly. The record of Dr. Pollak's experience as consulting social scientist at the Jewish Board of Guardians consequently is a timely account of experience in one specialized agency with implications for other agencies and individuals now working toward similar interdisciplinary cooperation.

The implications of this report are not limited to the field of child care and the health services. The Foundation, for example, is now cooperating in a variety of projects designed to aid in the improvement of the research-practice relationship in such major areas as education, penology, communication, housing, government, and intergroup relations, as well as in other projects in child welfare and health. Varied as these substantive areas may seem, in each of them there are the common problems of gaining better knowledge about the facts and principles of behavior and of putting it to effective use for the welfare of mankind. The record in any one area, such as that reported in *Social Science and Psychotherapy for Children*, has value for all.

The Foundation is indebted to the Jewish Board of Guardians for suggesting this exploration of social science-child guidance interrelationships and for its cooperation in carrying it to completion. It is a special pleasure to acknowledge the whole-hearted interest and pioneer perspective contributed to the venture by the agency under the leadership of Herschel Alt and Bertram J. Black.

December 20, 1951   DONALD YOUNG

Introduction

THIS BOOK is a report of exploration into the question of whether existing funds of social science knowledge can be adapted to psychotherapy practiced in a child guidance setting. That it should be made at this stage in the growth of professional social work and out of the experience of the Jewish Board of Guardians is a reflection of important developments in social work generally, as well as of specific trends in that agency.

It is sometimes said that developments in social institutions follow a circular path and return periodically to approximately the same form and structure they left some years before. This path is not similar to a circle, however, but rather to a spiral; by the time it has completed a turn, modification has occurred which represents the absorption of newer knowledge and understanding. The relationship between social work and the social sciences has followed such a spiral. Many leading social workers can recollect the days when social work looked upon itself as an applied form of the social sciences, a growing profession utilizing an artistry based on concepts and understanding of the social sciences of several decades ago. The swing of social work around the spiral later brought into focus newer concepts and understanding from psychology, psychiatry, and psychoanalysis, and the tie to the previous scientific background appeared to become thinner and more distant. Now the turn has come again and social work is interested anew in the relationship of its methods to a social science base.[1] In the analogy of the spiral, it begins again to see at least part of its underpinning in the social sciences. At the same time it recognizes that while practice was swinging

[1] See, for example, Davies, Stanley P., "The Relation of Social Science to Social Welfare," *Social Work Journal*, vol. 31, January, 1950, pp. 20–26, 32; Hoey, Jane M., "Social Work: Its Base, Skills, and Relation to Other Fields," *Social Casework*, vol. 31, December, 1950, pp. 399–410; Mayo, Leonard W., "Putting Our Present Knowledge to Work," *Social Work Journal*, vol. 32, January, 1951, pp. 4–8, 33.

around the spiral, the social sciences did not remain static but moved as well.

To an interesting degree the development of the program of the Jewish Board of Guardians has followed just such a spiral. The child guidance treatment approach of the agency, which has developed over the past three decades, originated from a concern with protective services to adults and children and from a desire to establish scientific methods for the treatment and prevention of juvenile delinquency. A chart of the changing methods of social work and clinical practice and of professional disciplines used would parallel closely the changing concepts of the cause and effect of delinquent behavior. The agency has gone through stages of utilizing religious teaching and moral persuasion as a treatment and preventive method. It has lived through the period in which the administration of good recreational outlets was thought to be the best preventive of delinquent behavior.

In the middle 1920's began a turn in the spiral which focused attention on a clinical psychiatric approach to the treatment of delinquency. More and more consideration was given to the psychological understanding of the child referred for treatment, and the social workers were required to absorb a greater fund of knowledge of psychodynamics, psychopathology, and general psychoanalytic theory. It should be noted that a similar trend has occurred in most social work agencies concerned with giving casework service of a high professional standard.

The acquisition of psychiatric understanding is slow and laborious, and perhaps because of this, as time and energy were taxed in revealing the intrapersonal life of the patient, there was less and less emphasis on the interpersonal. What had been part of the social worker's field of interest in the social, cultural, and economic environment of the child remained more as an attitude on the part of individual workers and supervisors than as conscious agency practice. By the middle 1940's only the Group Therapy and Volunteer Departments of the agency remained exceptions to the trend, for the very nature of their programs forced constant attention on the peer group associations of the child and contact with his larger environment.

Since the 1940's the major growth in the treatment services of the Jewish Board of Guardians has been in the field of child guidance. Under the leadership of the late Dr. Johan H. W. van Ophuijsen as chief psychiatrist, the agency developed a method of treatment for children who exhibit the symptoms of their emotional disorder by hitting out against their environment. This treatment process involved the fusion of psychotherapeutic techniques derived from psychiatry with approaches which clearly have their origin in social casework. In time similar specific treatment methods for the withdrawn and neurotic child were evolved. It was Dr. van Ophuijsen's insistence that treatment depended for its adequacy upon clear and full differential diagnosis, and over the years he devoted a great deal of time and effort to training the caseworkers in diagnostic procedures. He was much concerned with the tools for diagnosis, and together with Dr. Nathan W. Ackerman, who became chief psychiatrist when Dr. van Ophuijsen took on more definitely the role of teacher and chief consultant, developed a diagnostic outline for differential diagnosis. While this diagnostic summary made provision for putting down a picture of the interpersonal relations of the patient as well as the intrapersonal factors, the concern, in practice, was with the psychodynamic and psychopathological data which were considered in the diagnosis and treatment plan. It was expected that the social casework education and experience of the therapists would somehow ensure adequate inclusion of the environmental factors in diagnosis and treatment. This assumption, though, lost sight of the fact that the curricula of schools of social work, too, were emphasizing psychoanalytic psychology, and that the psychiatric clinical experience from which the more mature workers were recruited followed the same approach.

Under the stimulation of the executive director, Herschel Alt, and the guidance of Dr. van Ophuijsen, Dr. Nathan W. Ackerman, and Dr. Maurice R. Friend, the present clinical director, the child guidance service has become more clearly defined as a clinical program. In 1946 the Child Guidance Institute was established, separating child guidance from the traditional services to prisoners, children in juvenile courts, unmarried mothers, and so on; and the in-service training program since has stressed special preparation for psychotherapy in child guidance.

At present the Child Guidance Institute operates through three clinic offices. Each office has a number of professional "teams," composed of psychiatrist, clinical psychologist, supervisor, and four or five psychiatric social workers. With the exception of a small number of cases, therapy is carried on by the social workers, which will explain the interchangeable use of the terms "worker" and "therapist" in this book. The psychiatrist provides the medical control, and carries responsibility for the diagnostic supervision and treatment planning. He is also a teacher and conducts a continuous case seminar with his team. In this the supervisor shares teaching duties, as well as the more traditional individual casework supervision of the workers. The psychologist provides psychometric and projective testing as required in diagnosis and treatment planning.

The Child Guidance Institute, while a division of a social agency, is a recognized psychiatric treatment clinic. It is a member of the American Association of Psychiatric Clinics for Children and has been certified by the American Board of Psychiatry and Neurology for residency training in psychiatric treatment of children. For the Institute, as well as other psychiatric programs, the Jewish Board of Guardians is licensed by the New York State Department of Mental Hygiene.

It is interesting that the clarification of the child guidance function was accompanied by an increased interest in the environmental factors affecting the treatment of children with emotional disorders. Training seminars and interstaff discussions raised questions as to the scientific bases for the type of treatment provided. The therapists, particularly under the stimulation of Dr. van Ophuijsen and Dr. Ackerman, began to experiment with filling out more completely those sections of the diagnostic or evaluative summaries dealing with interpersonal factors. In relating group therapy and volunteer services to a better defined child guidance program concern was aroused as to the meaning of group relations and the wider environment in the total treatment of the child. This awakening interest in matters which have long been the concern of the various social sciences may have stemmed in part from trends outside the agency.

Social work and child guidance practice were not alone in making use of newer understanding and knowledge evolving from the development of psychiatry and psychoanalytic psychology. Other professions and arts have borrowed heavily from these developments and some social scientists have themselves turned to psychoanalytic concepts for a deeper understanding and clarification of the nature of many phenomena falling within their spheres of investigation. Interest in psychological motivations on the part of sociologists,[1] anthropological explanations of primitive symbolism in psychoanalytic terms,[2] and awareness of personal drives of men in power as occasionally expressed by political scientists[3] are all examples of the way in which these new psychologies are fast becoming noticeable in social science publications.

In return, both psychiatry, as a helping practice, and social work had begun to pay more attention to the propositions and findings of the social sciences. Psychiatrists first seemed to become interested in the approach of cultural anthropology because the anthropologists could turn up with primitive cultures and differing social settings in which the apparent validity of psychoanalytic explanations might be tested. More recently they have become interested in the cultural concepts which various anthropologists have found it possible to translate into terminology understandable and acceptable to the psychoanalytic field. Various psychiatric groups have recently been focusing their attention upon the formulations available from the students of group dynamics.

[1] See, for example, Dollard, John, *Caste and Class in a Southern Town*, Institute of Human Relations, Yale University Press, New Haven, 1937; Parsons, Talcott, "Psychoanalysis and the Social Structure," *The Psychoanalytic Quarterly*, vol. 19, 1950, pp. 371–384.

[2] See, for example, Hallowell, A. Irving, "Myth, Culture, and Personality," *American Anthropologist*, new series, vol. 49, 1947, pp. 544–556.

[3] See, for example, Lasswell, Harold D., *Psychopathology and Politics*, University of Chicago Press, Chicago, 1930; Idem, *World Politics and Personal Insecurity*, McGraw-Hill Book Co., New York, 1935.

Social work has followed suit in its interest, first in cultural anthropology, broadening this concern somewhat, however, to an interest in modern ethnic groupings, and has, particularly now in professional group work practice, begun to lean heavily on the field of group dynamics for an explanation of various group phenomena.

The difficulty, however, has been in translating this interest in social science into some meaningful form for utilization in social practice. That concern alone is not sufficient to bridge the gap is illustrated by an experience of the Jewish Board of Guardians during 1948 and 1949. Early in 1948 a plan developed to have some member or members of the staff prepare a manuscript describing the scientific base on which child guidance practice rests. Discussions within the agency, however, brought out the difficulty of preparing such a report without much background research and the idea became retranslated into another form. This was the suggestion that Dr. van Ophuijsen be asked to prepare a book on psychotherapy which would incorporate the psychiatric understanding upon which this agency's child guidance practice is founded, and which, in turn, might serve as a text for teaching others the fundamentals of psychotherapeutic practice. To this end Dr. van Ophuijsen delivered a series of lectures to the senior professional staff during 1948–1949. His death prevented him from carrying this project to the point of elaboration in textbook form. It is hoped, however, that in time these lectures can be developed into a pamphlet in his memory.

It is significant that with all the interest in examining the scientific understructure for social practice there was also much resistance to actually facing the problem. There was willingness to set down in writing the psychiatric underpinnings of child guidance therapy, but no one in the agency felt secure in attempting to delineate the funds of social science knowledge, if any, which conditioned the therapy.

There could be little question as to the interest, however, in social science materials at all levels of the professional staff. Many references to anthropology, cultural factors, environmental manipulation, family diagnosis appear in the minutes of staff meetings and seminars. There was even discussion of including representatives of other professional disciplines as consultants to the treatment team, but no affirmative action seemed possible at that time.

The announcement in 1948 by Russell Sage Foundation of its particular interest in the integration of social science knowledge and practice presented an opportunity of which the agency leadership was happy to avail itself. During the summer of 1949 the Foundation and the Jewish Board of Guardians agreed to enter into a joint experiment. For two years Dr. Otto Pollak, of the faculty of the University of Pennsylvania, has been made available to the agency as consulting social scientist. Dr. Pollak's responsibilities included efforts toward two objectives—first, to identify specific funds of knowledge in the social sciences which might be put to use in child guidance, and second, to see how far experience in child guidance may yield stimulation for social science research. This book can be looked upon as a preliminary report on the first objective.

In the chapter which follows Dr. Pollak describes in some detail the procedures followed in arriving at the findings of this report. They will prove of interest both to social scientists and to social practitioners.

There is now great desire throughout the clinical staff to test the extent to which the conceptions identified can be utilized routinely in treatment. To this end Russell Sage Foundation has agreed to cooperate for another period, during which one of the treatment teams will be set up with a social scientist as an integral member, and other social scientists will be made available for consultation on specific case situations. For the first year of the project Dr. Pollak will assume the role of the social scientist on the team.

It is extremely interesting to note some changes which have taken place in the milieu of the agency since this project was initiated. Whether these can all be credited to the introduction of a social scientist is not entirely clear, but that they represent a certain merging, in thought at least, of social science and social practice can hardly be questioned. At a conference of the professional planning staff held in December, 1949, great emphasis was placed upon the necessity of focusing treatment on the interpersonal factors in the child's life as well as the intrapersonal. In several staff meetings and training seminars attention has been given to the effect of cultural differences in the predisposition to emotional ills, of the culture differential between patient and therapist in the treatment process. There has been discussion of the effect of family interaction, of the sociological aspects of child development, of the importance of the standards of the cultural environment in relation to treatment goals, of the concept of the total personality.

There has been greater recognition of the fact that the therapist's interest in environment is nearly synonymous with the sociologist's interest in all the primary groups of which the child is a member, the interaction of these groups and their relationship to society.

It has seemed to this writer that during the past two years those members of the staff responsible for other treatment approaches than the clinical have received increasing recognition. Supervision of volunteers, casework service in the summer camp setting, school and family counseling, and guidance group service are being given a specialized status in the eyes of the professional staff, rather than being treated as fringe or auxiliary services as in former years.

All of this can be related as well to an interest in providing a broadening of the didactic material included in the training program for caseworkers and psychiatrists. For some years the Jewish Board of Guardians has invested heavily in in-service training for a twofold purpose. One is to train psychiatric social caseworkers to be child therapists. The other is to develop in the course of this training program a psychiatric speciality in the treatment of children. For its work in these two areas the agency is recognized as a training center for advanced fellows in psychiatric casework by the National Institute of Mental Health. In this connection the agency provides advanced field work training for such leading schools of social work as the New York School, Smith College, Fordham University, and Adelphi College.

The change in the training curriculum from that of earlier years is profound. Formerly the course content included such items as Diagnosis, Psychodynamics, Psychotherapy, Treatment Seminars, Special Seminars on Group Therapy as a Clinical Practice. In April, 1950, a new curriculum plan was drawn up. In that plan the fields to be covered included:

Science of Child Development
Psychoanalytic Psychology of the Total Personality
Clinical Psychiatry
General and Special Psychotherapy
Sociology and Cultural Anthropology, e.g., the sociological aspects of the family, the cultural aspects of child rearing and education, the group dynamics of wider social groups like the religious, the ethnic community, the school, recreational groups, and so forth.

To quote from the recommendations in this curriculum plan: "A large part of the required knowledge and skill is ready to be taught didactically and through supervised practical application. Another part may be made available in the future through methodical study of the applicability and usefulness of the findings of such sciences as sociology, cultural anthropology, psychology of learning. Still another part, for instance, the dynamics of family life, the psychodynamic aspects of learning psychology, of education, of child rearing, needs yet to be acquired through a combination of research and practice of our own. Effective environmental treatment methods which utilize all this knowledge are in need of further development through re-evaluation of present practice and experimentation."

It follows from this curriculum plan that the role of the social scientist in training and planning is now established in the agency. Whether the outcome of the cooperative project will also establish the role of a social scientist as a member of the treatment team remains to be seen. Its next phase should help to determine this.

The developments within the agency since the initiation of this project seem to have two implications. The first is that the coming together of social science and social practice affords an opportunity for expanding the horizons in the team approach to child guidance treatment. Such an expansion will produce changes in the treatment plan that will systematically take into account other aspects of the life of the patient, as well as his unconscious or personality structure. The subjecting of practice methods and techniques to scientific observation should lead to the design of more objective tools for better diagnosis of emotional and social ills and to more clearly established goals for treatment.

The second implication of these developments seems to this writer to be the following. It is presented with the reservation that this is a purely personal opinion. The relating of social science concepts to social casework practice will return status to the social caseworker as a professional practitioner distinct from the psychiatrist, the psychologist, or the educator. There is a good deal of evidence available that in the swing around the spiral, referred to earlier, social casework was rapidly losing an identity as a professional practice with its own underpinnings of scientific understanding. The social sciences, particularly sociology, cultural anthropology, and social psychology are the major scientific bases for social casework. What has been learned from clinical psychology and psychiatry should not be lost. Just as what was learned from economics at an earlier stage of the profession's development remains important, so will these scientific bases have to be retained. The social sciences, however, must be turned to for future professional growth.

In the relating of social science to social practice it should be kept in mind that bias is possible in the very selection of the concepts for examination. Care must be taken, especially at this stage of scientific knowledge, to invite as wide interdisciplinary attention as is possible to the bringing together of scientific thought and practical experience. An example of this concern might be the viewing of the environment of the child. "Environment" is looked upon differently from the vantage point of each of the social sciences and even within a particular discipline. The environment of one scientist may be skewed from that of another. To see the whole picture, it must be viewed from more than one angle.

Further attention must be paid to the concept of cultural difference between the treater and the treated if the most effective social service is to be rendered the clientele. This concept bears research examination by the social scientists, as well as careful evaluation administratively in its effect upon practice.

The social agency that serves as the framework within which social practice is carried on is a peculiar social institution in its own right and needs scientific examination. It has its own social stratification, its own problems of group interaction, its dynamics of role and status, all of which condition to some extent the effectiveness of treatment and the purposes and goals.

If social science and social practice are to continue explorations of significance to both, these are areas which will have to be studied in the near future.

December 20, 1951   BERTRAM J. BLACK

CHAPTER ONE

Adapting Social Science to Child Guidance Practice

IN INITIATING this study of the opportunities for closer liaison between the social sciences and the field of child guidance, Russell Sage Foundation and the Jewish Board of Guardians mapped out only two general lines of inquiry. One was to ascertain whether there were already in existence specific funds of social science knowledge that could be constructively adapted to use in child guidance practice. The other was to investigate needs for information experienced by child guidance practitioners that could be met by social science research.

The relative vagueness of the original design was intentional. In order to be truly exploratory, any venture to bring social science and social practice into closer relationship must be free from preconceived expectations of findings. Identification of specific points of interest in the early stages of such a project may secure certain foci of attention but only at the risk of excluding other points of interest. Thus there was in the beginning considerable freedom of exploration. In order to produce tangible results, however, it was found necessary stepwise to define and increasingly to specify its nature as the project passed from the planning stage into actual execution. By doing so it was possible to arrive at a number of specific findings. In their totality they represent an affirmative and detailed, although by no means complete or definitive, answer to the question: Are there presently available funds of knowledge in social science that could be usefully adapted to child guidance practice in the Jewish Board of Guardians?

The venture posed many problems. First of all, a decision had to be made as to whether the exploration should be limited to

BY OTTO POLLAK

a specific social science discipline or extended to several. Since the task was to investigate the possibilities of closer liaison between child guidance practice and the social sciences in general, the decision was made to include the fields of sociology, social psychology, cultural anthropology, and psychology of learning in the inquiry.

The next decision to make was with which of the services of the Jewish Board of Guardians to work first. When the project was initiated, the agency included a psychoanalytically oriented child guidance clinic, with a special group therapy department and a volunteer department; a department for unmarried mothers; an institution for maladjusted boys and girls in the adolescent age group—the Hawthorne-Cedar Knolls School; and a department of protective services to child and adult offenders and their families. It also operated three therapeutic camps for children and was responsible for the professional direction of the Council Child Development Center of New York City, a psychiatric clinic and nursery center for study and treatment of emotionally disturbed children of preschool age. As suggested in the Introduction, trends of overt or latent interest in a social science approach to the practice problems of the agency existed in its child guidance clinic, as well as in its other departments. However, at once the suggestion was made that the exploration might be most promisingly begun in the Hawthorne-Cedar Knolls School, since so much of social science is concerned with groups rather than with individuals and group phenomena play a greater role in an institutional setting than in a clinic. The agency's therapeutic camps might have been suggested as a starting point for the same reason, except for the fact that they are operated only in the summer and the project was to begin in the fall.

Although in all probability work in both of these settings would have been rewarding, neither was given favorable consideration for two reasons: First, it might have jeopardized a meaningful solution of the task if preexisting notions had been accepted as to where a social scientist could make his best contribution to practice problems. It might have vitiated the careful planning which had gone into the provision of an open field of exploration by tying the possible outcome of this exploration to the *status quo*, at least so far as those areas were concerned within which no particular usefulness of social science knowledge could be foreseen by practitioners.

The second reason was that the child guidance clinic of the Jewish Board of Guardians represented the most strongly emphasized service branch of the agency, if not the core of its service structure. As such it seemed best suited as a testing ground for an exploration of the potential usefulness of social science liaison with child guidance practice. In the light of these considerations the project was centered in the clinic.

Because of the twofold nature of the assignment a judgment had then to be reached as to which part should be carried out first. As this book reveals, it was decided to focus effort on adapting existing social science knowledge to practice. Concentration on the research part of the assignment, it was feared, would lend support to the not uncommon belief that the strength of social science lies more in the development of research techniques than in the practical usefulness of the findings already made. Also it might have increased the tendency in the practice field to initiate research projects which in view of preexisting knowledge in the social sciences are unnecessary. Finally, it might have strengthened a certain inclination among some social scientists to accept such assignments without questioning.

However, this decision is not to be taken as an expression of opinion that research by social scientists into questions encountered by practitioners would not be highly worthwhile. Rather is it a definition of the role of a social science consultant in a practice setting at the present stage of interdisciplinary contacts between the two fields in terms of need for priority. It seems desirable that every social scientist called into a consulting job in a practice organization should carefully consider whether it is not at least part of his function to scrutinize the funds of substantive knowledge already at his disposal for their contribution potential to practice before he accepts a research assignment, and if possible to suggest the utilization of such knowledge. To do so, however, he needs a certain type of attitudinal equipment which, in the experience gained in carrying out this project, has proved conducive to successful functioning in a practice setting.

In our era of specialization scientific gains are frequently made by a continuous narrowing of the field of inquiry. A social scientist, trained in psychology, sociology, or anthropology, who has established himself in any one of the subdivisions of these various disciplines might attempt the solution of a problem as a whole with specialized knowledge of only one of its aspects. By doing so he is likely to decrease his contribution potential, because in adding specialized knowledge he might exclude other equally important information. He might also antagonize the professional members of the agency which he has been asked to serve. A sociologist, for instance, would be a failure as a consultant in a psychoanalytically oriented child guidance clinic if he believed that application of sociological knowledge would make application of psychoanalytic knowledge unnecessary.

Also important is willingness on the part of a consultant to become intimately acquainted with the problems of practice before he tries to contribute to their solution. His funds of social science knowledge may not be readily applicable to a particular task and adaptation may be possible only if he thoroughly understands the existing practice scheme. A considerable amount of social science research is not immediately related to practice. Thus the knowledge accumulated in the various disciplines of social science frequently will require some rethinking before it can be applied to practice problems. And before the social scientist can begin such rethinking, he must become acquainted with the manifestations of these problems to practitioners.

A social scientist must realize that his power of communication with practitioners may be severely limited unless he learns their technical terminology. This does not mean that he has to sacrifice his own. Actually, as will be shown later, his own terminology may be of decisive importance in contributing knowledge to the practice area in which he operates. But before he can introduce his own terminology he must be able to use the technical language of those whom he serves as a consultant. He must again remain free from any spirit of replacement and must strive for a synthesis of scientific terminology rather than for substitution. Without such readiness to adjustment in terms of scientific communication, he will find it exceedingly difficult to become a functioning member of a team devoted to interdisciplinary effort.

Finally, it should be noted that a social science consultant in a practice setting is by definition not a decision maker. However valuable his contribution may seem to him, it has the nature of a proposal and only that. The decision regarding its incorporation and application remains with the practitioners and policymakers. He will increase his effectiveness, therefore, if he is able to enlist their cooperation in the development and formulation of his suggestions.

In the case of this project the considerations mentioned above led to the following steps in establishing liaison service between social science and child guidance practice. A period of several months was devoted to the consultant's getting acquainted with the work of the clinic and learning the technical terminology used by the practitioners. This resulted in the formulation of a tentative list of ideas as to how funds of social science knowledge could be adapted to child guidance practice. In formulating these ideas special emphasis was put on two areas of concern. One was to respect the body of professional knowledge upon which the staff of the clinic largely depends in its work, namely, the dynamic psychology developed in psychoanalysis. The other was to try to show how a synthesis of this area of knowledge with social science knowledge could be achieved. This twofold emphasis increased the meaningfulness of social science for the practitioners and protected such knowledge from the implications of incompetence which might have been created had the consultant set himself up as a judge of the validity of propositions made in a field not his own.

In the course of this exploratory period the impression was gained that a potentially fruitful adaptation of social science knowledge to child guidance practice could best be achieved if such efforts were connected with certain areas of professional discomfort about the clinic's diagnostic and therapeutic procedures. These areas of discomfort antedated the initiation of the project and suggested possible points of receptivity on the part of the practitioners to new ideas and approaches. There was, for instance, some dissatisfaction with concentrating diagnostic and therapeutic effort upon the mother and the child. The chief executive, Herschel Alt, the clinical director, Dr. Maurice R. Friend, and other executives questioned whether such environmental factors as neighborhood and school conditions received sufficient consideration by the therapists. Very frequently it was found that unfavorable reactions of key persons in the child's environment interfered with the successful continuation of treatment. These were due to behavior changes resulting from the child's responding to psychotherapy in a way not expected by his family. Some of the executives and supervisors felt concern about disregard of cultural material by inexperienced workers, and others felt concern about socially unacceptable behavior ("acting out") of adolescents during treatment. Others, again including the clinical director, felt that permissiveness and passivity on the part of some therapists were extended beyond the periods of treatment in which they seemed therapeutically indicated.

Theoretically, there were three ways of bringing social science knowledge into contact with attempts to alleviate these discomforts. The first possibility was to share with the therapists the general approach of social science, with its emphasis on environmental factors in their totality rather than on a selective basis; the second was to introduce specific social science concepts; the third was to acquaint the therapists with the results of statistical observations and the nature of theorems developed in social science. It was decided to make use only of the first two possibilities and to postpone use of the third. Utilization of the first possibility seemed indicated because the interest in environmental phenomena existing in the clinic was not evenly expressed and lacked consistency in application. Group therapy, volunteer services, interest in Jewishness, concern with the patient's reaction to his wider environment are only a few of the instances of the consideration given by certain departments or individual therapists to environmental factors. An integrated approach, however, taking into account the availability of these various services and the potential importance of these points of consideration in all cases did not seem to exist. Consequently a solidification of these interests by presenting the general social science approach in one or the other of its theoretical formulations offered promise.

The consultant introduced, therefore, with some adaptations, *the situational approach*, postulated for social science research by W. I. Thomas and currently reemphasized by Leonard S. Cottrell, Jr. In this approach Thomas saw basically a research orientation for social scientists which might help them avoid the pitfalls of selective consideration of certain specific factors in the explanation of human behavior.

> The situation in which the person finds himself is taken as containing the configuration of factors conditioning the behavior reaction. Of course, it is not the spatial material situation which is meant, but the situation of social relationships. It involves all the institutions and mores—family, gang, church, school, the press, the movies, and the attitudes and values of other persons with which his own come in conflict or cooperation.[1]

He also saw in the situational approach the closest approximation possible in social science research to the techniques of controlled experimentation used in the natural sciences.

> A study of the concrete situations which the individual encounters, into which he is forced, or which he creates will disclose the character of his adaptive strivings and the processes of adjustment. The study of the situation, the behavior in the situation, the changes brought about in the situation, and the resulting change in behavior represent the nearest approach the social scientist is able to make to the use of experiment in social research. . . .[2]

Roughly twenty years after Thomas had formulated these thoughts for a general seminar on problems of research methodology arranged by the Brookings Institution, Cottrell found it

[1] Volkart, Edmund H., editor, *Social Behavior and Personality:* Contributions by W. I. Thomas to Theory and Social Research. Social Science Research Council, New York, 1951, p. 87.

[2] *Ibid.*, p. 88.

necessary to reemphasize them, taking as the occasion his presidential address to the American Sociological Society in September, 1950.

> It is difficult to imagine . . . that any alert graduate student or junior staff member in our major centers of social psychological training and research could get very far with a research project on traits or attributes of persons or groups without redefining the problem in dynamic situational terms. Nor will a morale branch agency in World War III fail to give as much or more time and skill in precisely specifying the dynamic situational contexts it studies as it will to the measurement of the specific items of behavior and attitude.[1]

Thus in the consultant's own field an approach had been stressed which the practice of the agency, particularly its child guidance clinic, seemed to need and for which it was prepared by historical development. However, this approach in social science was related to research and had now to become related to practice if it was to serve the therapeutic tasks of child guidance directly. The bridge for achieving this adaptation seemed to lie in one of the two basic functions of the therapists—diagnosis and treatment. In a sense, diagnosis can be visualized as case history research. It was thus relatively easy to point out the value of the situational approach for diagnostic procedure. Once this connection was established, it proved possible also to adapt the situational approach to the treatment process itself. Since treatment in the clinic is based on diagnosis, as soon as the situational approach was accepted for the latter it was bound to make itself felt in the former. For instance, once it was accepted that in a specific situation a father's behavior should be investigated in terms of its influence on the behavior difficulty of the child, it followed easily that such a broadening in scope of the diagnostic inquiry would call for inclusion of the father in the range of possible patients. To what degree this basic idea could be carried out will be seen in the chapters that follow, since the implications of the situational approach are presented there in terms of both diagnosis and treatment.

[1] Cottrell, Leonard S., Jr., "Some Neglected Problems in Social Psychology," *American Sociological Review*, vol. 15, December, 1950, p. 706.

Essentially the situational approach with its emphasis on all environmental stimuli to which a person reacts, in combination with the emphasis of psychoanalytically oriented psychiatry on motivation and affect, seemed to have the following implications for theory and practice: (1) that individuals with the same basic personality structure may react differently in different situations; (2) that different situational experiences would produce differences in basic personality structure. As a practical consequence of these theoretical implications, the situational approach seemed to provide, first, a balance wheel and safeguard not against the use of psychodynamic understanding in child guidance but against overlooking significant psychological experiences in the child's development which were not in areas some therapists had come to consider exclusively in a more or less routinized practice. Specifically it promised to extend an understanding of pathological influences beyond the family circle. Second, it promised to bring in cultural understanding not as a hobby or an individual concern of some workers with private motivations, but as an essential tool in finding out about the client's emotional life. Third, it promised to suggest a broadening of the potential range of patients and a more cautious expectation of positive results of the therapeutic effort than routinized practice seemed to contain. Finally, it promised to integrate more closely group therapy and utilization of volunteers with individual psychotherapy for children.

Even greater emphasis was put on introducing *specific social science concepts* with which the therapists had not been familiar. This was done for a number of reasons. One stemmed from the following interesting observation. Although a broader environmental approach was frequently suggested by the consulting psychiatrists in individual case consultations, the therapists did not appear to follow this part of the psychiatric consultation with the same degree of interest and application with which they applied the psychodynamic part. In view of the fact that the therapists looked to the psychiatric consultants as their guides in treatment and authorities in evaluating its success, this presented a puzzling phenomenon. They seemed to use the gist of the psychiatric consultation only selectively, applying with emotional understanding and intellectual interest the psychodynamic interpretation but frequently disregarding advice to consider environmental factors. At least they appeared to be unable to transfer guidance for the utilization of environmental factors given by psychiatrists in one case to another. Thus they might have followed specific suggestions of the psychiatrist, such as inviting a father in one case, but continued to apply the routinized consideration of only mother and child in another case where the father seemed to be of equal importance.

Upon closer inspection of the material discussed in the psychiatric consultations, however, at least a partial solution seemed to suggest itself. When the psychiatrist spoke about psychodynamics, he used *concepts* which made it possible for the worker to understand the phenomena referred to and, unless blocked by emotional factors, to transfer the knowledge so imparted to other situations to which it was equally applicable. When the psychiatrist spoke of environmental factors, he spoke with wisdom but did not use conceptualized language. Since concepts are an important tool in "learning to respond to a situational feature or a set of features irrespective of the particular circumstances in which they may be found,"[1] this differential between reference to psychodynamic and reference to environmental material on the part of the psychiatrist seemed to explain, at least in part, the differential in the worker's receptivity to and utilization of his guidance. The decision, therefore, was made to provide the consideration of environmental factors in child guidance practice with as much conceptualization as existing social science theory and the receptivity of the therapists seemed to permit.

That the need for conceptualization of environmental influences has been felt also by physicians can be seen, for instance, in Henry B. Richardson's *Patients Have Families*.[2] According to Dr. Richardson, an understanding of illness requires a combina-

---

[1] Boring, Langfeld, Weld, *Introduction to Psychology*, John Wiley and Sons, New York, 1939, p. 404. As to other writers expressing the same point see, for instance, Dashiell, John Frederick, *Fundamentals of General Psychology*, Houghton Mifflin and Co., Boston, 1937, pp. 558, 560.

[2] Commonwealth Fund, New York, 1945, pp. xviii, 408.

tion of approaches and a consideration of a plurality of physical and emotional, as well as of interpersonal, factors. From that point of view certain constellations of family living must be taken into account if cures and prevention of certain diseases are to be achieved. Part of the volume deals with concepts related to family constellations found useful in medical work. Among others mention is made of imitation, identification, focus or sense of direction of the family, and patterns of dominance and submission in the family. The presentation of these concepts reveals a high degree of insight into the structure of human interaction within the family circle. Dr. Richardson and his coworkers appear to have believed, however, that they identified and conceptualized these phenomena for the first time. They do not seem to have been aware of the fact that sociologists had preceded them in doing so.[1]

Thus in Dr. Richardson's book there is a recognition of the need for conceptualization of environmental factors on the part of a representative of the medical profession but at the same time also an indication of a danger of duplicated effort. The experience of teamwork between social science consultant and therapists gained in the joint project of Russell Sage Foundation and the Jewish Board of Guardians suggests that such needs for conceptualization of environmental factors can be satisfied without the wastefulness of duplication in theoretical and practical efforts.

An incorporation of social science concepts into the theory underlying child guidance practice promised to support the application of the situational approach by achieving the following results. It promised a widening of perception on the part of the workers for significant factors in pathogenesis and therapy, because "what we perceive, or overlook, in the field of our potential experience depends on the framework of concepts which we have in our minds."[2] It is interesting to note in this formulation of Ichheiser's that concepts not only help perception but also exclude perception of things not conceptualized. If utilization of

[1] *Ibid.*, pp. 79–90, 321–325.
[2] Ichheiser, Gustav, *Misunderstandings in Human Relations.* Special Issue of the American Journal of Sociology, vol. 55, September, 1949, Part 2, p. 2.

social science concepts had been proposed with the idea of replacing the psychodynamic concepts currently used by the practitioners of the agency, and even if such a proposal would have been accepted, there would have been no widening of perception on the part of the therapists, but merely a shift in perception. Since an attempt was made to synthesize the funds of knowledge available in social science with those available in psychoanalytic theory and practice, this danger was avoided.

Furthermore introduction of these additional concepts promised not only to increase the perceptual range of the therapists but also to lay the foundation for a broader scientific base of child guidance work. Concepts are both the essential tools of perception and the building blocks from which theorems and laws—that is, statements about the constant aspects of relationships between phenomena—are formed.[1]

There was also a promise of special usefulness for training purposes. Being logical constructs which "through signs or symbols or both" are "transferable from situation to situation and communicable from person to person,"[2] concepts are obviously of great help in psychiatric consultation as well as in supervision. They make it possible to transfer knowledge during the training process instead of relying on the trainee's acquiring wisdom by experience. As indicated, the use of concepts for psychodynamic phenomena had proved its training value for the clinic staff. The use of social science concepts for environmental phenomena could be expected to do the same.

Concepts particularly selected were the *family of orientation, social interaction, socialization, cultural relativity, culture conflict, social roles, status, youth culture,* and *reinforcement* in *stimulus response learning.* All of these were discussed in a number of meetings with the department and district heads of the child guidance clinic. In the discussion an attempt was made to elucidate the relationships of the phenomena designated by these social science concepts to psychodynamic phenomena encountered in patients and

[1] Woodworth, Robert S., and Donald G. Marquis, *Psychology.* Henry Holt and Co., New York, 5th ed., 1949, p. 601.

[2] Heidbreder, Edna, "The Attainment of Concepts: I, Terminology and Methodology," *The Journal of General Psychology,* vol. 35, October, 1946, p. 173.

workers. After agreement on their meaningfulness had been achieved, the potential impact of these relationships on diagnosis and therapy was deductively determined. These logical deductions, combined with illustrations of their potential usefulness by case analysis, were then elaborated in detail and before final formulation discussed with the clinical director. Thus it was agreed that serious application of these concepts required changes in routine and operations. In summary, the introduction of the situational approach and the social science concepts mentioned above seems to have produced two basic results for therapeutic practice—a new type of perceptivity and tools for an ordering of reality.

The decision to postpone exploration of the possible contribution which statistical observations and quantitative expressions of theorems may have for child guidance practice was based on the following consideration. Training and therapeutic experience both seem to lead many therapists to mistrust quantified statements about human relationships. Presentation of social science knowledge in such form might have created reluctance on the part of a considerable number of workers to find use for it. Introduction of knowledge expressed in tabulations and formulas, therefore, was intentionally omitted for the time being. This decision applied to quantitative research in psychology and sociology generally, as well as quantitative research in child development centers as presented, for instance, in the works of Harold E. Jones and Willard C. Olson.[1]

It may be anticipated, however, that, with clarification of concepts and theories in the clinical field on the one hand and a growing interest among experimentalists in the phenomena which are significant for the clinician on the other, we may see an increasing utilization by the latter of relevant, quantitatively expressed research findings. An example in point is S. R. Slavson's use of such material in his contribution to this volume.

In this report social science concepts are discussed in connection with a relatively large number of quotations from published

[1] Jones, Harold E., *Motor Performance and Growth*, University of California Press, Berkeley, 1949, p. 181; Olson, Willard C., *Child Development*, D. C. Heath and Co., Boston, 1949, pp. xiii, 417.

works. On the other hand, the chapters are rich in clinical illustrations. Both of these aspects of the presentation, it is hoped, will facilitate mutual acquaintance between social scientists and practitioners of psychotherapy with children. Footnote references and theoretical discussions are poor mediators of acquaintance. If not provided with samples of social science thinking formulated by leading theoreticians and research scientists, practitioners may be easily misled into thinking that those social scientists who have become known outside their own field are necessarily representative and that their writings give a clear indication of the contribution potential existing in these disciplines. Social scientists in turn, accustomed as they are to the analysis of mass data, may fail to get the breadth and complexity of actual clinical work with individual child patients suffering from mental disorders. Hearing about one or the other symptom, they may be inclined to think that their knowledge of mass phenomena may furnish easy explanations of the whole difficulty. The samples provided by the quotations from social science literature and illustrations of specific cases are intended to prevent pitfalls which threaten sincere attempts on both sides to get acquainted. It should be stressed, however, that they are introduced to accomplish only that. The references quoted do not pretend to include all source material which conceivably could be introduced. To do so would have been impossible within the framework of this project, which represents only a step in the direction of closer liaison between social science and child guidance practice. In turn, the clinical material in the case illustrations is worked up only to the degree of showing the practical usefulness of specific social science concepts in the theoretical equipment of practitioners of psychotherapy with children.

The findings presented in the following chapters may impress some readers as obvious and, therefore, as not requiring elaboration by social science concepts. Comments to that effect may come from various quarters. They may come from social scientists engaged in intricate quantification and prediction research. Appraising the social science content discussed here, such scientists may feel that only the most elementary part of the specialized knowledge existing in their fields has been utilized. Such comments would overlook the fact that liaison between social science and a practice field requires in its initial phase quickly demonstrable utility and easy accessibility to the new material presented as a contribution.

Experienced therapists, secure in their own performance, may feel confident that they have been and are considering all the phenomena to which the social science concepts here discussed refer. They may think, therefore, that their introduction into the theoretical equipment underlying their work is not necessary and may voice the opinion that what this book proposes to achieve is already being done in "good therapy." Therapists who would comment in this vein would overlook, however, the time it took them to acquire this security of performance and also the good fortune which they may have had in being gifted with more than average powers of discernment. Therapists may also contend that what this conceptual elaboration tries to prevent is merely mistakes in practice which could have been corrected without such concepts in the process of supervision and psychiatric consultation.

All such expressions of judgment would disregard the point made at considerable length in the preceding pages; namely, that wisdom without concepts cannot be taught, but that formalized and conceptualized knowledge can. Wisdom acquired by experience in combination with a personal gift for discernment will always remain the good fortune of a few. Formalization and conceptualized information can be made the possession of many. The demand for mental health services in our society cannot be met by depending on the wisdom of a necessarily limited number of superior therapists. The essence of such wisdom has to be spread in the manner of science, which perhaps is less inspiring but more accessible to large numbers of professional helpers. In this sense, science pays the price of modesty for the reward of usefulness.

There is still another reason suggesting the advisability of introducing these social science concepts into the theoretical equipment of child therapists, which is based on an interesting and by no means obvious phenomenon. Many therapists select from their training in psychodynamics only a limited number of theoretical propositions. The selection seems to be guided by their personal emotional responses to these propositions, on the basis of individual experiences which often have become submerged in their unconscious. If these emotions are satisfying, the propositions which aroused them take on exaggerated qualities. They seem to explain every case. Thus they come to be regarded as of such vital importance that hardly anything else needs to be considered. Therapists with such convictions tend to disregard the realities of individual patient situations. The easily understandable concepts discussed in the following chapters may provide therapists of this type with at least some intellectual safeguards against such fallacies and the resulting treatment failures. They may also be utilized by supervisors and consulting psychiatrists to tie up a therapist's disregard of the phenomenon which they designate with the particular emotional reasons accounting for it. Thus these concepts may be of assistance not only in the intellectual but also in the emotional and dynamic aspects of supervision and consultation. It is this twofold impact of their utilization which holds the greatest promise.

Before presenting the material mention should be again made that this report does not purport to represent definitive conclusions. The conclusions reached are tentative and will require controlled observations of practical results.

CHAPTER TWO

The Concept of Family of Orientation in Diagnosis and Therapy

ACCORDING to current practice in the child guidance clinic of the Jewish Board of Guardians, the main source for diagnostic information, in addition to the child himself, is his mother. She is the person from whom the basic data about the child's symptom picture, his developmental history, and his family background are gathered. Routinely the child is seen for diagnostic observation after his mother, and on the basis of the material collected from these two sources in interviews covering an intake period of about six weeks, an initial summary is prepared for the diagnostic conference with the consulting psychiatrist.[1] In cases which have been referred through schools, hospitals, or social welfare agencies, information supplied by them is, of course, included in that summary. Only in a minority of cases is the child's father also seen as part of the initial diagnostic contact. When this happens, the reason usually is that he has taken the initiative in the referral stage. In such a case both parents may be invited to the intake interview, but sometimes even though the father is the parent who has approached the agency only the mother is asked to the initial interview regarding the child's difficulties.

Similarly it is basically only the mother who is regarded as a potential patient besides the child, although as treatment progresses the father may also be seen for therapy. In such cases it is usually a request on the part of the mother that brings about the contact between the worker and the father. It may be due to

By OTTO POLLAK IN CONSULTATION WITH BETTINA LEHNERT

[1] Until the completion of this stage the case is carried by a so-called "intake worker"; after the first diagnostic conference the case is assigned for therapy to a worker frequently referred to as "therapist."

initiative taken by the father himself. It hardly ever occurs as a consequence of initiative taken by a worker. Siblings may occasionally be considered potential foci of therapeutic effort but the decision as to whether a sibling should be included in the treatment process is left entirely to the parents. Other family members, such as grandmothers, grandfathers, aunts, and uncles, are never regarded as potential recipients of therapy.

Several reasons may account for this phenomenon. The division of labor in our society which assigns the task of infant care and early child rearing primarily to the mother may furnish considerable justification for considering the mother the best available source of information regarding the child's developmental history. In some cases, however, it may be necessary to see the father as well. Thus the diagnostic contact should not be stereotyped to seeing only the mother and the child. Where there is any suggestion of the father's importance for an understanding of the pathogenesis of the child, the *situational approach* would suggest that he also should be seen.

The strategical position of the mother in the growth pattern of the child makes it probable that his behavior difficulties and affect disturbances may largely be due to the interaction between him and his mother. The physical absence of the father from the home during working hours may make him appear a relatively remote factor in the development of the child. Such reasoning, however, does not seem to furnish an explanation for practice in a psychoanalytically oriented child guidance clinic because an understanding of the oedipal conflicts of children certainly does not permit a discounting of the father as an important factor in child development.

Since most of the workers at the clinic are women, a certain preference for contact with a parent of the same sex may exist. The workers may question whether the father will be ready to accept professional authority from a woman therapist. The father's own shortcomings or the mother's unconscious hostilities may also serve to increase the worker's tendency to satisfy the mother's desire to become, together with the child, the only focus of clinic interest. Unsatisfied maternal longings of childless women workers, or the emotional tendencies of workers who have difficulties with their own husbands may lead them to identification with the mother to the exclusion of the father. Another factor may be pressure to produce as large a volume of cases as possible. This may account for some reluctance on the part of intake workers to take the time required for including fathers in the diagnostic contact. Furthermore it may explain a shortage of workers available for assignment when family members other than the mother and child seem also to need treatment.

Besides these reasons, the inclination of child guidance practitioners to concentrate their diagnostic inquiry and therapeutic efforts upon the mother and the child may be due to the fact that inexperienced therapists discuss emotional phenomena in terms of individuals rather than in terms of family constellations.

The soundness of this emphasis on the child and his biological mother has been questioned repeatedly within the agency. In a paper read at the Thirty-seventh Annual Meeting of the American Psychopathological Association, held in New York City in June, 1947, Dr. Nathan W. Ackerman and Dr. Peter B. Neubauer expressed their opinion regarding this practice as follows:

> The fundamental closeness of child to mother is a recognized factor. Nevertheless, this is one example of oversimplification which sometimes leads to failure in treatment. If the therapy of the environment is to be child oriented, the primary need is an intimate knowledge of the relationship of each parent to the child. The father's personality, as well as the mother's, must be understood, and the emotional interaction between these two persons must be dealt with. Often, the father must receive treatment as well as the mother, if adequate results are to be achieved. It is necessary, of course, to recognize the practical obstacles which often stand in the way of such a program. Nevertheless, the relevant issues must be clearly seen, if success in therapy is to be assured. . . .
>
> In most cases, since the mother is usually the one who brings the child, it is possible to achieve earlier and easier access to her problem than to that of the father. Therefore, one may easily overlook the pathology in the father.[1]

[1] Ackerman, Nathan W., and Peter B. Neubauer, "Failures in the Psychotherapy of Children," *Failures in Psychiatric Treatment*, edited by Paul H. Hoch. Grune and Stratton, New York, 1948, pp. 86–87, 88.

Similarly Gordon Hamilton, in her study of the principles of psychotherapy as practiced in the Child Guidance Institute of the Jewish Board of Guardians, expressed herself in favor of bringing fathers and siblings more actively into the treatment relationship.

> Treatment of the parental situation . . . has become not merely one angle for treating the child, but an integral part of the therapeutic process. Theoretically, both parents should be brought into the treatment relationship, but in American culture, since the mother, especially when there are young children, is more involved, it is usually she who is most actively engaged in the process. In the family guidance of the future, more effort must be made to bring fathers actively into treatment. Siblings come into focus both as individual patients and as an environment for the chief patient.[1]

Although these opinions have been expressed by persons who in their field, as well as in the agency, hold the status of professional leaders, agency practice has remained relatively unaffected by them. Only a few indications of practice changes with regard to fathers have occurred. In one of the district offices of the clinic a committee was organized to study the advisability of including fathers in the treatment process. A primary conclusion reached by this committee was that "when treatment has already begun with mother and child, it is imperative to appropriately time the father's introduction into the treatment situation." The committee also found that "in excluding fathers from treatment, too close ties between mother and child were often unwittingly cemented." Therefore the committee concluded that "an early recognition of his [the father's] role and its use in treatment may well lead to greater economy in therapy."[2]

Still, compared with the fervor with which the workers at the Child Guidance Institute are following the principles of clinical psychiatry and advanced casework in other areas, their response to suggestions of broadening the range of diagnostic inquiry and selection of persons other than the mother and child for therapy

[1] Hamilton, Gordon, *Psychotherapy in Child Guidance*. Columbia University Press, New York, 1947, p. 282.

[2] "Father Comes of Age," *J. B. G. Spotlight*, published by the volunteers of the Jewish Board of Guardians, vol. 3, November, 1950, p. 1.

has not been so strong as might be expected. Diagnosis and treatment of the child in clinic practice are still largely concentrated on the child and his mother.

This is a point at which the *situational approach* to the study of the family should be of considerable help in improving diagnosis and therapy along the lines pointed out by Dr. Ackerman, Dr. Neubauer, and Dr. Hamilton. Its emphasis on all environmental stimuli to which persons react, in combination with the psychoanalytic emphasis on motivation and affect development, should help to strengthen the perceptual equipment of the therapists of the clinic for interpersonal relationships affecting the child, other than the mother-child relationship. Consequently it should make it less likely to overlook interpersonal relationships which are of importance in the growth process of a child patient.

The practical application of such an approach will be facilitated by the incorporation of sociological concepts into the professional equipment of child guidance therapists. In this respect it would be important to introduce the concept of *family structure* and the distinction between the *family of procreation* and the *family of orientation*.[1] The structure of a family has various implications for child therapy. It implies, first of all, different power positions of the various family members in relation to one another. Thus it furnishes a key for the prediction as to what action or decision will be taken when there is disagreement within the family group. It further implies a division of functions among the various family members which may indicate the nature and the frequency of contacts among them. Finally, it indicates lines of communication among the family members, as well as between them and the outside world, which may be important to consider in building a relationship between the family and the clinic.

[1] Bossard, James H. S., *The Sociology of Child Development*. Harper and Bros., New York, 1948, pp. 40, 55.
Attention is drawn to the fact that these terms as used by Bossard and in this volume have a slightly different connotation from their usage by W. Lloyd Warner and his research associates. The latter introduced these concepts and utilized them for purposes of status analyses within the class structure of society. See *The Status System of a Modern Community* by W. Lloyd Warner and Paul S. Hunt, Yale University Press, New Haven, 1942, p. 16; and *Social Class in America* by W. Lloyd Warner, Marcia Meeker, and Kenneth Eells, Science Research Associates, Chicago, 1949, pp. 86-87.

There seems to be very little recognition, and even less acceptance, in diagnostic and therapeutic emphasis, of the fact that the *family of procreation*—the biological and reproductive unit of the parents and child—need not be identical with the *family of orientation*—the sum total of persons who form continuing members of the household in which the child grows up, that is, the primary group at the home. There may be aunts and uncles, grandparents, or even boarders, who are in daily-living contact with the child for periods extending over the whole stretch of his formative years.

Perhaps the basic fact about the presence of "other persons" in the home is that they are not acceptable equally to all members of the family of procreation. They may be acceptable to the child, or to the parents, or to one parent and the child, and so on, but not to the other or others. The presence of an adult relative, particularly if childless, invariably means the presence of an active competitor with the parent of the same sex as the relative for the child's affection. This competition may be overt or it may be subtle or insidious. Or the adult relative is not included in the rules or regime which the parent imposes upon the others in the family; hence this adult, no matter how circumspect his behavior may be, appears to the child as a challenge to the parent's authority, or as a refuge or comfort which the child may seek. A good many domestic situations might be summarized in the statement that the presence of a younger adult in the family means a potential competitor for the affection of the child; and the presence of an older person, a potential competitor for his control. The problem, of course, is often less simple than such a summary suggests. Adults who live with other families tend often to be problem adults. A parent's brother or sister who is not married, or who has been married but not successfully, or who cannot get along with other people, or who is too sick or too feeble to live by himself—these constitute a good proportion of the adults who live with "their" families. Taking in a relative is often the assumption of a burden and a problem. Parents may assume such an obligation with the philosophy of maturity or the resignation of despair, but to the child the newcomer is as he is, without the comfort of compensating philosophy.[1]

This may arise particularly in situations where a member of the family of orientation, such as an old and feeble grandfather,

[1] Bossard, James H. S., *op. cit.*, pp. 59-60.

competes with the child for the attention and care of the mother and thus actually starts something equivalent to sibling rivalry between himself and the grandchild.

Thus in psychodynamic terms all members of the family of orientation may become partners to emotionally significant inter-relationships with the child and influence his growth process. Dynamic consideration of all persons living in the household in which the child grows up may give a now lacking measure of assurance that an important relationship is not overlooked, minimized, or perceived in its full impact only after considerable treatment time has been lost. Of course, treatment of the child's environment must admit the treatment needs of such persons as well as the treatment needs of the mother.

In its adaptation to child guidance practice the situational approach to the study and treatment of disturbances in child development has two major implications. First, it requires in every diagnostic study consideration of the possibility that an interpersonal relationship other than that between the child and his mother may play a part in the pathogenesis of the child's difficulties. This seems to be theoretically accepted by the workers, but the necessary conclusions for the diagnostic process are not drawn. It is not recognized, for instance, that because of this theoretical insight direct contact should be made with family members other than the mother and the child, if not in routine fashion, at least in all cases in which material produced by the mother or the child suggests the implication of such persons in pathogenesis. Long-distance diagnoses have obvious dangers. The workers would certainly object to making a diagnostic de-cision on the basis of only the statements of the mother without seeing the child. If the situational approach to family diagnosis with its implication of possible pathogenic influences resulting from the relationship between the child and family members other than his mother is accepted, direct contact between the diagnostician and these other persons becomes a *sine qua non* of diagnostic concern.

Second, if such diagnostic investigations should reveal that a personal interrelationship between the father and the child, or between a sibling and a child, plays a role in his developmental difficulties, these persons should be regarded as potential patients as well as the child himself and his mother. The diagnostic process will then have to lead to a decision as to which relationship or combination of relationships causes the disturbance. In other words, the diagnostician must identify the significant problem. At the present time diagnostic consideration may pay attention to factors other than the mother-child relationship, but current clinic practice indicates that the practitioners believe that the basic problem can lie only in the mother-child relationship. The situational approach would require the conception of the possibility that the problem may be differently located, or that the problem lies in a combination of human factors involving more than two persons, and thus presents a constellation problem. If that is so, persons other than the mother may have to be considered for treatment, either instead of or in addition to her.

Two cases are presented to illustrate the possible occurrence of situations where the relationship between father and child, or that between the child and the oldest sibling, in combination with the mother-child relationship, seemingly accounts to an appreciable degree for the pathogenesis of the child's difficulties. The changes in diagnostic procedure and selection of patients for therapy which the situational approach in synthesis with psychodynamic interpretation would require in such situations will be pointed out in both instances.

One week after Sam, age seven, had begun his second year in the grade school of a Yeshiva, he refused to attend classes upon learning that he would be required to spend three hours there each Sunday morning. From then on, regardless of threats or actual punishment, he would not go to school even on weekdays.

Actually this was the climax of a series of earlier difficulties which centered around school attendance. After half a year in kindergarten, Sam had refused to stay. At the beginning of his first year in grade school, he objected to remaining unless his mother stayed with him. However, his resistance was eventually overcome in these instances.

The child's developmental history contained, among others, the following facts: Because of the war Sam's father had been away from home since Sam was nine months old and did not return until he was three years old. Nine months after the father's return the mother gave birth to a baby girl. The boy developed strong feelings of rivalry with his little sister, but this rivalry centered around the father. The latter actually preferred his daughter and Sam reacted violently to the affection which his father showered on the little girl.

There were also indications that Sam felt strongly in competition with his mother for his father's affection. During the year before referral, almost every night he went into the bedroom of his parents, although he showed no fear of the dark, and invariably got into their bed at the father's side. Reprimands were of no avail. The parents were very demonstrative in their affection for each other, and Sam would frequently tell his mother to go away from his father, saying, "He is my daddy."

Sam's need for affection from his father was frustrated because the latter worked as a window display decorator during the day and went to school at night, which left him little time to be with his son. He also discouraged Sam from various developmental ventures, such as participation in a handicraft contest, because of a perfectionistic emphasis on standards of achievement. The doll play of the boy revealed strong ambivalence toward his father. Outstanding in it was the child's emphasis on his relationship to the father and a dearth of material regarding the mother.

Having been without the assistance of her husband and therefore under considerable strain during the second and third years of her son's life, the mother had brought up the child to be relatively independent even of her physical care and had come to assume mostly the role of disciplinarian. She was a rather punitive person, frequently using corporal punishment. She herself reported Sam saying accusingly to her, "You are always hitting me."

Pushed into independence by a mother whom he experienced mainly as a punishing agent, and frustrated in his reaching out for his father as a source of emotional warmth and acceptance, the boy became increasingly guilty about his feelings of hostility toward his parents. Relatively early in the contact he revealed that he was afraid that they would arrange in his absence to send him away from home, and that this was the reason he did not want to go to school. In this connection it should be noted that Sam's father, in spite of his double work load of job and night school, on occasions came home during working hours in order to get materials for his job and was always home on Sunday. Thus the second-grade schedule of the Yeshiva, more than any other school schedule Sam had ever experienced, deprived him of opportunity to be at home when he knew his father would be there.

The psychiatric diagnosis in this case was beginning psycho-neurosis. The psychodynamic interpretation given by the consulting psychiatrist stressed the fact that part of Sam's conflict was his relationship to his father, which indicated accentuation of the inverted oedipal situation.

Although a great deal of pertinent material indicating the importance of Sam's father among the factors determining the child's difficulties was obtained in the first interview with the mother, it was not considered necessary to see the father at that stage of the contact. Particularly the information regarding the father's absence during two of the boy's formative years and the boy's constant attempts to get into his parents' bed at the father's side should have made it appear desirable to establish contact with the father at that stage. It might have been helpful had the worker explained to him right at the beginning how important he was in working out his son's difficulties, and how much Sam needed identification with him as a condition of his normal growth. Probably it might have been also helpful to give this father an opportunity to discuss his own difficult position after his return from army service, during which he and his son had become completely estranged.

It is true that the therapist recognized the possibility of the father's contribution to the child's difficulties and asked to see him, but not until two months after the first intake interview with the mother. In the interview with the father the following items of diagnostic information were brought out:

> Sam's father had always felt that he and his son had a very good relationship. It appeared that he had been unable to attend college before the war because of his family's economic situation and was now extremely happy that the G.I. Bill of Rights permitted him to realize his ambition. It was impossible for him to accept the fact that his son refused to attend school. He also mentioned that because of this he was particularly troubled and confused about Sam's behavior, had become inconsistent in his approach to him, and had even resorted to corporal punishment. Toward the end of the interview, he expressed considerable guilt over having possibly contributed to his son's difficulties by his own absorption with night school. On the whole, it appeared that he was not aware of the impact which his

wartime absence from home and his demonstrative show of affection to his wife and daughter on the one hand, and his rejection of his son on the other, seemed to have on Sam.

Although the interview had produced significant material for the formulation of a family diagnosis and indicated this father's need for therapeutic contact with the clinic, the worker felt obligated to apologize for having arranged it and did not squarely face the father's need for treatment, as is apparent from the following recording:

> In response to inquiry and also because of my own feeling that it was helpful, I did give a few rather specific suggestions and recommendations to the father about the handling of the school problem, and in essence it is my feeling that he does not perceive himself as coming in here for any continuous contact with me but that, as he put it, when he feels that he can't cope with the problem, he'd be very happy to see me again. *I felt that it was very worthwhile to see him if only to give him the feeling of participation and also to give me a clearer picture of his personality constellation.*

Treatment of Sam's father was not attempted until five months had elapsed since he had first been seen and seven months since the first intake interview with Sam's mother. Even then it did not come about in a planned fashion, resulting from the diagnostic conclusions. It developed rather as a result of the father's having come on his own initiative to see the therapist in order to check upon the development of his son in treatment. At the end of that interview the responsibility for arranging another appointment was again left with him. He called the following week and came for six weekly interviews before treatment ended for the summer. The case was closed in the fall because the family moved to another city.

In her contacts with this father the therapist was able to achieve the following improvements in the growth conditions surrounding the child: As a result of the first and, according to the worker's intention, purely diagnostic contact with the father, a significant change occurred in the management of the child by the parents. They became consistent in refusing to let him sleep in their bedroom. The therapist originally had tried to achieve this simply by discussing it with the mother, but without success. A few weeks after this suggestion had been made to Sam's father, however, the mother reported with considerable relief that she and her husband had consistently put Sam back into his own room at night when he came into theirs, and he had finally stopped trying to sleep with them. The emotional reasons that may have prompted this father to become consistent in restricting his son and to help his wife in being so could not be established on that level of contact. The fact remains that the contact was helpful in improving the growth conditions of the child. In the therapeutic contacts with the father, which occurred later, the worker was able to help him reduce some of his perfectionistic standards for Sam, so that the latter would feel that his father was interested in *him* and not only in his achievements. It also proved possible to help this father understand that he would meet with failure in his attempts to approach Sam's difficulties if he relied only on reason in dealing with them and disregarded the emotional meaning of his interaction with his son.

In spite of these therapeutic results, however, the worker found it necessary in the closing summary to make the following statement:

> The father was drawn into treatment at a point where both child and mother seemed secure in their relationship with the worker. Because of the moralistic, punitive, and rigid defense system of this man, it was not possible to work with him on an analytical, interpretive level, but rather with the material that was consciously available to him.

This statement shows the pitfalls which the traditional emphasis of the clinic practice on the mother-child relationship can create even for workers who perceive diagnostic resources and treatment needs generally not considered under the current system. First of all, it should be noted that the father was not *drawn* into treatment, but was only *admitted* into treatment when he approached the clinic on his own initiative. Second, one might wonder about the principle that fathers can be treated only after the worker's relations with mother and child are secure. The clinic has never postponed treatment of a mother until the child was secure in his relationship with the therapist. Finally, in her statement about the father's untreatability on an insight level the worker overlooked the fact that the agency had always treated mothers of the same personality type on an insight level. It would seem necessary for therapists to realize the necessity of having both parents *participate* in the treatment of the child, no matter which of them is seen regularly in treatment. The attitudes and behavior of the other parent are meaningful for the treatment process whether he is actually treated or not.

In summary, this case suggests that diagnostic and therapeutic contacts with fathers—where indicated by the family constellation—should be approached as a normal requirement of the child guidance process. They should not be considered adventures requiring apology and extreme caution in fitting them into the contacts with the mother and the child, and they should not be approached with more diffidence than contacts with the mother or the child. Once the situational approach to family diagnosis and family treatment is accepted in the practice of the clinic, it will become easier in the training and supervisory process to spot such therapeutic concerns as phenomena of personal mechanisms of defense on the part of the workers. At present they can easily assume the cover of clinic practice, and thus escape supervisory notice, to the detriment both of the patient and of the professional development of the therapist.

The situational approach would also suggest that the siblings of child patients should be similarly included in the diagnostic and therapeutic contact. Current clinic practice accepts the decision of the parents as to which one of two siblings should become the focus of the child guidance process. It is theoretically accepted by the clinic staff that pathology in one sibling may lead to reactive behavior disturbance in the other, and that for some reason the parents may be more concerned with the second pathology than with the first. No attempt is being made, however, to make parental attention to this problem a condition of therapy, to require diagnostic contact with all siblings involved, and to make the parents see that their concern for the child brought to the clinic for treatment may demand the treatment of the other child. This does not mean that the workers in their psycho-dynamic interpretations remain unaware of the pathogenic in-fluence of a sibling upon the patient, but supported by current agency practice, they exhibit a completely fatalistic attitude toward the situation. When parents mention the difficulties of a child other than the one brought for treatment, the therapists deal with such material as if that were the consideration of an-other case. There is apparently little realization that it is a facet of the case already in treatment and perhaps the most important. Consequently when parents show concern about the difficulties of a sibling not yet in treatment but feel that he would not want treatment, the therapists may offer to make contact with him if the parents should wish it. They do not point out, however, that the two situations are interdependent and that treatment of the child not yet in therapy may be a condition of therapeutic success for the one already treated. Again a combination of the situa-tional approach with psychodynamic understanding would seem to promise certain definite practice changes in such cases. It would require: (1) direct diagnostic contact with the siblings of a child patient in all instances in which there is an indication of pathogenic relationships between them; (2) a decision regarding selection of a sibling for therapy according to the total constella-tion of the interrelationships rather than according to the decision of the parents, or inclusion of all siblings involved in the patho-genic constellation. Of course, it may be necessary in the begin-ning to accept that sibling for therapy whom the parents have brought to the clinic, but such an initial decision need not remain binding during the whole course of the therapeutic process.

The following case highlights the possible nexus of develop-mental problems among siblings:

Harry, age eight and the younger of two siblings, was referred to the agency because he did not work up to capacity in school, was unable to concentrate, could not get along with children, and was hyperactive. He would disappear from his home for hours and would be seen climbing roofs and telephone poles. His disappearance from home caused his family a great deal of anxiety and they had to spend a lot of time trying to find him.

Harry's mother had been a nurse before her marriage and it was revealed later in the contact that she had always liked to take care of sick persons. His father was a scholar, who through external circumstances had been forced to become a textile salesman. Charles, Harry's six-year-older brother, caused the mother considerable concern because he was moody and jealous of the younger boy. The mother had preferred Charles until Harry began to develop difficulties. She had placed both children in a children's institution once for a year when the family encountered economic difficulties and she felt she had to go outside her home to work. At the time of that placement Harry was two years old.

From the beginning of the contact there were indications that Charles was an important factor in Harry's difficulties. The mother brought Charles again and again into the discussions with Harry's therapist. She felt that Charles suffered under the shifting of her attention to the younger boy and mentioned that Charles showed considerable aggression and hostility toward Harry. She also felt that the older boy's depressive moods upset Harry, who shared a room with him and was, therefore, permanently exposed to the emotional impact of his brother's expressions of negative affect. Repeatedly the mother raised the question whether the clinic could not also treat Charles, but in the same breath showed considerable ambivalence about having Charles come.

In one of the initial sessions of the contact, Harry became interested in the dictaphone in the worker's office and asked to have its use explained. Picking up the receiver he screamed, "Hello, you stinker. Charles is a stinker." Later on in the contact he expressed his resentment against his older brother in other forms. As the case continued, it became increasingly clear that the relationship between the two boys was greatly disturbed and that the mother infantilized both of them.

The psychiatric diagnosis for Harry was primary behavior disorder, with some question about the possibility of a beginning psychoneurosis.

Although the diagnostic considerations contained in the record indicate clearly that the consulting psychiatrist and the intake worker were aware of the harmfulness of the mother's relationships with her sons, their interdependence and the harmfulness of the resulting sibling relationship, clinic practice apparently did not permit either diagnostic or therapeutic contact with the older boy unless his mother referred him on her own initiative.

The intake worker raised the question of accepting Charles as a client during the diagnostic conference with the consulting psychiatrist, but the latter felt that this would be too threatening to the boys' mother at this time and that she might terminate the contact if this point were pressed. That risk may indeed have existed. It was not realized, however, that the decision not to try to take Charles into treatment exposed the chances of helping Harry also to serious risk. Actually the idea of taking Charles into treatment was completely abandoned, and the case, after four years of treatment, ended unsuccessfully.

Consideration should be given to the question of whether the psychodynamic and social constellation of the mother and the two boys would not have suggested other alternatives than those visualized in the decision not to treat Charles; namely, (1) treatment of the mother and both boys, (2) acceptance of the untreatability of the case as long as the mother's anxieties prevented the dynamically indicated range of patients, or (3) treatment of the mother alone until such time as she could accept the treatment need of both boys.

Of special importance for diagnostic and therapeutic consideration among the members of the *family of orientation* are also those persons who assume the role of parent substitutes. With regard to mother substitutes, we again quote Dr. Ackerman and Dr. Neubauer.

> In passing, it is desirable to mention the importance of working therapeutically with mother surrogates. In certain sections of middle-class society the maternal function is in actuality a shared responsibility. The cultural pattern is such that the maternal responsibility is not assumed exclusively by the real mother, but is shared with or delegated to auxiliary mother persons, the grandparent, the aunt, the governess, maid or teacher.[1]

In our society, with its tendency to open up wider and wider employment opportunities for women and its increasing divorce rate which forces more and more women to avail themselves of these opportunities,[2] the mother substitute becomes so frequent

---

[1] Ackerman and Neubauer, *op. cit.*, p. 90.

[2] Burgess, Ernest W., and Harvey J. Locke, *The Family:* From Institution to Companionship. American Book Co., New York, 1950, pp. 503-504, 514-515.

a social phenomenon that child guidance work which focuses only on the biological mother of the child appears somewhat unrelated to the times.

Similarly more attention might be paid by child guidance workers to the phenomenon that a broken family in our society is usually one in which the father is missing.[1] The void thus created may be filled by other male persons in the living environment of the child, such as grandfathers, uncles, and the male friends of the mother, particularly if they are regarded by her as potential husbands or at least integrated into her life on a more or less permanent basis without conscious contemplation of marriage.

The following cases are presented for purposes of illustrating the dynamic importance of such persons among the growth conditions of a child and of the practice changes which their involvement in the pathogenesis of his difficulties may suggest.

Johnny, age eight, was referred to the clinic because of disobedience at home, lack of friends, and poor adjustment in school. He had poor eating habits, nibbling between meals and gulping his food, and was overweight. He had many fears—of the lake or ocean, of a sharp turn on a highway while driving, of riding on elevated trains, of going up in an airplane, and of movies which involved crime or violence. He was also a nailbiter.

He and his mother, who had been deserted by her husband in the third month of pregnancy, lived with the maternal grandparents. The mother was employed as an office worker and the grandparents took care of Johnny while she was away from home. Actually the grandparents supported both mother and child so that the mother could use her income more or less for her own personal needs.

Johnny's mother was a rigid woman with paranoid tendencies, who felt extreme hostility toward the grandmother. At the same time she was unwilling to free herself from her dependence on both grandparents. To Johnny, she was punitive to the degree of cruelty and at the same time sexually seductive. Her sadistically disciplinary attitude toward him expressed itself, for instance, in handling one of his symptoms, vomiting, by rubbing his face in the vomit. On the other hand, she used to wake him in the morning by tickling him and con-

[1] Sutherland, Edwin H., *Principles of Criminology.* J. B. Lippincott Co., Philadelphia, 3d ed., 1939, p. 159. (This point has been omitted from later editions of this book.)

tinued to bathe him in spite of his age. Recently she had begun to share a bed with him.

She described Johnny's grandmother as overprotective, restricting and infantilizing the boy. Reports from the "Y" and the school, as well as the therapist's observations of her handling of Johnny in the waiting room when she brought him to the clinic confirmed the mother's statement that the boy's grandmother's behavior toward him was actually controlling and nagging. The grandmother insisted that his mother get after him about his homework. When he sat on his mother's lap, the grandmother made fun of him, but on the other hand, when his mother tried to get him to assume some responsibility for himself, or be helpful around the house, the grandmother protested that his mother was abusing him.

A very negative picture of Johnny's father, whom he had seen only a few times, was drawn by the grandparents. Although he knew about the separation of his parents, he told the neighborhood children that his father had been killed in the war. To his mother, however, he said that his father was mean, because he never visited or showed any interest in him.

The grandfather, whom Johnny's mother described as a very passive individual, disliked the boy, and the latter in turn expressed violent hostility toward his grandfather.

The consulting psychiatrist diagnosed the case as anxiety hysteria with phobias and conduct disturbances, and pointed out that to a great extent the boy's provocative, aggressive, and assaultive behavior represented a direct protest against the ego-inhibiting, infantilizing attitude of his grandmother. He also indicated that the grandfather of this socially fatherless boy failed to provide an adequate male figure with whom the boy could identify, and that as a result Johnny felt greatly threatened by the two powerful masculine women in the home. Finally, he interpreted that the seductive attitude of Johnny's mother had stimulated sexual tensions in her son beyond his threshold of tolerance, with the result that his phobic symptoms had to be invoked in an attempt to control these tensions.

Thus this was a three-generation family in which the oldest generation financially and functionally represented the top layer of the whole family structure. In this setting there were the following pathogenic influences at work, which in their constellation brought about the behavior difficulties of the boy. There was, first, the simultaneously seductive and punitive behavior of his mother, increasing his sexual stimulation as well as his hostility and, consequently, his anxiety beyond his repressive power. Second, there was the infantilizing and frustrating behavior of his grandmother; and third, the rejecting behavior of his grandfather, who was the only male figure in the boy's environment, but because of his attitude and affect tone was unable to furnish an appropriate figure of male identification for him.

The need for full psychodynamic information in terms of the situational approach certainly would have required diagnostic contact with the grandparents as well as with the mother. The power constellation in the structure of this child's family of orientation would have also required therapeutic work with the grandparents, directed at getting at least their cooperation in the treatment effort, if not a basic change in their behavior toward the child. Actually no effort was made in either direction. The diagnostic contacts were confined to the mother and the child, and so were the treatment efforts. The status of the grandmother in the structure of that family—although dynamically considered in the diagnostic evaluation of the case—was disregarded in the course of therapy and actually mismanaged. The grandmother, as a natural consequence of her function as mother substitute, was frequently called upon to escort the child to the clinic. To do so was necessary because of the mother's employment and the unusual difficulties which the worker had in getting volunteer services for this child. During the first year of treatment, the grandmother brought Johnny to the agency ten times. In every instance the worker met her in the waiting room but not once was she given an opportunity to feel part of the clinic contact, or to receive attention as the mother substitute of Johnny, which she actually was. Never was she asked a question about him. Never did it enter the therapist's perceptual grasp of the family situation that this woman was the most powerful person in the child's environment.

In other words, the family boss—and mother substitute—was treated by the therapist as a servant, who was permitted to bring the child to the clinic when nobody else was available but had to remain in the waiting room without ever being asked a single question about her opinion concerning, and her feelings toward, the child and the clinic. In contrast, it is agency practice to ask every volunteer who escorts a child to write reports about him and to give the volunteer a chance to work out his feelings with regard to the child in interviews with the professional staff.

Only after more than a year of treatment had elapsed, when the child's mother proved unable to go through with a placement plan for him because the grandmother opposed it, was an effort made to establish interview contact with her. By that time, however, it was too late. The grandmother paid the clinic back in kind. She refused to give her approval to the placement of Johnny, made his mother submit to her wishes in this matter, and treatment had to be terminated. Of course, it is possible that even an early contact with this grandmother would have failed to overcome her antagonism to the child's treatment at the clinic. However, the fact remains that no effort was made in the beginning to enlist her cooperation, and it should be stressed that nothing in the current practice of the clinic could have guided the therapist to perceive the need for, or even the desirability of, a contact with the mother substitute—in this case the grandmother—because this concept does not seem to be included in the theoretical framework underlying the agency's child guidance practice. Thus this case cannot be regarded as an instance of bad therapy, but must be understood as the normal reflection of agency emphasis. Involvement of the grandmother in the diagnostic or early therapeutic contact would have been pioneering, but not an expression of clinic practice.

A case which shows such pioneering, as well as the psychodynamic importance of an aunt in the pathogenesis of a child's difficulties, is the following:

> Lillian, a nine-year-old girl, was referred by her aunt, at the suggestion of the school, for disruptive behavior in the classroom, extreme restlessness, poor eating habits, general feelings of insecurity, and frequent temper tantrums. At the same time the child's father had made application at another district of the clinic.

Thus the nature of these referral sources indicated conspicuously the emotional absence of the mother from the concern area around the child. In spite of this, the normal pattern of agency practice with its focus on the mother asserted itself, as can be seen from the opening recording:

> The aunt explained to . . . the receptionist that the child's mother works and that she, the aunt, takes care of the girl during the day. She explained that the mother isn't well and goes to business in order to be away from the home. The receptionist told the aunt it would be necessary for us to see the child's mother, and she said she supposed the mother could take time off for an early morning appointment. However, at the same time, the aunt said that she felt she could handle this herself and seemed somewhat reluctant for us to see the mother. . . .
>
> Upon clearing this case with the central office, the receptionist of the district with which the aunt had established contact discovered that the X office was also clearing it. . . .
>
> The receptionist of X office called the father and told him of the aunt's having made application in the Y office. The father agreed to come to the Y office and said he would like to come in with the mother for an appointment.
>
> Wrote appointment letter to Mr. and Mrs. . . .

This handling of the aunt's and the father's referral contacts with the clinic shows tellingly the need for a broadening of the conceptual framework of agency practice by including the concept of the family of orientation. In spite of the initiative taken by this child's aunt, and her specific request to be interviewed, the receptionist insisted that the mother had to be seen, obviously unaware that this very move taken by the aunt marked her as an interesting and probably powerful factor among the child's living conditions, a person who should not be disregarded and certainly not antagonized. Similarly the father's approaching the clinic on behalf of his daughter did not give him access to the intake worker as a matter of course; he had to ask specifically to be interviewed together with the child's mother, who otherwise would have been invited alone, although she was apparently the only one who had not expressed an interest in the agency contact.

> Lillian's mother was a very immature and narcissistic person, who showed maladjustment especially in the area of marriage and motherhood. Having been a chronic truant from school in her own

childhood, and being obsessed by the fear that Lillian had inherited this tendency from her, she was very demanding and punitive toward Lillian in order to achieve a greater degree of conforming behavior from the child than she had exhibited herself. Eight months before the family had made the contact with the clinic, she had gone to work on a full-time basis and given the daytime care of her daughter to her younger sister, because she felt completely frustrated in her attempts to handle her.

The father was a rather perfectionistic type of person, who was preoccupied with the emotional disturbances of his wife and sought full compliance with his demands from his daughter. He had no real feelings of warmth for her and spent very little time with her. However, the child admired him greatly and longed for more attention from him.

The child's aunt, in whose house Lillian spent the hours after school, had only an intellectual understanding of her needs for warmth and attention. She had a little boy of her own, whom she naturally preferred to her sister's daughter. Beneath a surface of concern she was a cold person and was very scornful of her sister's inadequacies as a wife and mother. She aroused a high degree of hostility and suppressed aggression in Lillian, who envied her little cousin the love and attention he received.

Lillian's grandmother, who also occasionally assumed functions normally fulfilled by a child's mother, was hard in her criticism of the girl's behavior. The child felt the intense hostility which her grandmother had toward her and reciprocated emotionally. Because of unresolved oedipal conflicts, the child experienced her relationships with her mother, her grandmother, and her aunt in a period of considerable sexual confusion, and her aggression against these women took on a pronounced sexual tinge.

The diagnosis was behavior disorder, oedipal type. The disorder was explained as a reaction to the emotional starvation to which the child had been exposed by her parents, as well as by her aunt and grandmother, who had felt compelled to assume mother functions.

In contrast to the handling of the preceding case, the child's therapist, who was one of the consulting psychiatrists, had occasional contact with all members of the family of orientation. He never seemed to treat any one of them merely as a person who facilitated the transportation of Lillian to the clinic but had no claim to his attention. In his own closing summary the therapist stated his position in this respect as follows:

This therapist had occasional contacts with both parents, and with the maternal grandmother and aunt, which were fruitful in that they made him thoroughly familiar with the negative qualities in the child's environment even though these persons were unable to change significantly (with the exception of the mother in response to her own treatment) in consequence of these contacts.

It might be questioned whether these contacts actually did not prove of more than diagnostic and prognostic value to the therapist. He perhaps unconsciously, but apparently effectively, considered the status needs of the members of the child's family of orientation. Thus he kept the family positively related to the whole therapeutic process. The therapist's readiness to talk to them and his attempt to involve the father in treatment, at least by interpretation and advice, gave the entire family a feeling of worth which prevented them from becoming antagonistic to the agency and the treatment of the child.

Compared with the case of Johnny, where the grandmother was treated like a servant, this case reveals great strength of diagnostic and therapeutic procedure. It suggests that incorporation of the concept of the family of orientation in clinic practice would not only imply that persons other than the biological mother might have to be involved in the diagnostic and therapeutic contact. Apparently it would also imply that at least readiness for contact with these other family members might keep the emotional attitudes of all persons who are influential in his upbringing positively inclined toward the treatment of the child. This becomes increasingly important as the child in the course of treatment shows behavior changes which deprive the members of his family of the secondary gains they derived from caring for him previously.

CHAPTER THREE

Social Interaction and Therapy

AN EFFORT will be made in this chapter to show that concern with interpersonal relationships should be extended from diagnostic considerations of the past to diagnostic considerations of the future. Interpersonal relationships should be evaluated not only in terms of pathogenic conditions but also in terms of the total results which an attempt to change these conditions in the course of therapy may produce. In other words, interpersonal relationships not only appear as factors which may have created a need for treating a child and certain persons in his environment; they may change during the process of treatment in such a way as to present obstacles to the achievement or retention of therapeutic gains. On the other hand, these changes may open up resources for strengthening the therapeutic influence, which, if considered in the course of treatment, may accelerate the attainment of the treatment goal.

Dr. Ackerman and Dr. Neubauer have drawn attention to the negative aspects of this nexus of phenomena in their discussion of "Failures in the Psychotherapy of Children":

> Another frequent occurrence is that as a child improves in response to therapy, the parent becomes noticeably worse. One need not seek far for the explanation. Since the mother and child form a psychic unit, any change in the child's behavior mobilizes more anxiety in the mother and forces a shift in her usual defense pattern. As a means of combating this anxiety, the parent sometimes tends to sabotage the child's treatment.[1]

Dr. Mittelmann has reported similar observations in the course of treatment of partners to intimate relationships.[2] The impor-

By Otto Pollak in consultation with Bettina Lehnert

[1] Ackerman, Nathan W., and Peter B. Neubauer, "Failures in the Psychotherapy of Children," *Failures in Psychiatric Treatment*, edited by Paul H. Hoch. Grune and Stratton, New York, 1948, p. 89.

[2] Mittelmann, Bela, "Complementary Neurotic Reactions in Intimate Relationships," *Psychoanalytic Quarterly*, vol. 13, October, 1944, pp. 482–483.

tance of considering the possibility of such negative developments in therapeutic planning was pointed out by Anna Freud
as early as the 1920's.

> Where analysis of the child cannot be organically one with other
> living conditions, but like a foreign body is injected into other rela-
> tionships which are thereby disordered, one will probably create for
> the child more conflicts than treatment in the other direction will
> be able to dissolve.[1]

Thus therapists frequently have to contend with reaction on
the part of persons in the patient's environment which counter-
acts the treatment effort. Obviously such situations should be
avoided in the interest primarily of preventing a possible deterioration in the patient's condition but also of preventing un-
productive financial outlay for either the patient or the community. That they should be avoided as well in order to save
therapeutic time seems equally important, in view of the frequently unmet need for mental health services. This requires
supplementing the diagnostic understanding of the past by
a prognosis of the future. It involves a problem of prediction,
which extends beyond the behavior changes to be expected of the
patients to all persons with whom they have meaningful relationships. In that sense a *family* prognosis becomes necessary, and in
the case of patients old enough to have significant contact with
persons outside the family circle a *social* prognosis is required.
Such prognoses present another opportunity for constructively
bringing together psychoanalytically oriented psychiatry and
sociological theory. Psychoanalytic theory has indicated the importance of these phenomena and sociology has so conceptualized
them that their identification appears transferable from the level
of wisdom and experience to the level of theory and training.
Underlying all situations of unfavorable, as well as favorable,
reactions of family members, schoolteachers, and agemates to
the behavior changes of the client in treatment is the phenomenon
of *social interaction*, which presents a key concept of sociological

[1] Freud, Anna, *Introduction to the Technic of Child Analysis*. Nervous and Mental
Disease Publishing Co., New York, 1928, p. 56.

thought.[1] In a relatively recent formulation this concept has been defined as:

> *The reciprocal interplay of personalities within a given social environment,* keeping in mind the fact that this process is distinguished by the following characteristics, *viz.:*
> a. The unique background histories of the personalities involved. . . .
> b. The reciprocal effects upon personalities which this interaction produces;
> c. The anticipations and expectations which each interactive situation produces;
> d. The chief forms which interaction may take, i.e.:
> (1) Accommodation
> (2) Adjustment
> (3) Competition
> (4) Conflict[2]

To anyone acquainted with child guidance practice specifically and with psychotherapy in general it will occur immediately that the characteristics mentioned in the definition under *a*, *b*, and *d* constitute an essential part of the professional concern of the therapist. This, however, is not true for point *c*. Although the very setting of a treatment goal and the clinic's general concern with prevention are related to the future, the "anticipations and expectations which each interactive situation produces" are not always given sufficient consideration in therapeutic planning. This is particularly so with regard to its potentially negative aspects. Among the reasons are probably the following: Psychoanalytically trained therapists center their interest on the patient, believing that changes in him which produce increased conflict for his associates will lead the latter to seek help if they are inca-

[1] Simmel, Georg, "The Problem of Sociology," translated by Albion W. Small, *The American Journal of Sociology,* vol. 15, November, 1909, p. 296; Cooley, Charles Horton, *Social Process,* Charles Scribner's Sons, New York, 1918, pp. 8–9; Park, Robert E., and Ernest W. Burgess, *Introduction to the Science of Sociology,* University of Chicago Press, 1931, pp. 339–434; Waller, Willard, *The Family: A Dynamic Interpretation,* The Cordon Co., New York, 1938, 621 pp.; Lundberg, George A., *Foundations of Sociology,* The Macmillan Co., New York, 1939, p. 311; Bales, Robert F., "A Set of Categories for the Analysis of Small Group Interaction," *American Sociological Review,* vol. 15, April, 1950, pp. 257–263; Bernard, Jessie, "Where Is the Modern Sociology of Conflict?" *The American Journal of Sociology,* vol. 56, July, 1950, p. 11.

[2] Bloch, Herbert A., "A Synthetic View of the Social Individual as a Primary Datum in Sociology," *American Sociological Review,* vol. 8, October, 1943, p. 506.

pable of arriving at constructive readjustments by themselves. As a consequence such therapists are more concerned with curing the patient than with the problems that the process may create for the patient's associates. Thus they do not consider sufficiently the possibility that increased conflict for the patient's associates may not lead these persons to make constructive readjustments by themselves or to seek help but simply may produce negative social interaction between them and the person under treatment. Furthermore the idea that therapeutic gains can be counteracted from the outside may be a frustration of the narcissistic need of some individual therapists to succeed. Against this frustration they may defend themselves by disregard, a form of counter-transference. By stressing the future-oriented characteristics of social interaction resulting from behavior changes brought about in therapy, the concept might counteract these tendencies of disregard and become a useful tool both in therapeutic planning and in training therapists.

The importance of this concept for understanding the family has been demonstrated by Willard Waller, who based his whole analysis of that institution on the proposition, originally made by E. W. Burgess, that the family is "a unity of interacting personalities."[1] In Waller's formulation the behavior of each family member is "cause and effect in relation to the behavior" of other family members.[2]

To effect changes in the behavior of one member of a family, therefore, will not only incidentally but necessarily, and with regard to all members, change the interpersonal relationships in the family circle. Recognition of this generally valid phenomenon, if incorporated into the theoretical thinking underlying child guidance practice, might put treatment planning, as well as treatment results, on a less hazardous basis. It may thus become possible to avoid problem creation by problem solution.

The concept of social interaction may also serve to broaden the perceptual range of workers beyond the range of family reactions. The interplay of personalities, which is designated by this con-

[1] Burgess, E. W., "The Family as a Unity of Interacting Personalities," *The Family*, vol. 7, March, 1926, pp. 3–9.

[2] Waller, Willard, *op. cit.*, p. 16.

cept, takes place whenever an interchange of experience is operative.[1] Everybody with whom the child has meaningful contact will be affected and in turn affect the expression of personality change in the child.

Finally, this concept may prove helpful in clarifying the always important fact that the child and the persons in his environment will interact not only with one another but also with the therapist, both as a person and as a representative of the agency. As far as the relationship between therapist and patient is concerned, that would appear to be a statement of the obvious. It is one of the main foci of supervisory concern and is conceptualized in professional casework and psychoanalytic literature under the headings relationship, transference, and countertransference. With respect to members of the patient's family not included in the treatment, and teachers and other persons who may play a role in the life of the patient, however, social interaction between them and the therapist is not always clearly perceived. Allusion to this important aspect of human relations in therapy already has been made in Chapter 2, where the disregard of a powerful grandmother by one therapist was contrasted with the considerate treatment of an aunt by another.

Emphasis on the future-oriented aspects of the concept of social interaction may be helpful even in those cases in which the therapist is justified in expecting that the patient's associates will be led by an increase of conflict to seek help of their own accord or show manifestations of constructive readjustment. Treatment of a child and the appearance of behavior changes on his part may lead a parent, originally not accessible to treatment, to recognize that he may benefit by therapy himself. An increase in femininity on the part of a mother as a result of therapy may give her husband a chance to assert his own male role and thus enable him to furnish a more suitable object of identification for his son. Thus resources for strengthening the growth conditions in the environment of the child may open up as a result of initially treating only him. In the mental atmosphere of child guidance,

[1] Dawson, Carl A., and Warner E. Gettys, *An Introduction to Sociology*. The Ronald Press, New York, 1935, p. 205.

which continually sensitizes the perception of the workers to liabilities rather than to assets among the developmental determinants surrounding the child, this aspect of social interaction deserves emphasis. It can help the worker perceive readiness for treatment on the part of family members who formerly may have been inaccessible; also it may make them aware of developmental resources outside the worker-patient relationship which may be utilized for bolstering therapeutic experiences.

A further contribution potential of the concept of social interaction may lie in the direction it may give to planful selection of the patient. If, for instance, in a family constellation both parents have personality difficulties, it may happen that one shows promise to react positively to the improvement of his spouse and child, and the other to react negatively. An assessment of their probable future interaction along such lines could provide a basis for deciding which one, besides the child, should be taken into treatment.

Negative social interaction between family members and the patient in the course of therapy may express itself, first of all, in their reactions to an increase in his aggressiveness. Since such an increase usually accompanies the release of formerly suppressed hostility, the reactions of family members to this concomitant of therapy frequently present a problem of management. The case of Robert discussed below illustrates how such reactions may disturb the home environment while the worker is trying to help the patient overcome a specific symptom. This case is believed to have particular demonstrative value because Robert's presenting symptom was stuttering and because patients who stutter frequently act out tremendous aggression at home while their main symptom under the impact of treatment gradually disappears. Consideration in the therapeutic planning of the possible consequences of such a development may suggest that the parents might not be able to tolerate it unless they are included in the treatment process, and perhaps not even then.

At the suggestion of a speech clinic Robert, age fourteen years and six months, was referred to the child guidance clinic by his step-mother. He stuttered severely, this symptom being accompanied by facial contortions and eye blinking. He was very arrogant and stubborn, showed no respect for adults, had temper tantrums, ate excessively, was overweight, did not work up to capacity in school, was not interested in his personal appearance or hygiene, and spent hours just lying on his bed or sleeping in the afternoon. He liked to be alone and had no friends. Robert's mother had died when he was eleven, and his father had remarried a year later.

The stepmother appeared to be an extremely domineering and hostile woman. It seemed that she had some unconscious seductive feelings for Robert, and that part of her controlling attitude might have been an attempt to deny her own libidinal wishes toward him. Although treatment of the stepmother was not discussed with her at intake and was felt not to be desirable by the intake worker, the boy's therapist later suggested assigning her to another worker. However, this was not possible because none was available. As to the father, who was also seen at intake and whose treatment was suggested by the intake worker, the boy's therapist, who saw him once, felt that he needed treatment much less than his highly tense and neurotic wife. Consequently neither the mother nor the father was taken into treatment.

While the boy had been provocative with his stepmother before treatment began, his behavior had not been seriously threatening to her and had not expressed itself in physical, aggressive action. During treatment the therapist allowed the boy to express many hostile feelings, verbally and through play material, without showing any negative countertransference toward him. From his stepmother, however, he encountered tremendous hostility when his aggressiveness began to increase at home. Also she constantly tried to frustrate his wishes, particularly on the oral level, by not buying him the special things to eat which he wanted. He eventually became physically violent at times, throwing his stepmother's wrist watch on the floor or threatening to throw a chair at her. When weeks of silence followed such a scene and the stepmother called the boy's worker, all the latter could do was to try to explain the boy's behavior to her on the telephone. To arrange an appointment for her with the boy's therapist seemed undesirable at the time because Robert had shown feelings against this, and disregard of them might have interfered with the treatment relationship.

As the treatment progressed, the boy's stuttering lessened appreciably and even disappeared for a period of several weeks. Interestingly enough, just at this turn of the treatment process, the mother felt the need to telephone the worker again, making new complaints about Robert. She said she was at her wits' end and feared she would have a mental breakdown like her own mother, because she could not tolerate the boy's aggression any longer. At this point the therapist explained to the mother anew that the gradual disappearance of Robert's stuttering could only be brought about by a release of his tremendous aggression. He was being helped to gain such a release in the treatment, and the resulting behavior changes at home were only temporary. The therapist also promised the mother to give her and her husband an appointment as soon as Robert's resistance to this could be worked out.

The social interaction between the stepmother and child in this case appeared to be an effect of his gradual maturation resulting from the treatment process. Robert's aggressiveness, except for its physical expression, took on more adult manifestations which his stepmother could bear even less well than its previous childish and neurotic forms. His self-assertion and overt expression of hostility taxed her frustration tolerance even more than his former stuttering, overeating, laziness, and neglect of his personal appearance. Consideration of the possibility of such a development might have suggested the need for preparing the parents for the boy's probable increase in overt aggressiveness and for evaluating the flexibility of the home environment in relation to expected behavior changes. Consequently a decision as to whether concurrent treatment of the stepmother should be arranged or the case refused for treatment altogether ought to have been made part of the therapeutic planning. The latter decision might have been indicated because of worker shortage or poor prospects of treating the stepmother successfully. As this situation was permitted to develop, however, therapeutic efforts were invested and at the same time the boy's chances of retaining his therapeutic gains potentially lessened.

The following case shows the deterioration of a parent not as a result of his child's temporary increase of behavior difficulties during treatment but as a result of definite personality gains which the child achieved in therapy. It is presented here in order to dispel the notion that social interaction in its negative aspects may exist only as a temporary concomitant of unfinished therapy. The case of Ruth shows that the trust of a worker in completed therapy as a necessary resolvent of all difficulties developed during treatment may be unfounded. In this situation the father deteriorated the more his child improved, his negative reaction to her therapeutic gains reaching its height at the time when she no longer needed treatment.

Ruth was referred to the child guidance clinic at the age of six and one-half because she could not get along with other children, was lethargic, and took punishment and denial from her mother without resistance. This represented a complete change from the hyperactive and aggressive behavior which she had previously exhibited. The change came about when her mother gave birth to a baby boy. On that occasion Ruth was sent to camp because the mother, faced with the care of an infant, felt she would be unable to cope with her during the first weeks after the baby's birth. There was also trouble in school, where the child did not conform; she demanded special attention constantly from the teacher and misbehaved when it was not given.

Ruth's mother had always felt unloved and inadequate, particularly in comparison with her sisters. She was subject to depressive moods, which for a time had incapacitated her to a very high degree. During one of these, she had found it impossible to get out of bed before noon, letting Ruth go without any breakfast each morning. At that time the child was about two years old.

The father was also a much disturbed person, who experienced recurrent difficulties in keeping jobs, tended to be negativistic, and had many problems centering around food. A great deal of marital friction existed between the parents, who were sexually incompatible. The mother felt that her husband would not have married her if she had not become pregnant with Ruth, that he had never had any love for her, and might still abandon her.

The consulting psychiatrist diagnosed Ruth's condition as primary behavior disorder and recommended that treatment consist in helping her understand and express her feelings, particularly in relationship to the worker. No definite diagnosis was reached regarding the mother, but treatment was undertaken, first at the agency and later by a psychiatrist, simultaneously with the treatment of the child.

Ruth improved relatively quickly and was able to maintain and increase her therapeutic gains. At the end of treatment the range of improvement extended over the following areas: She got along exceedingly well with other children, had developed what appeared to be real affection for her young brother, had stopped being demanding and lethargic at home, and behaved well in school. Significant also was the fact that although her difficulties had become apparent in connection with a camp experience in the summer before referral, two camp experiences arranged by the agency in the second and third years of treatment proved successful.

Toward the end of treatment Ruth herself spoke of the gains which she had made in therapy, telling the worker that she remembered when she had been seen by the psychiatrist. At that time she used to throw things around, mark up the walls of the clinic, and quarrel with everyone. Now she did not do these things and people liked her more. Ruth's mother also showed therapeutic gains. Her relationship with Ruth had improved more than she had ever anticipated and for the first time she was experiencing the feeling of having some things under control. Thus in relation to members of the family who had received therapeutic help the case had the appearance of success. The child's father, however, reacted definitely unfavorably to the gains made by his wife and daughter.

The first change in his behavior after Ruth had been taken into treatment revealed itself in uncontrolled physical punishment of the child. As the treatment proceeded and Ruth improved, he became increasingly depressed and his financial situation, which had always been tenuous, became worse. When treatment was tapering off, the mother reported that he yelled and screamed at Ruth, and seemed to make her the butt of his aggression. She said, however, that Ruth seemed to bear up exceedingly well under this stress at home and that she also had been able to adjust to a very difficult teacher in school. Thus in view of the child's development of adaptive capacities, the case was closed.

Since in this case the father was never interviewed, a full explanation of his reactive behavior to the treatment gains made by Ruth and his wife cannot be attempted. It appears significant, however, that his disturbance increased in violence and concentrated on Ruth as the receiver of his aggression. This suggests that her difficulties had satisfied some unconscious emotional need on his part and that, deprived of this as a result of her treatment, he became increasingly disturbed. At any rate consideration of social interaction in formulating the treatment plan might have made it appear desirable to evaluate beforehand whether so disturbed a father could, without help, react positively to successful treatment of his child and wife. By planning help for this father one might perhaps have avoided what actually happened—his deterioration and the exposure of the successfully treated child to his channelized and intensified aggression.

Social interaction which may interfere with the achievement of the treatment goal or the retention of therapeutic gains can occur also between the patient and persons who are not members of his family. This deserves particular attention because of the emphasis which psychoanalytically oriented therapy rightly puts on family relationships. However, workers should not feel that they should exclude persons other than family members from the therapeutic contact. That such exclusions do occur even in cases where social interaction between nonfamily members and the patient may be of greatest importance for the development of the therapeutic process is illustrated by an incident in the course of treatment of Deborah.

Deborah, sixteen and one-half years old, and an only child, was referred to the clinic by her school counselor because of difficulties experienced at school and at home. She had lost interest in her appearance, had begun to truant, and had stopped working to capacity in school. She had periods of depression and the school counselor indicated that she had problems relating to her father but seemed unable to talk about them.

In her first contact with the intake worker Deborah talked in very positive terms about her mother and sister, but failed to mention her father. When questioned about this omission, her eyes filled with tears and she stated that once he had done something terrible to her but she could not talk about it. In the course of further contacts, Deborah was able to tell the worker that her father had attempted to have relations with her when she was about thirteen and that she had concealed this from her mother for some time.

Although Deborah first said that she had no understanding of what was happening to her, she revealed later that she had been seductive to her father and had become extremely guilt-ridden when he had responded. As a consequence she refused to have anything further to do with him, withdrew from the home, and fell in with a number of girls who were not interested in school, were wearing heavy makeup and loud dresses, and were hanging around boys' clubs and street corners.

In one of these clubs she met a boy named Francis, to whom she became attached. Her parents, however, objected to him for several reasons. He was not Jewish; he had a sister in prison; and there was much illness in his family. When Deborah was fourteen, Francis joined the United States Merchant Marine and after his departure she became friendly with Morton, a promising young salesman, who wanted to marry her and was more acceptable to her family. However, she did not forget Francis, who occasionally wrote to her and visited her.

During the initial phases of the treatment Deborah thought that she would marry Morton, with whom she had been going out for two years. She had told him about the incident with her father and he had insisted that she tell her mother about it. He indicated his abhorrence, but still wanted to marry her.

During most of the treatment, which continued for more than a year, Deborah vacillated in her emotions between the two boys, partly because of the exploration of her feelings with the worker and partly because Francis had renewed his interest in her. As her psychological mechanisms and related experience became clearer, it appeared that Francis, although generally engaging in sexual experiences with girls, had always respected Deborah. On the other hand, it appeared that she had had a physical relationship with Morton for some time and that this relationship had been encouraged by her parents.

The psychodynamic interpretation given by the consulting psychiatrist was that these two boys represented to Deborah a split father ego image. His penetrating analysis showed that, although the social backgrounds of the two boys would have suggested the opposite, it was actually Francis who, not having had sexual relations with her, played the role of the superego part of the father, while Morton, who had had relations with her and had continually attempted to bring home to her the incident with her father, thus counteracting her repressive tendency, played the role of the incestuous father.

In view of this situation it seemed questionable whether Deborah was ready to marry anyone at that time. The purpose of the treatment was to help her work out her difficulties before taking such a step. However, after the summer vacation, which followed the first year of treatment, the mother informed the agency that Deborah was about to marry Morton and the case was closed.

In the course of Deborah's treatment an incident occurred which illustrates the importance of extending therapeutic consideration of the phenomenon of social interaction beyond the members of the family circle. At a time when Deborah still thought that she was going to marry Morton, the therapist asked her why in all the discussions of her fiancé she had never mentioned being in love with him. She did so in order to help the girl become aware of her ambivalence toward Morton. A short time later Deborah met Francis, who had been released from the Merchant Marine. Probably under the impact of these circumstances, Deborah suddenly realized that she did not want to marry Morton and told him so. Morton became much disturbed and, knowing about her contact with the agency, telephoned Deborah's worker, asking in great excitement for an appointment in terms of help for himself. Probably involved in strong countertransference and supported in its expression by stereotyped practice, the worker failed to sense the phenomenon of social interaction operating here and refused to see Morton. She recorded her process of thinking as follows:

> It was necessary for the worker to deny Morton the possibility of seeing her, not only on the basis of the inadvisability of involving the boy in treatment here, but also because of his tendency to dominate the complete home situation, which continued to reveal itself as extremely pathological.

It must be questioned on what basis Morton's contact with the clinic could have appeared inadvisable. The worker knew about Deborah's telling Morton that she had decided not to marry him. She also knew that Morton was extremely upset. Moreover, because of the close relationship between him and Deborah, his reactions to her decision were certainly of importance. Especially since the worker felt that he was not the right husband for Deborah and that the girl was not yet ready for marriage with anyone, everything pointed to the desirability of seeing the boy and helping him along lines conducive to the therapeutic plan. If, in order to keep the therapeutic relationship between herself and Deborah undisturbed, the worker felt that it was not advisable for her to see Morton, she should have arranged for his being seen by another worker. By refusing his request for an appointment altogether she antagonized him and created an enemy, whose importance to the outcome of the case, as later events proved, should not have been underestimated. Actually Deborah yielded to his pursuit and finally decided to marry him.

Also consideration should be given to the question whether tendencies to dominate on the part of a person connected with the life situation of a client are a reason for denying his request to be seen. Assuming that the dominance pattern of such a person is a negative influence, one might well wonder what reaction the denial of his request would produce. It would seem reasonable to suppose that it would increase his desire to dominate and thus add to the difficulties which his behavior tendencies present in the patient's life. In addition, it might turn these attitudes toward the agency and thus against the success of the therapy being attempted.

The cases discussed so far have illustrated social interaction primarily, although not exclusively, between persons in the living environment of the patient and the latter himself. The case material now presented will demonstrate the existence and therapeutic implications of this phenomenon between such persons and the agency. Parents, siblings, mother substitutes, friends, and teachers interact not only with the patient, but also with the representatives of the agency with whom they come in contact. If the workers create negative interaction between these persons and the agency, the patient's chances of getting therapeutic help or of retaining therapeutic gains may be seriously impaired. If they create positive interaction, additional resources for improving the patient's growth conditions may be activated and his general environmental atmosphere made favorable to the treatment experience.

The cases of Freddy and Phil, presented below, show negative social interaction or loss of opportunities to create positive social interaction between fathers of patients and the clinic. Their illustrative value is considered of particular importance because the behavior of workers in handling father contacts may more frequently have a reinforcing effect upon pathogenic conditions and obstacles to therapeutic developments than their contacts with persons outside the parental circle.

In many instances an outstanding phenomenon among the factors interfering with the growth process of a boy is a certain dominance and masculinity pattern in the personality of his mother. If in such a situation the child's father makes the referral and is neglected in the diagnostic or treatment procedure, the clinic, which is usually represented by a female worker, assumes the role of an extension of the dominant wife and mother. The clinic in essence does what the mother has done. It prevents the father from becoming a proper object of masculine identification for the boy. If the father has ego strength, he will become antagonistic to the clinic and use such strength to defeat the therapeutic effort; if he is so weak that he takes such an experience without reacting unfavorably, he will become constantly weaker and less able to be an object of masculine identification for the patient. Moreover, he may be prevented from utilizing help which he himself might need. The case of Freddy illustrates this particular situation.

> Freddy, age eleven, was referred to the agency by his father on suggestion of a counselor at a "Y" because of excessive daydreaming both at school and at home, disrupting the classroom routine by singing or whistling under his breath, and because of inability to play with other children. Another symptom elicited in intake was excessive sensitivity to reprimands, which manifested itself in spasmodic coughing and crying.

The disregard of the father's role in the referral can be seen from the following recording:

> Referred by: Father in office through counselor. . . .
> Problem: Excessive daydreaming. . . .
> Telephone call to Mrs. X making an appointment for. . . .
> Mr. and Mrs. X in office. In view of the fact that I thought it advisable to see the parents individually, I suggested to Mr. X that I would see him later, in about an hour, and see Mrs. X first. I had expected Mr. X to wait but Mrs. X instead turned to him, suggesting that he go back to the store and remarking that he would be able to see me after she had returned. I noticed that Mr. X scowled and when I suggested my interest in seeing him later, he nodded curtly and without a word left the office.

Before discussing the psychodynamic implications of this handling of the father contact, let us say that he never visited the agency again and that during the whole course of the treatment no effort was made to see him.

One might question whether the very fact that the intake worker invited only the mother, although the referral was made by the father, was not bound to start negative feelings on his part toward the clinic. At any rate he appeared with his wife to discuss his child's problems. However, whatever desire he still might have had to perform his father function in concert with the agency and to express his father concern in this matter to the worker was doomed to another frustration. Instead of inviting both parents to come into her office, the worker disregarded the fact that the father had taken the initiative in referral and his need for recognition by asking to see the mother first. The mother in turn used this opportunity to exert her dominance pattern by sending the father away and asking him to come back later. The record does not indicate what took place between the parents after the mother came from the interview, but the father did not go to the clinic again. By permitting this to happen the worker lost an opportunity to cultivate a resource of desirable influence on the growth conditions of the boy and to make the father accessible to therapeutic help, which he later needed.

In the diagnostic investigation of this case it became clear that Freddy's mother was a very domineering woman, who managed a business in which she had the controlling interest. Her husband and brother worked in that enterprise also, the husband as an employe and the brother as a junior partner. Freddy suffered from rejection by his mother and, like his father, was prevented by her from expressing his masculinity. Because of his mother's dominating and threatening him, he had developed a tendency to turn his aggressive tendencies upon himself in the form of daydreaming, phobic fears, and proneness to accident.

Thus Freddy needed support in expressing socially acceptable aggressiveness. That the father might have provided a resource for this should have been apparent from the fact that he took the initiative in the referral. It might also have been recognized later when he took an active interest in Freddy's Boy Scout activities, in which under the influence of therapy Freddy had become able to participate. The father took the scouts in his truck to outings and helped his son achieve derived status by establishing himself almost as an associate leader of the group. This suggests that with encouragement from the agency he might also in other respects have been able to help the boy express his masculine drives but that possibility was never explored.

In addition to not using the father as a treatment resource, the worker by rejecting him made it impossible for him to get therapeutic help when he was under great stress.

> At a later stage of the treatment process his wife bought out her brother's share of the business. Under the impact of this event, which to him was threatening, the father suffered attacks of gastroenteritis, diarrhea, vomiting, and so on, which were diagnosed by his doctor as of a psychogenic nature.

That the development of such anxiety disturbances in reaction to the step taken by Freddy's mother did not make him a more adequate father figure for a son, who was already suffering from anxiety conditions caused by his mother, requires no elaboration. Nothing, however, could be done then by the worker to help, because the opportunity of establishing a contact and of creating in the father a feeling that in the clinic he would find recognition and understanding was lost.

Negative social interaction between father and agency, however, can also arise from the fact that failure to establish direct contact with him may permit a mother to give her husband the impression that he is disregarded and even disapproved of by the clinic. This occurred in the case of Phil.

> Phil was referred at the age of seven because of enuresis. His father telephoned to arrange an early appointment for Phil's mother and the child. No effort was made by the clinic to see the child's father until two months after the treatment had begun, when he began to question the treatment and objected to paying the fee. The psychiatrist, who was consulted because of the worker's concern over the father's interference, pointed out that such interference could have been anticipated as a result of the worker's failure to draw him into contact with the clinic. In effect this indicated that the clinic disregarded him as the father of the child and that the mother and the clinic would assume entire responsibility for the boy. Inasmuch as it was the father who had insisted upon the child's coming into treatment, and had been eager to shorten the waiting period, he should have been made part of the contact. The psychiatrist predicted that as long as this was not done, the mother would continue doing what

she had begun to do, namely, to exploit anything the worker said, turning it against her husband and thus making him antagonistic to the clinic.

As a result of this psychiatric consultation, the father was seen by another worker. After some initial show of antagonism, the father was able to receive the interpretation given him of the probably temporary nature of the behavior changes in his son and wife which had given him concern. During the interview he became increasingly more accepting of the services of the clinic. Yet no permanent contact with him was established, partly because he did not show any interest in receiving therapy and partly because of a shortage of workers.

Soon after this interview, Mrs. X began again to report that her husband questioned the value of the treatment. Material which she produced in this connection, however, indicated that she did what the consulting psychiatrist had predicted. Wanting to convince her husband of the desirability of their having another child, she used the agency as a club, indicating that the worker agreed with her. When the father was seen again, he appeared full of resentment and reported among other complaints that his wife had told him that her worker had suggested they should give Phil up for adoption. Learning that no such suggestion had been made, he was tremendously relieved and again reacted positively to an interpretation of the therapeutic work done with his son and wife.

This case shows clearly how negative social interaction between a family member of the patient and the agency can be produced by the patient's abuse of the lack of contact between that family member and the agency. If this situation had not been clarified, the father's antagonism might have combined with the resistance of the mother to break up the treatment process. Such occurrences suggest that periodic contacts with fathers might prove to be a valuable practice even when the occasion does not specifically demand it.

Actually there can be little doubt that interaction between the patient in treatment and all meaningful persons in his life circle will be better predicted and perceived if the therapist establishes some kind of observational contact with these persons directly or through volunteers.

CHAPTER FOUR

Extrafamilial Influences in Pathogenesis

BEYOND the family is the world. This fact parents, educators, and therapists have increasingly realized as essential to the progressive development of the child. While the family is a very important foundation, ultimately one's life-sphere is extended beyond the family by gradual stages in an ever-widening circle. As important as harmony in the family is, adequate adaptation to the total social setting constitutes true mental health.

It is inevitable and natural that the child's first interests and preoccupations should be centered around himself, which Freud designated as the "ego-libido," or narcissism. But in the orderly development of his personality he becomes aware of the importance of other persons in his life and in his survival. His interests and preoccupations are therefore directed toward them and the libido becomes in part attached to other objects. This is designated as "object-libido," which forms the basis for all sound human relations.

At first these objects are members of the immediate circle, the family, but as the child matures and his perceptions increase and his field of awareness widens, individuals other than members of the family become important. Among these are other relatives, playmates, schoolmates, friends, and later professional, political, special interest, and other numerous chance or permanent, perfunctory or profound relationships. Loyalties and attachments can center upon persons, interests, ideas, and ideals beyond the confines of locality and even nation. Development in these areas of intellectual and emotional attachments and interests may continue or may have already reached a point of comparative stability at a certain age.

By S. R. SLAVSON

This change from inward to outward interests, from preoccupation with self to concern with outer realities, can be described as the *centrifugal* movement of the libido, as contrasted with its earlier *centripetal* direction, when the infant was the center of his own attachment. This outward movement begins in the pre-oedipal stage but one of its high points occurs after the oedipal stage and during latency. If he has worked out adequately his relationship with his parents, both as individuals and as a couple, the child can now partially repress his sexual drives and some of his energies (libido) are transmuted into nonsexual interests and social channels. To the extent to which the oedipal conflict has not been resolved, to that degree social adaptations are inadequate. Discussing the process from an environmental point of view, Kurt Lewin formulates it as follows:

> In child psychology . . . the same physical environment must be quite differently characterized according to the ego, the individual character, and the momentary condition of the child. The "life-space" of the infant is extremely small and undifferentiated. This is just as true of its perceptual as of its effective space. . . . With the gradual extension and differentiation of the child's life-space, a larger environment and essentially different facts acquire psychological existence, and this is true also with respect to dynamic factors. The child learns in increasing degree to "control" the environment. At the same time—and no less important—it becomes psychologically *dependent* upon a growing circle of environmental events.[1]

Since biological survival in modern society no longer holds the risks and dangers of past ages, man's preoccupation is now predominantly with his social survival or acquisition of status and of group acceptance. Failures in these respects are a source of great anxiety. It is becoming increasingly more evident that survival is not entirely the individual's struggle for existence. It is achieved rather by the group and through the group. In fact, the higher the scale of evolutionary development, the greater is the importance of the group. Protection against danger and the creation of a milieu essential to survival are the product of the group as a

[1] Lewin, Kurt, "Environmental Forces," in *A Handbook of Child Psychology*, edited by Carl Murchison. Clark University Press, Worcester, Mass., 1933, pp. 594–595.

whole rather than a single individual. This is particularly characteristic of man. Individual survival is to an unalterable extent
group survival and individual human existence is irrevocably
intertwined with the existence of the group. Moreover, the more
democratic a society is, the more is individual achievement a
reflection of the vigor, strength, and prosperity of the group as a
whole. The individual can achieve the full fruition of his powers
in our society only by adapting himself to various groups, each
having its special significance in his development and in satisfactory social functioning.

Elsewhere[1] I have described these various groups as the family,
nursery and play groups, school, one-sex groups, heterosexual
groups, occupational groups, adult voluntary groups, and the
family in which one becomes the parent. Successful experience
in each of these groups has a major contribution to make to
the growth process of the individual. Among the major contributions of the family to the child, although by no means the only
one, is a feeling of acceptance and unconditional love. The contribution of the play group consists in providing an opportunity
for social experimentation of a wider scope and content than the
home. The school follows in order of the progressive phases of
development and meets the child's needs for creative expression
and mastery. The chief value of the voluntary one-sex group in
the period of latency and puberty is identification, an increased
acceptance of one's own biological destiny, and acquiring the
ability to conform to the demands of that destiny. In late adolescence and early adulthood the heterosexual peer group replaces
the one-sex group and serves to prepare the individual for heterosexual adjustment. At this stage the individual becomes concerned about gainful work as a preparation, psychologically and
materially to discharge adequately the functions of parent and
member of adult society. Through the occupational groups one
experiences that measure of socioeconomic adequacy which in
our society is a *sine qua non* for the socially well-adjusted man, and
with increasing frequency also for a socially well-adjusted woman.

[1] Slavson, S. R., "The Group in Development and Therapy," *Proceedings of the National Conference of Social Work, 1938*, pp. 334-343.

In an adult voluntary group an individual gains further assurance of his social adequacy. In discussing this topic Cooley has the following to say:

> By primary groups I mean those characterized by intimate face-to-face association and cooperation. They are primary in several senses, but chiefly in that they are fundamental in forming the social nature and ideals of the individual. The result of intimate association, psychologically, is a certain fusion of individualities in a common whole, so that one's very self, for many purposes at least, is the common life and purpose of the group.[1]

Failure in these groups may frequently lead to subsequent failure in one's total adjustment. Failure in one's family may lead to failure in school and later in recreational and occupational groups, as well as in the family in which one becomes the parent. Such failure is likely to interfere with the development of a healthy self-image; it tends to engender feelings of inadequacy, to undermine wholesome self-esteem, and to result in general depression. Feelings of inadequacy lead to socially unacceptable reactions and emotional maladjustment. Clinical experience suggests the great extent to which failure in the family begets fantasies of being unworthy of love and of enjoying advantages in life, that may result in many character problems. Another area of social failure is that in relation to siblings, where a brother or sister is either, for some reason, preferred by the parents or is more successful. This, too, may give rise in turn to feelings of inadequacy and insecurity, which are accompanied by either strong self-effacing trends or aggressive behavior. A case in point is that of Steven.

> Steven, an eleven-and-one-half-year-old boy, was referred by the school because he disturbed the classroom routine. He was unstable, uncooperative, and belonged to a neighborhood gang, the members of which had frequently committed small thefts. Steven once took his teacher's purse, but returned it. There were also some stealing incidents at home. Other symptoms were dawdling, thumb sucking, nailbiting and strong feelings of guilt, expressed in repeated state-

[1] Cooley, Charles Horton, *Social Organization*. Charles Scribner's Sons, New York, 1909, p. 23.

ments that he was "bad." The mother expressed considerable concern about Steven's friends.

The mother was overprotective, and, because of her own low status, expected from her son high achievements. When he failed to come up to her standards, she nagged him. The father was openly hostile and punitive to the boy, and both parents seemed to prefer his five-year-older sister, who in turn disliked Steven. The boy slept in the room with his sister and seemed sexually overstimulated and preoccupied with matters pertaining to sex. Later Steven gave up stealing but began to use profane language with a sexual content, in which he freely indulged both in school and in the home.

Steven is a child whose relations in the home caused tensions which he could not master. Because he was not accepted at home he sought such acceptance from his agemates on their own level. This also served to express his retaliatory impulses against his family. The association with a gang of boys who engaged in thefts and profanity, the response of his schoolmates to his "showing off," coupled with the sexual overstimulation at home, culminated in his behavior difficulties.

The social import of the school in our present society is of such a nature that it becomes as exaggerated in the eyes of the child as it is with adults. However, there are realistic bases for the fear and anxiety attached to school failure. In school the child is placed on probation. His parents, relatives, teachers, and other children expect him to make good in terms of the standards set. If he fails, he is considered inadequate and different from others in his age group. This constitutes a true failure which overshadows all others, for by his own standards he has proved himself inadequate, and his self-esteem is damaged as a result. This serious failure in his real and most important peer culture often gives rise to types of reactive behavior patterns that may serve as an escape from the situation, or as a means of preventing or diminishing anxiety, or of retaliating against the persons whom he sees as the cause of this failure.

The school pressures are such that the more timid children react by withdrawal and repress their hostilities, only to act them out in their social milieu or against themselves. The less diffident act out against the school itself. Whatever the response, the school, instead of mitigating the child's problems and reducing tension under which he lives, frequently adds to his difficulties.

In this connection the conclusion drawn from a statistical study of the adjustment of fifth- and sixth-grade pupils in the public schools of a city in central New York State is significant. The pupils were studied with regard to three factors: family disorganization, school situation, and behavior.

> Undesirable behavior is most likely to appear . . . among children who are unfavorably situated both in home and school. The data suggest that a *relationship exists between the child's behavior and both his home and school situations.*

The findings of a similar study, which was made of a group of 114 children who had appeared in children's courts on delinquency petitions following a 1946 survey of 5,299 children in grades three through eight, revealed that:

> . . . 67 per cent of the delinquents were from unfavorable home situations and that 51 per cent were from unfavorable school situations. One third of the delinquents had been in adverse settings both in home and school. Only 17 per cent were not affected by handicaps either in home or school. This finding tends to confirm the concept that the basic causes of delinquency lie in unintelligent practices in the school as well as in the home.
>
> These data on the relative influences of home and school on children's behavior are encouraging from the point of view of delinquency reduction. They suggest the desirability of strengthening our schools so as to provide havens of security wherein children can develop emotionally as well as intellectually. The data are encouraging because it is *relatively* easy to improve a school whereas the improvement of family life is a very difficult and complex task.[1]

Failure and anxiety about failure in school is in many instances the last straw that leads a child to the path of social maladjustment. Children who otherwise could carry the emotional tensions to which they are subjected in the home and to which they have adapted themselves as they grew older break down in the face of school failure. Here they are directly pitted against others

[1] Clarke, Daniel P., and Dorothy Gray, "School Surveys and Delinquency Prediction," *Journal of Educational Sociology*, vol. 24, September, 1950, pp. 21–23.

in a competitive relation where they have to make optimum effort and where failure always stares them in the face. It is understandable that children who have been exposed to emotional stress would have lower reserves to meet the school's intellectual demands. The drain on their ego strength impedes intellectual activity and alertness. In a state of tension and conflict the availability of psychic energies for intellectual pursuits as well as for social relations is of necessity limited. It is equally evident that a child reared in an unfavorable emotional setting needs release in appropriate aggressive and creative effort with as little restriction, as few demands, and as little threat of failure as is compatible with orderly social living. Being placed in an artificial, heterogeneous group in a setting of physical confinement and restrictions, with fear of failure and of being rejected, further increases tension and the psychic instability of the child who already labors under many difficulties.

Saul, age eleven, was referred to the agency by the school because he could not get along with children. He was a fat, blond boy with a continual grin on his face, who had sustained some birth injuries to his arm and left eye. The eye had been operated upon twice and a third operation was recommended. Although the eye was opened after the second operation, a heavy and droopy appearance in the eyelid remained (ptosis). On a purely physiological basis the boy was therefore handicapped in attaining a satisfactory self-image and acceptance by others.

The parents were tired people in their fifties, who were unresponsive to the child's demands. They had four children besides Saul. He had been conceived by the mother relatively late in life upon recommendation of her doctor. The siblings were all adults.

In school the children picked on Saul, called him names, and derided his appearance. He was not able to defend himself, but in turn was demanding and provocative, egotistical and intolerant. He complained that he always came in contact with "tough kids," while he was interested only in intellectual things.

After a period of activity group therapy and two summers in a therapeutic camp, Saul got along with children, accepted their teasing calmly, which subsided as a result, and when attacked was able to defend himself at least verbally.

*   *   *   *   *

Alfred, ten years old, was referred by the mother because he was difficult to handle at home and in school. He seemed nervous and sensitive and felt that nobody loved him. In school he did not pay attention and seemed always to be distracted. He daydreamed a great deal and did not get along with children. For the most part all he could do was to watch other children at play. When he did play, he ordered his playmates around and demanded that they do his bidding. The mother stated that the father did not really accept the child, ridiculed him, and was derisive toward him. Also in the neighborhood Alfred was rejected and beaten by children who would gang up on him, but despite this the boy expressed a great desire to have friends. He gave the impression of being fearful and lonely.

After two years in activity group therapy, Alfred was reported as having made a "remarkable improvement." He was able to mix readily with other children, engaged in some roughhouse activities, and showed improvement in the home as well. He later joined the Boy Scouts and seemed to be making a good adjustment there. He no longer got into conflict with children in the neighborhood. The mother said that Alfred could be "reasoned with," while formerly he had dominated the whole household. His relationship to his younger sibling had improved as well.

Here we have two situations where pathology or constitutional disposition and unresponsive parents combined with the rejection of the peer group create behavior difficulties in children who have been frustrated in their desire for belonging in the outside world. The fact that in both cases group therapy exclusively brought about improvement, indicates again how acceptance by a peer culture can be helpful in the growth process of a child even if the family background and the family atmosphere are unfavorable. These cases demonstrate the positive effects of a favorable group environment which can be marshaled in therapeutic efforts to counteract negative interpersonal relationships and unfavorable character organization.

An even clearer case of the effect on a boy of inappropriate school placement is that of Frank.

Frank, a ten-year-old boy, was referred to the agency on the suggestion of the family physician because he was nervous and jumpy, had difficulties about eating, was extremely slow in dressing, and was always in trouble at school. He was fearful of other children and offered no resistance when they beat him. He seemed to have no friends and engaged in a great deal of daydreaming. He had not yet learned to read or write properly, or even to sign his name.

In intake at the clinic it was established that Frank suffered from progressive myopia. The mother said she had taken the boy from one doctor to another, with little benefit. At about the time Frank started school, an eye specialist suggested that he be put in a sight conservation class, but the mother was very much opposed to this. After consulting various persons she finally found an eye clinic, where she was told that a special class was not indicated for Frank. He was therefore entered into a normal class at public school, but for two and a half years learned nothing.

Being tall for his age, he was put in the back row, from which he could not see the writing on the blackboard. As a result he gave up all effort at learning. His teacher finally convinced the mother that she would have to overcome her resistance to a sight conservation class, and Frank was finally put into such a class. After that his learning improved, but he never caught up with the other children, either socially or educationally.

His mother, who was foreign born, felt resentment against her own parents because they had taken her out of grade school before graduation and wanted Frank to achieve in life everything she had been deprived of. She experienced Frank's difficulties as a narcissistic wound. She blamed the teachers for all his difficulties at school, and did not see herself as a factor in the child's problems. In her relationship to the boy, she was rigid, tense, and nagging.

The father, a housepainter by occupation, seemed to have little understanding of his son's difficulties, and having many opportunities through his job for observing other children was bewildered by Frank's behavior.

Frank had a younger sister, a bright child, who easily excelled her handicapped brother, and who, in Frank's feelings, and probably also in reality, was preferred in the home.

In treatment it was found that Frank perceived the world as essentially hostile and that he had strong feelings of inadequacy and inferiority. His asset was a gift for craftwork and he liked to work with his hands. He also liked his typing classes at school and applied himself there apparently because his near-sightedness was no handicap. Frank's behavior difficulties appeared when he entered school.

In Frank's case the contribution of the school to a child's behavior difficulties is unusually clear. He had been exposed to the demands of the school and agemates which he could not possibly meet because of a physical handicap. He was placed in a situation in which he was bound to fail. He fell behind and gave up all effort at learning, and social failure inevitably followed in its wake.

Here we have a case where unfavorable conditions in the school environment aggravate an already unfavorable attitude on the part of the mother and a faulty self-image developed by the child with resultant hostile and aggressive trends.

Among the individuals to whom the child turns in his evolutionary unfoldment are children of his own age, his peers. This peer group is of great significance in his orientation to the world. The acceptance or rejection by peers is strongly charged with feeling and indelibly affects ego development, self-esteem, and self-identity. Survival as an acceptable member of the group cannot be overestimated, for it is charged with intense feeling.

One of the child's major periods of stress is during this reality testing, that is, when he pits himself against the outer world and the people in it. His adequacy and ego strength are put to test and are conditioned by these experiences with and reactions from outer reality. In this process the peer culture is especially important, for self-awareness and self-confidence are largely determined by success and failure in it. If it is tolerably favorable and friendly, manners and values are accepted and incorporated; when antagonistic, they are rejected. The tendency toward imitation and the need to be like others in order to be acceptable to them are the motives for assuming the characteristics and values of one's culture.

> Exclusive dependence on adult models can have unfortunate consequences. Almost characteristic is the plight of the child who is without brother or sister and is isolated because of the social setting from other children. Under such circumstances the child must depend in large part on adult models, who, although they may be satisfactory up to a point, are incapable of providing the child with those social adjustment techniques that are suggested by the term "good fellow."
>
> Strive as they will, the best of parents cannot be good playmates for their children. When the adult plays with the child, the relationship is never that of equals in stature; either the adult bends down, or the child looks up. In the latter case, the child may get some

exercise; but he cannot acquire much in the way of new adjustment patterns. In the former case, when the playing adult gets down on hands and knees to romp with a child, he may amuse himself. About all the child can learn from this, however, is some elementary points for getting along with playful elders.

Play is more than exercise; it is a process of socialization. For the complex, subtle, and necessary modes of behavior involved in the give and take of social life are acquired by the child mainly through association with other children.[1]

Among the clientele of child guidance clinics and social agencies are a considerable number of children whose difficulties are found to stem from the fact that the child of a minority group is rejected by the children in the neighborhood and cannot find playmates. In many instances children are afraid to pass through certain streets or to go out at night because of their fear of being attacked. These fears do not remain separated in the psychic organization, but rather have repercussions in the formation of the total personality. They give rise to feelings of inadequacy, unacceptability, and inferiority, and the total self-image and ego-development are affected negatively.

A case in point is that of Abe.

Abe, a Jewish boy, eleven years old, was referred by his mother at the suggestion of a municipal welfare bureau investigator because of the boy's babyish behavior, excessive clinging and dependency on the mother, inability to fight back when attacked, feminine activities, such as cutting out paper dolls and designing clothes for them. He played with children younger than himself, had fears of various kinds, and some respiratory difficulties that suggested asthma. Abe was also a nailbiter. His father had been in prison for some time, having served a prison term once before, and, therefore, was absent from home. The mother appeared to be a helpless and dependent person who used the child for her own psychologic needs.

The mother stated that Abe was afraid to make friends because of the neighborhood. There were many Negroes and Gentiles who were given to rough and aggressive behavior, and Abe was not one to be aggressive, she added. This opinion of the mother's in regard to neighborhood influence was maintained during the course of the treatment of over three years' duration.

[1] LaPiere, Richard T., and Paul R. Farnsworth, *Social Psychology*. McGraw-Hill Book Co., New York, 3d ed., 1949, p. 133.

It was clear that the neighborhood conditions intensified the boy's fears and prevented him from developing and testing his masculine drives and assertive trends. The social environment helped perpetuate in Abe the feminine traits acquired in the family setting by isolating him from growth-producing experiences in the larger world with his peers. Abe was referred to activity group therapy and treated by this method exclusively.

In the group he was described as being definitely effeminate both in appearance and in actions. His "mannerisms were girlish, his voice high-pitched and sometimes squeaky, his choice of language was on occasion characteristically effeminate." However, from the start he related well to the therapy group for the following reasons: The boys did not fully recognize at first Abe's inability to fight. Since he was physically better developed and taller than the rest, he was given a breathing spell before they became aggressive toward him. During that period of grace Abe was able to experience the gratifications of craftwork, which utilized his special skills and interests. This gave him an opportunity to enter into more masculine pursuits to which he reacted positively. For example, once when he sawed a piece of wood he exclaimed with glee, "The first time I sawed!"

After a number of sessions, however, the boys caught on to him and he soon became the butt of their aggression. They began to call him "nut," "moron," and similar derogatory names. The group therapist remarked in his report after four months that this treatment appeared to be familiar to Abe, judging by the way he received it. Even the smallest boy in the group found that he could very effectively assert himself against Abe, who was much taller. Although visibly frightened, Abe managed to endure these attacks without being driven to withdraw from the sessions because the activities seemed to give him great satisfaction. He continued to come. After months of struggle, Abe stopped jumping on chairs and yelling for help from the therapist when attacked and he did not seem to be so frightened.

The group therapist reported about a year later that Abe had made definite progress. The boy had developed skills and managed to remain in the group in spite of the pressures placed upon him by the other boys. Because he received support through his relationship with the therapist, Abe was able to take part in group activities. A "follow-up" interview with Abe's mother at about the same time revealed that the boy was able on occasion to play with boys of his own age on the street. He had become interested in sports, such as ball playing and roller skating, which was a completely new development for him.

In the progress summary dated six months later, Abe was reported to have become aggressive toward boys in the neighborhood. This increased security was apparent also in the group. Once he had splashed paint on and scratched another group's supply cabinet because he had been told that members of this group had abused the cabinet of his own club.

More progress was revealed in the summary for summer camp, another six months later, that is, two years after treatment was initiated, and in the follow-up interviews with Abe's mother. The mother stated that Abe spent most of his free time playing games with boys in the neighborhood. He also stood up for his rights in the group and argued when attacked by some of his fellow-members. During that period Abe was observed for the first time to engage in actual physical combat with boys. This development began when he joined a fellow-member in a game of "cops and robbers," in the course of which there was some wrestling. When Abe discovered that he was physically stronger than his adversary, and was in a position to subdue him, he seemed to derive a great deal of pleasure from provoking the latter into more fights. A few weeks later he accepted a challenge from a boy to a wrestling match and seemed astonished when he had won out. He now became fully aware of his newly discovered strength to fight back without fear. In line with these changes, Abe's status in the group was enhanced. He no longer was teased and fully participated in all group activities and discussions.

The change in Abe's personality was consistent. He continued to be assertive, free, and cooperative in his relations with his fellow group members and toward the end of treatment was reported as having become more masculine. In an interview before the case was closed, the boy acknowledged gains from the "club" and recognized that it gave him sufficient confidence to make friends of his own and to engage in sports.

As we compare the neighborhood situation with the special therapy group setting, it is evident that the beneficial effects of the group in changing Abe's character were derived from the contrast of the two. The neighborhood had pathogenic effects on him which the group successfully counteracted, because he felt a part of it and was accepted by his fellow-members.

The feeling of difference from others and rejection by them, particularly if they represent the larger community, as in the case of members of various minority groups, increases the distance between them. It engenders insecurity and discomfort in the less favored group. Mental health requires that one feel a part of his milieu and that one be not so different as to set himself off from others. The feeling of difference begets fears of being rejected, stigmatized, inadequate, and weak that usually result in withdrawal and diffidence, or compensatory overaggression and overassertiveness, behind which lurk strong feelings of inadequacy and insecurity.

> Tied into this part of the problem is the issue of security for any child of a minority race. . . . At first he feels threatened, not because he belongs any the less in his own family but because he finds himself in a situation which he "can't do anything about." At this early time the picture is largely one of the child's bewilderment over the fact that his social status (the things he's allowed to do, the names he's called, etc.) is affected by something completely beyond his control or making. As he grows older this goes over into a pervasive feeling that everything that is done to him, every attitude that is built about him, is because of his race (e.g., "because I am a Jew"). . . . My theory is that once racial insecurity has been really experienced, it never disappears. . . .
>
> The child of a minority race may show insecurity due to racial status, even though he has plentiful security in his own family. So the clinician sees the anxiety and panic of insecurity bobbing up in full intensity at times and disappearing at others. . . . Each of these children is very soon faced with the paradox that the parents to whom he must, and does, look for security are the very ones who are responsible for his insecurity, from a racial point of view. This ambivalence means that resentment and punishment are wreaked against those whom the child recognizes as his mainstays.[1]

The following case illustrates some of Dr. Plant's statement with particular vividness.

> Dave, a ten and one-half-year-old boy, the oldest of three siblings, was referred for treatment by his father because Dave did not get along with children and had a tendency to be effeminate. Being afraid that he would be beaten, he preferred playing by himself. Occasionally he would play with girls. Other presenting symptoms

[1] Reprinted by permission of the publishers and The Commonwealth Fund from James S. Plant's *The Envelope*, Cambridge, Mass.: Harvard University Press, 1950, pp. 14, 15, 160.

were a "nervous" cough, developed during the year preceding treatment; stuttering, which had started at the age of five; awkwardness in running, slovenliness, arbitrariness in eating, and food fads.

Dave was the son of a Jewish father and his Gentile wife who were divorced after a rather hectic relation, punctuated by a series of separations and reconciliations. Dave had two sisters, three and four years younger, respectively. When the boy was five years old, the father was sent overseas and the mother placed the children in foster homes—the two girls in one and Dave in another. It was at this time that Dave began to stutter. When the parents were divorced Dave was seven years old; the father then placed the boy with his parents. For a period Dave also lived with the maternal non-Jewish grandparents on a farm. Later he went to live with his father and stepmother in a large metropolitan city.

During the treatment interviews Dave expressed the wish that his parents had not been divorced and believed the explanation given to him by his father that they could not get along together to be untrue. He thought the problem was that his mother was a Protestant and his father a Jew. He did not know what he wanted to be himself, but wished his children to be Protestants. He said that "normal" kids did not like Jewish people so well as they liked Gentiles. He wanted to live in the country when he was older and his people to be Christians because most people in the country are Christians. For the present he had only one wish, which he hoped the agency would help him to fulfill, namely, to be sent back where he could live like a "normal" boy.

If he could not live with his mother and his sisters, he felt he could at least live with his maternal grandparents. He felt he knew enough about farming, could take care of the corn, and help his grandfather manage the farm.

Dave also complained about his grandparents' disparaging his Jewish countenance. He particularly complained about his thick lips and reported that the boys in school told him he looked like a "slob." He did not want to look like his father, who was very Jewish in appearance.

In addition to those extrafamilial factors in personality development already enumerated, namely, the school, friends, and free-time occupations, the ego-ideals, the objects of identification in any given culture, and its values are preeminent. The individual adopts the values of his culture at a very early stage by imitation, identification, and through the need to be like others and acceptable to them. To become acceptable to others, one must not be at too great variance from them; to feel a sense of unity and oneness with peers one must be like them, for homogeneity and likeness are highly important cementing forces among people.

Values and ideals vary not only in groups and cultures, but also at different stages of childhood and adolescence within a given culture. Identifications in the preoedipal stage are derived from the family circle, which is later widened in the postoedipal and latency periods. In latency, especially, identifications are fluid and changeable and are strongly endowed with affect, for it is the period of the so-called "hero-worship." It is from the many influences, ideals, and heroic personalities that the individual finally molds his visions, hopes, desires, and strivings. They leave indelible imprints upon his psyche and determine the current of his development, his social images, and his values. Society's values and the cultural climate are filtered through to the child's world and into his evolving psyche. Cultural harmony, tensions, and conflict are all reflected in the structure of his personality.

Culture conflict is not confined to extrafamilial relations, however. It occurs also within the home and is equally destructive. Many homes are characterized by the conflict between cultures represented by members of different generations. The mores and practices of parents and grandparents may conflict with the child's peer values, which he of necessity brings into the home, and which are of great significance in his personal and social adjustment. When the system of values of his progenitors is at variance with that of his peers, conflict invariably arises. This conflict does not always emanate from the differences in old and new world values and ways of living. It also exists where the parents have been brought up in a different locality in the same country or when they adhere to outmoded concepts unsuitable to a new social milieu. Frequently the resulting tensions require the attention of a psychotherapist or guidance counselor. Recent experiments in family psychotherapy, that is, where the whole family is treated together as a unit, may be a step toward alleviating this situation.

The case of Murray treated at the child guidance clinic of the Jewish Board of Guardians represents a constellation of pathogenic factors in the home, in minority status, in neighborhood influences, and in culture conflict.

Murray was referred for treatment at the age of eight and one-half years by his mother because he was uncontrollable. He had to be fed and dressed; he played with baby toys, was disobedient, and was in continuous violent conflict with a sister, fourteen years old. There was also difficulty in getting him to go to school.

Murray, whose father had died, was the youngest in the family of three children. The two older siblings were girls, one three years and the other about five years older than Murray. The father died when the boy was five years of age. The mother, an uneducated immigrant, dull and harassed, had little warmth for any of her children. She felt that the difficulties in the home stemmed from the violent conflict between the oldest girl and herself, on the one hand, and Murray, on the other.

In the early contact with the caseworker Murray stated spontaneously that he went to Yeshiva and that he learned Hebrew and Yiddish there. In a later interview he mentioned that he had quit the Yeshiva and now attended a public school. In that connection he mentioned that what he liked about the public school was that he got out of school earlier in the afternoon. The thing he did not like so much about it was that the children there were all Italian and Spanish and that he and another boy were the only Jews in his class. The other kids all talked to each other in Spanish and Italian and he felt left out. He had felt better in the Yeshiva. The principal there had been a good man. There was noted an interesting effort at conformity with his Gentile surroundings. Murray was fingerpainting and mentioned that brown was his favorite color. He said that he used to like blue but all his "friends," the Spaniards and Italians, liked brown, so he thought he should like what everyone else liked. Now he, too, liked brown.

In this interview immediately after he had expressed his feelings about being left out by the other boys and had called the Spanish and Italian children his friends, he mentioned a friend, ten years old, whom he called "dumb." He was a Catholic and only in class 3B. He liked that friend, even though he was dumb.

The reaching out for Gentile friends appeared again one day when Murray played with toy soldiers. Explaining his game, he said they were only practicing shooting at the "enemy." He did not say who the enemy was but that three Jews were fighting their enemy. He finally changed his mind and said that one soldier was a Protestant, one a Catholic, and one a Jew. In the same interview he mentioned a neighborhood group of five children and that he was the only Jewish member. He expressed ambivalent feelings about a boy who was the leader, calling him mean, but still found it necessary to justify the latter's behavior. When talking about other groups in the neighborhood, Murray called them gangs, while he called his own group a club, saying that most of the gangs around his way consisted of Negroes and Spaniards. A week later Murray again played with soldiers; one Catholic, one Protestant, and one Jew together were shooting at the "enemy." The soldier, whom he designated as Jewish, was lying on his stomach and the Protestant and Catholic were standing up.

Some five months later Murray talked about his camp experiences of the preceding summer. He spoke of colored boys. The worker said that he mentioned colored people in many of his interviews, but she did not know why. Murray said that colored people really were nice, but the caseworker registered an undertone of fear in the boy connected with Negro people.

When Murray discussed the counselors in camp for the coming summer, he asked whether they were "mixed." The worker stated that she did not know what he meant. Murray went on to say that "Christians are all right; they're human beings, too. They're just as good as Jews. They're like Jews. There's no difference. Are there going to be Christian counselors?" He later asked if there were only Jews in camp. The caseworker asked how he felt about it. Murray immediately said he did not care.

Seven months later Murray mentioned that Negroes fought dirty when they boxed. There was a boxing match between a Negro and a Jew, in which the Jew won even though the Negro did not fight fair. During the same interview Murray told the caseworker that his teacher was Jewish but was married to a Catholic; that her husband had been in the Army and one day he had come to school and told his class what war was like. A month later Murray walked up to the toy shelf, picked up an airplane, and said he wanted to be a pilot. Then he remarked that Jews were discriminated against in the Air Corps. However, if he joined the Seabees, things would be different. They treated Jews wonderfully. He would like to join the Seabees when he was eighteen years old. Two weeks later he spoke of the persecution of the Jewish people in Europe and how terrible it was.

In another interview Murray said that he was on a team of all white boys and that they had played a team of Negroes. They had played the Negroes twice and had been beaten both times. The day before, a team consisting of Negroes, Jews, and Irish had played and they had persistently asked Murray whether he would like to play with them. After some prompting about his feelings and upon questioning by the caseworker whether he had felt proud, Murray nodded slightly but suggested that it was just a neighborhood game and they needed somebody to play.

Murray's reactions to Jewishness became clearer about two years after treatment was initiated. At that time he attended Hebrew school in the afternoon for religious instruction, because he had to prepare for his Bar Mitzvah (confirmation). Talking about his difficulties, he said:

"There was a rabbi who taught me in Hebrew school. This rabbi was a very superstitious man, and he told the kids lots of things that would bother them. He told them that if they didn't go to sleep at night with a cap on their heads, they would die when they awoke in the morning." Murray laughed a little nervously, and said, "Of course, this was just superstition." The caseworker remarked that maybe it was pretty difficult for him to go to sleep at night, because he might wonder whether he would wake up in the morning. Murray nodded, and said that sometimes when he woke in the morning, he thought he was already in Paradise. There would be angels around, and he would be among them. And then he would realize that he was actually at home and in bed. It did make him very nervous to have this feeling, but he felt that since it was just a superstition he would get over it. The rabbi had also told the children that if they dropped a Jewish book, and did not kiss it when they picked it up, God would be very angry with them and they would never go to Heaven. They would just wander around forever restlessly in space and never have any place to go. This rabbi was an old man and he was finally removed from his position in the school. Now they had a young rabbi, who did not fill them with all these superstitions. The caseworker agreed with him that they were superstitions, but remarked that perhaps he still felt that there was some truth in them, and that it worried him a little. Murray giggled slightly, shrugged his shoulders and said, "Maybe that's right," and added that he had "day troubles" as well as "night troubles."

His feelings about Jewishness were brought out with more clarity when he talked of his desire to go to baseball games. He mentioned that he would prefer to go with his (therapy) group leader if they should be going at the same time as his Hebrew school classmates. He did not like to go with the latter because the teacher was too strict. They had to wear hats; even when the Star Spangled Banner was sung one of the boys did not remove his hat. Murray did not like this. They were not allowed to eat frankfurters and the teacher always told them that if they did not abide by the rules and regulations of the Jewish law, something might happen to them. There was a time when he was very much scared about this but he was not afraid any more. He did not care so much now; he was not so religious. The group leader gave them much more freedom than the Hebrew school teacher, and that was why he thought he preferred to go with him than with the Hebrew school group.

The idea connected with Bar Mitzvah was that now he would have to "become a man." This caused a great deal of apprehension. At first Murray claimed that he was proud. Then his feelings of fear, anxiety, and anger became obvious. Being the only boy in his family, he felt the responsibility even more. Everybody, especially his uncle and the rabbi, told him that now he was becoming a man and, not having a father, the responsibilities of the home devolved upon his shoulders. His mother also mentioned this to him. The uncle especially stressed the importance of his now being a man and taking the place of the man in the home. He would have to study hard so that he could do things well and would make his mother proud of him once, at least. Murray brought out in this connection that his mother was never proud of him; that she considered him a "bad boy" who did not work enough, was not obedient enough, was not considerate enough, and was frequently aggressive. He felt that now, if he were not a good Jew and did not do his Hebrew lessons and did not attend the religious services often enough, his mother would be very much disappointed.

Murray apparently took rather literally the statement of the rabbi and the uncle that he now would have to be a man. The caseworker explained to him at length that one does not become a man so suddenly and that even with Bar Mitzvah he would not actually be a man. In this discussion Murray, with rage and at the same time self-pity, brought out that he had been cheated all his life, that he had been cheated by not having a father, by having special responsibilities put upon him with regard to good behavior because his mother had so much work to do and was so poor, and that women meant such heavy responsibilities for a man. He would not marry for that reason.

In view of the fact that this outburst arose from the impact which the Jewish rite had upon him, one may wonder whether he did not imply that also by his Jewishness he was cheated out of things. It is significant to note in this connection that the change in the person of the group therapist from a Jew to a non-Jew gave Murray great concern because the latter did not understand the importance of the Bar Mitzvah lessons for him, which interfered with the group therapy sessions.

On a later occasion Murray expressed concern about Jewishness in relation to his Big Brother. He made the point that the Big Brother should be Jewish but again stressed that he did not actually mind if a person was not Jewish. He had non-Jewish friends. At the same time he stated that he felt closer to Jewish people. He thought that they understood his problems better, especially in connection with Bar Mitzvah, and that all his family members were interested in Jewish things. He was relieved when he learned that his caseworker was also Jewish.

Murray considered his Bar Mitzvah an event of major importance. He received great recognition and stimulation from it, but was worried as to whether he could live up to the new obligations that devolved upon him.

During interviews that followed he repeatedly mentioned positive reactions to Jewishness on the conscious level, such as feeling better understood by Jewish people; his interest in Jewish candidates for political office; his pride in the Jewish Board of Guardians being a Jewish organization; his feeling that Jews were more interested in having their children become good people than were Gentiles. He suggested that the group (therapeutic) sessions should include some Jewish instructions, some Hebrew or some knowledge about Palestine.

A year later he noticed a picture of Santa Claus on the wall in his caseworker's office and showed annoyance, since "this was a Jewish place." But his ambivalence about being Jewish reappeared on that occasion. With a note of mockery he stated that the caseworker, who was a woman, should become the chief rabbi of New York. Speaking of the things which she as the chief rabbi should do, he suggested her taking care of the Jews in New York, so that they would have the proper education and enough to eat; also give some thought to the Jews in Palestine and Europe. He mentioned that she would probably have more understanding because she (being an immigrant) knew what the Jews went through in Europe. It was evident from Murray's recounting the functions of a chief rabbi that he felt that there were great disadvantages in being a Jew, that Jews needed special care and protection.

In his conversations with his Big Brother, Murray expressed considerable antagonism toward Negroes and in his interviews with the caseworker brought out fears he had of Negroes as a result of several incidents in his neighborhood. He mentioned that he was especially afraid because an uncle of his had been attacked one evening by a Negro.

When discussing sex, Murray mentioned that many boys in his neighborhood had had sexual experience with Negro girls. He said that the boys wanted to try it out, and stated that maybe he, too, had had the same wish but never had acceded to it. Soon afterward he mentioned two boys in the neighborhood who had gone to the home of two sisters and slept with them in the nude. He mentioned that they were colored and apparently looked at such things differently from the way he did.

In the next set of interviews he reiterated his opinion that Jewish people take better care of their children than Gentiles. Referring to some Puerto Rican families in his neighborhood, he said that he thought this might be due to the fact that Jews have fewer children than Puerto Ricans and Negroes.

Later he expressed some fear that without the help of the agency he might be influenced by the children in the neighborhood. With irritation he said: "You don't know how bad the children are in our neighborhood. They don't live so comfortably as the social workers." He also mentioned that some boys in the neighborhood gambled, some formed gangs, and some stole.

In a recurrent dream Murray manifested his conflict between the restrictions of Jewishness and the freedom the Gentile world represents. The dream was that he saw Jesus Christ walking through a door. At first Murray was very much frightened, but when Jesus smiled and took his hand, Murray was less afraid. He felt it to be a strange dream for him, a Jewish boy. He did not actually know how it came about. He had had the same dream several times. Christ's face was a mixture of strictness and kindness, but after he smiled Murray had not felt so bad. Then Murray said: "After all, Jesus himself was a Jew, having been born of Jewish parents. He wasn't a Roman or a Gentile."

By way of interpretation it may be stated that in view of the neighborhood influence where power is associated with majority status, the sexual freedom of his agemates in the Negro group, his own sexual stimulation in a forbidding home environment, his shy attempts to be accepted by Gentiles in the neighborhood gangs, the threatening experience of the cultural impact of the Hebrew school and the Bar Mitzvah, we need not be surprised that the release which Murray received in therapy should have taken the form of a liberation by Christ.

It is quite clear from the above that children who come for treatment in child guidance or other clinics for emotional disturbances and social maladjustments must be regarded as persons upon whom influences outside the family may have been exerted which determined to varying degrees the problems with which they are faced. Disadvantages, other than those originating in the family, must be seen in the total setting of the child's life-sphere. Adaptations to, and relationships with, persons and groups outside the family, who may have significance in his life, need to be considered and the treatment plan should take cognizance of them. Corrective social experiences that serve to dissolve a destructive psychologic set toward people and groups are frequently essential.

It is because of these considerations that various forms of group psychotherapy have been added to the armamentarium of the psychotherapist. Their effect is to dissolve unwholesome attitudes toward persons—adults and peers—through substitute satisfactions and corrective relations in a group setting. Such conditioned group life affords strengthening of the ego, effects changes in character organization through identification and altered ego ideals, as well as through correction of superego restraints and improved self-image. Such a new life-setting can have a permanent effect upon young children who, being psychologically mobile, can absorb and assimilate experiences and make them a part of their personality structure. Being as yet free of serious ego tensions and rigid defenses and having ease in establishing new identifications, it is possible for them to gain such positive results from special groups. Experience shows that a very large number of prepubertal children who come for treatment can be helped through groups.

It must be noted, however, that where psychosexual distortions are intense and where the libido is strongly tied either to the patient's own body or to other persons, individual transference therapy is essential. But even in such cases the therapist's awareness of the additional pathogenic impact of extrafamilial influences upon the child may suggest environmental implementation of the direct therapeutic effort.

CHAPTER FIVE

Culture and Culture Conflict in Psychotherapy

THE QUESTION has sometimes been raised *whether anthropological information is of potential usefulness for an understanding of symptomatology in cases where the patient and therapist do not belong to the same cultural group.*[1] That is a problem which deserves special attention in the framework of this study because frequently the patients of the clinic come from subcultural milieux which are different from those of their therapists.

One of the significant contributions of cultural anthropology to an understanding of human behavior is its emphasis on *cultural relativity.* In essence this concept designates the phenomenon that the same basic needs can be satisfied in various ways and that the members of different societies actually do follow different patterns of behavior in satisfying them. As a means of counteracting ethnocentric misunderstandings, the concept of cultural relativity undoubtedly has a definite place in the professional equipment of social practitioners and deserves attention in psychotherapy. Unless cultural relativity is understood and considered in practice, the therapist may fall into the trap of assuming a standard of normality drawn from the culture pattern to which he belongs. In doing so he may remain untroubled by the possibility that the patient may come from a culture pattern in which different standards of culturally expected behavior apply.

BY OTTO POLLAK IN CONSULTATION WITH YONATA FELDMAN

[1] Clark, Elizabeth W., "The Challenge of Transplanted People for Casework," and Sandi, Peter W., "The Psychocultural Approach in Social Casework" in *New Emphasis on Cultural Factors.* Papers reprinted from *Journal of Social Casework,* Family Service Association of America, New York, 1946–1948, pp. 14–22; Gioseffi, William, "The Relationship of Culture to the Principles of Casework," *Social Casework,* vol. 32, May, 1951, pp. 190–196; Ginsburg, Sol Wiener, "The Impact of the Social Worker's Cultural Structure on Social Therapy," *Social Casework,* vol. 32, October, 1951, pp. 319–325.

This danger has been described by Ruth Benedict as follows:

> . . . We read of the behaviour of small children as it is moulded in our civilization and recorded in child clinics, as child psychology or the way in which the young human animal is bound to behave. It is the same whether it is a question of our ethics or of our family organization. It is the inevitability of each familiar motivation that we defend, attempting always to identify our own local ways of behaving with Behaviour, or our own socialized habits with Human Nature.[1]

A possible consequence of such cultural ethnocentrism may be an interpretation and evaluation of a patient's symptoms in terms of the cultural norms of the therapist. John Gillin has reported an instance of this, which came to his attention as consulting professor in the Department of Neuropsychiatry of the Duke University Medical School. The patient was

> . . . talking incessantly and in an intimate manner to Jesus; a young Northern intern assigned to the case concluded that a major dissociation or disorganization of the personality was evidenced and diagnosed schizophrenia. . . . Further investigation, however, revealed that the patient came from a rural Southern community where it was customary for every one to talk out loud to Jesus when in a crisis situation. The patient was actually suffering from . . . a mild situational neurosis, induced by being abandoned by her husband and by failure to obtain a job.[2]

Such situations are bound to arise, particularly when the patient belongs to a cultural group very different from that of the therapist. It is significant that the psychiatrists and social workers in the Lasker Mental Health Center in Jerusalem, reared and trained in Western civilization as they are, have recently felt the need of anthropological and sociological help in their diagnosis and prognosis of patients of Yemenite and Moroccan background. For this reason the Center started in 1950 a "Sociological

---

[1] Benedict, Ruth, *Patterns of Culture.* Houghton Mifflin Co., Boston, 1934, pp. 6–7.

[2] Gillin, John, *The Ways of Men:* An Introduction to Anthropology. D. Appleton-Century Co., New York, 1948, p. 577. Used by permission of Appleton-Century-Crofts, Inc.

Workshop" in order to gain more information regarding the social norms which governed the lives of these immigrants to Israel in their countries of origin.

It should be stated, however, that—important as an appreciation of cultural relativity may be for an understanding of symptomatology—it promises to be useful in diagnostic practice only in combination with psychodynamic understanding. An emphasis on anthropological information alone may lead to overlooking a symptom as easily as to preventing erroneous assumption of its existence. An example may serve to illustrate this.

Eli, thirteen and one-half years old, was brought up by Chassidic parents. According to the customs of their group, the parents were in continuous contact with their rabbi, going to him daily for advice and inspiration. On the surface Eli had adopted this pattern and insisted that he had to go to see the rabbi every day before he went to school. In order to do so he would get up every morning at five o'clock and create a terrific commotion in the home, disturbing his parents to a point where they begged him to give up his daily contacts with the rabbi. A purely anthropological approach might have tempted one to question the symptomatic character of the boy's behavior and to discount its element of annoyance to his father and mother because of the closeness of its appearance to the conduct of the parents themselves. Seen together, however, with the facts that Eli's parents never had given him any emotional warmth, that he was abusive toward his mother, stole from his parents and from children, truanted from school, where his parents wanted him to be a remarkable success, and was destructive at home, it appeared that in his attachment to the rabbi Eli was not simply practicing the culture of his parents but was abusing it in order to punish them for having rejected him.

Consequently diagnostic practice can receive significant help from cultural anthropology only along the lines mapped out by Edward Sapir who, in discussing the relationship between psychiatry and cultural anthropology, clarified the problem as follows:

We are not, therefore, to begin with a simple contrast between social patterns and individual behavior, whether normal or abnormal, but we are, rather, to ask what is the meaning of culture in

terms of individual behavior and whether the individual can, in a
sense, be looked upon as the effective carrier of the culture of his
group.[1]

This principle is based on the recognition that culture normally
serves the function of making life easier for the members of a society. If a person appears to rebel against his culture, or to submit
more slavishly to it than do the other members of his group, he
may be suffering from a behavior disorder, or a neurosis. In order
to make a correct diagnosis, the clinician needs to have, first, an
understanding of the normal expressions of culture, because only
such understanding will help him evaluate whether the actual
behavior of a patient deviates from the cultural norms active in
his environment either through rebellion or exaggerated submission. Second, the clinician must understand the meaning of this
deviant reaction of the patient to his culture in terms of his emotional life. Correspondingly in cases which show indications of
culture conflict, the question should be raised whether the conflict is one between conduct norms, which has been internalized
by the patient, or whether it is merely being used by him to express an interpersonal conflict. The phenomenon of internalized
culture conflict in pathogenesis has been discussed in the previous
chapter.[2]

The case of Lloyd illustrates how an apparent rebellion against
the religious orthodoxy practiced in this boy's home was actually
the expression of an unresolved oedipal conflict.

> Lloyd, age fourteen, was referred to the clinic by his mother be-
> cause of severe conflict with his father over the correct observance of
> Jewish ritual law, violent temper tantrums, threatening his mother
> with a knife, constant quarrels with his ten-year-old sister, and be-
> cause of his feeling that he was unloved by his family.
>
> According to the boy's mother, the main difficulty was the con-
> flict with his father. The latter, a strictly orthodox man, wanted
> Lloyd to say his prayers regularly and to keep the Sabbath strictly,
> not turning on the light or the radio on that day. Lloyd, however,
> wanted to listen to the radio and have a light in his room. Almost as

[1] Sapir, E., "Cultural Anthropology and Psychiatry," *The Journal of Abnormal
and Social Psychology*, vol. 37, October–December, 1932, p. 233.
[2] See particularly the case of Murray.

an aside, Lloyd's mother mentioned in the first interview that he was very much attached to her and although he was at times disobedient, always wanted to protect her; she said also that she had the feeling he wanted to be continuously with her and wished his father were out of the way.

When the boy in his first interview was questioned about the onset of the conflict between him and his father, he reported that he had been unhappy about this since he was seven or eight years old. He would frequently think about it and would slowly get away from the orthodox way of life. The final decision, however, came shortly after his Bar Mitzvah, when he went to camp. Although this camp was supposed to be for orthodox boys, Jewish law was not adhered to, and he began to think that people got along better, and enjoyed life more if they were not orthodox.

He also corroborated his mother's statement about his feelings toward her. Explaining why he felt that he did not need any help from the clinic, he reported that he had made up his mind to conform with his father's wishes in order to please his mother and to protect her from excitement. Later on in treatment he said that he had always felt that way about his mother, admitting, however, that more recently the relationship between him and her had not been undisturbed.

Six weeks after treatment had begun, Lloyd told the worker that he had arrived at a completely different conclusion regarding his home situation. He felt that his difficulties were not due to any differences between him and his father but were the fault of his sister. She was the one who caused all the trouble by playing up to their father and by getting him to side with her against Lloyd. However, that was nothing the father could be blamed for, since he was really fooled by his daughter. Moreover, Lloyd now felt that the many little arguments that he and his father had over turning on the light or the radio on the Sabbath were not important.

In the course of therapy, however, it became more and more apparent that Lloyd's statement regarding his sister's being at the core of his problems was a displacement and that his initial statements regarding his relationship to his mother and father were closer to the truth.

About one year after treatment had started, it developed that Lloyd had gone to stay with his uncle, who had invited him. The invitation had been given at the suggestion of Lloyd's father after Lloyd himself had indicated his interest in it. When the worker picked up the matter of Lloyd's father having suggested this move, Lloyd gradually brought out that his father for years had been suggesting to him that he go and stay somewhere else, with some relatives or some friends. Lloyd then revealed with considerable affect that this was a standing joke in the family. It had really been a serious remark of the father's at first, but it had later developed into a joke. Lloyd said he did not know the reason for this but he remembered his father saying to him on the occasion of some conflict when he was six years old, "Take your packl and go." For a few years this tended to be a seriously repeated, angry remark on the part of his father when the latter was dissatisfied with him. Questioned as to what he thought this had meant, Lloyd's reaction was that it implied two things— one, a threat, and, two, an indication of his father's desire to get rid of him. He revealed that he had been upset and angry about this as a child and even now it disturbed him greatly. When the worker pointed out to Lloyd that all this seemed to be covering up some conflict in him in terms of his feeling about his father, he was able to bring out that the real belief he had had since he was six was that his father did not love him.

In the latter part of the treatment Lloyd's inability to resolve the oedipal conflict, due to his father's rejecting attitude, came out clearly and was worked with directly. His behavior at home had improved but nevertheless there was constant friction, mainly with the father. Both the latter and Lloyd seemed to be acting out openly their rivalry on an almost equal level. This was heightened by the fact that Lloyd's mother seemed to be able to stand up better for herself and to act more like a mother and wife than she had been able to do previously. As the real oedipal conflict became more sharply outlined, Lloyd's hostility toward his sister decreased, and the conflict became consciously centralized around his father. Yet, despite the rivalry and the negative feelings, Lloyd's desire to be loved by his father and to have a good companionable relationship with him came out over and over again. The father, however, was unable to respond maturely to Lloyd and continued to react negatively to his pattern of provocation. The boy, in turn, was unable to give up his rivalry with the father and to accept his role as that of a son rather than competitor.

No attempt was made to draw the father into treatment and no positive emotional change on his part came into being as a result of social interaction with his wife and his son. Following one particularly violent conflict, Lloyd, on the suggestion of his uncle, was placed in a boarding school. There he did well scholastically but whenever he came home to visit, his conflict with his father flared up again and violent behavior outbursts took place.

This case material makes it necessary to consider two alternative interpretations of the nature of the boy's difficulties. It is of interest to note that the time at which the apparently basic conflict about observance of Jewish ritual law originated coincided not only with the onset of the latency period but also with the time at which the father began to show his rejection of the boy by his repeated utterance, "Take your packl and go."

The connection between the appearance of the boy's conflict with his father over orthodoxy and the onset of the latency period which brought him in contact with people practicing less restricting conduct norms makes it possible to think that this experience created his rebellion against the culture of his parent. The connection with the episode in which rejection by his father showed itself in the overt form of being told angrily to pack up and go, on the other hand, suggests the possibility that it was the disturbance of the basic relationship with this specific bearer of the orthodox Jewish culture which caused the boy to rebel against it.

Was it then the paternal rejection, or the experience of a more latitudinarian way of life than that of his orthodox father and the latter's effort to impose his orthodoxy on the child—that is, culture conflict—which created the difficulty? The answer is suggested by the following consideration. The boy's rebellion against his father's orthodoxy did not stand out as his one problem in an otherwise undisturbed development. It was not his only symptom. There were also his protective, albeit oscillating, attitude toward his mother and his constant quarrels with his sister. Looking for the psychological meaning of these various difficulties in their togetherness, we must come back to the boy's own point of view. From the beginning he expressed the conviction that his being disadvantaged in terms of his relationships within the family presented the significant problem. This suggests that Lloyd's rebellion against the culture of his home was only the manifest content of his oedipal conflict with a rejecting father.

Another point at which cultural understanding can be put into the service of the diagnostic and therapeutic task lies in the *communication value of cultural material* for purposes of conveying psychodynamic information. In their attempt to apply the principles of psychodynamics to child guidance practice, many workers have become accustomed to look for direct expressions of the emotional reactions of their patients to the key people in their family. In this quest they frequently have developed a tendency to regard production of cultural material by the patient as diagnostically and therapeutically insignificant. Such production is therefore frequently not utilized by the workers and remains more or less unrecorded. This situation came to light when the clinic initiated a study to find out whether the religious, ethnic, and subcultural background of its patients was in any way reflected in the case material. The study revealed that the clinical records contained almost no information of this kind. In only two or three cases had such material been perceived as significant, been utilized accordingly, and had found its way into the record. When these few cases were presented to the staff, more information of that type began to be recorded, but much more is still to be desired in this direction.

The study mentioned above suggested that many workers made a sharp distinction between the immediate family environment of the patient and his larger cultural environment, and that they considered only the former of significance for an understanding of pathogenesis. It has been pointed out in Chapter 4 that such an attitude probably presents an oversimplification of pathogenesis. Even from the point of view, however, that only an understanding of interpersonal relationships in the family circle is necessary for diagnosis and therapy, an attitude of disregard for cultural material may be self-defeating because it is based on a lack of understanding of the tie that exists between a patient's reactions to his culture and his reactions to his family. Actually this has become apparent in the case of Lloyd. In the analysis of that case however, the emphasis was put on a psychodynamic evaluation of a patient's reaction to the culture pattern presented in his family. In the discussion which follows, the emphasis will be put on the possible facilitation of communication between worker and patient regarding significant material.

An exposition of the concept of *culture* in its scientific usage will indicate that the readiness to listen and to analyze cultural material produced by the patient might open up and shorten the procedure of gaining significant information about interpersonal relationships between the patient and members of his family. There seems to be a tendency among workers not acquainted with cultural anthropology to think that the term "culture" designates material objects and ways of doing things as distinguished from feelings about persons in one's own life circle. This, however, is a misconception. It should be noted that affect is not something that falls outside of the cultural orbit.

> Culture is a way of thinking, feeling, believing. . . . By more or less adhering to a system of related designs for carrying out of the acts of living, a group of men and women feel themselves linked together by a powerful chain of sentiments.[1]

Thus one of the functions of culture is the creation of a feeling of belongingness or, in other words, a creation of security and positive affect toward one another in the members of a society.[2]

> What really binds men together is their culture—the ideas and the standards they have in common.[3]

It should also be noted that culture is not something that has its existence outside the individual, mystically or perhaps only inaccurately perceived to be a characteristic of a group, the same for all members of that group, and thus of unconcern for those who deal with individuals and their personal difficulties.

> For each individual the commonly accepted fund of meanings and values tends to be powerfully specialized, or emphasized or contradicted by types of experience and modes of interpretation that are far from being the property of all men. If we consider that these specialized cultural participations are partly the result of contact with limited traditions and techniques, partly the result of identification with such biologically and socially imposed groups as the family or the class in school or the club, we can begin to see how inevitable it is that the true psychological locus of a culture is *the individual* or *a specifically enumerated list of individuals*, not an economically or politically or socially defined group of individuals. "Individual," however,

[1] Kluckhohn, Clyde, *Mirror for Man*. Whittlesey House, New York, 1949, pp. 23, 27.
[2] See Chapter 4.
[3] Benedict, Ruth, *op. cit.*, p. 16.

here means not simply a biologically defined organism maintaining itself through physical impacts and symbolic substitutes of such impacts, but that total world of form, meaning and implication of symbolic behavior which a given individual partly knows and directs, partly intuits and yields to, partly is ignorant of and is swayed by.[1]

Thus when a patient talks about cultural material, such as religious beliefs, problems of being Jewish in a Gentile society, folkways practiced in his neighborhood, and so on, he really talks about himself. The fact that in doing so he is "touching common interests so far as this particular culture pattern is concerned,"[2] must not conceal this fact. In producing cultural material the patient engages in a process of self-revelation which may be diagnostically and therapeutically of high significance.

In talking about cultural material the patient may not even be talking only about himself; he may also be talking about those persons who transmit his culture to him. In our society at least the first, and because of their strategic advantage most important, transmitters of culture are the parents of a child. What they regard as cultural demands becomes attached in the child's mind to their person, or to the child's image of their person. Consequently the child's feelings about culture are determined by his culture transmitters. It can readily be seen that a child's production of cultural material may open up for the worker avenues of understanding concerning those feelings in which the workers, with their psychoanalytical training, are basically interested. When a child expresses negative reactions to his parents' culture, the worker may be faced with the child's only way of giving vent to his feelings about his parents because of a taboo which prohibits the direct verbalization of negative feelings toward one's father and mother.

In the last analysis every person must take the means of expressing his emotions from his culture. To discuss them in such terms as love and hate for one's parents, guilt over one's own behavior, and anger toward the therapist, is in itself using the

[1] Sapir, E., op. cit., p. 238.
[2] Ibid., p. 240.

symbols of a special culture which is in process of formation in our present-day society. This subculture has been created by the impact of psychoanalysis upon the modes of expression of therapists and adult members of the middle class to whose intellectual equipment this terminology has come to belong. Many patients, however, may try to express these emotions in different terms and according to their conception of appropriate behavior, which is less direct than the one created by contact with psychoanalytic theory and practice. Thus there may occur culture conflict between therapist and patient regarding the norms governing forms and content of communication.

To break into or to disregard the patient's verbalization of cultural material may prevent him from developing a line of association which may lead directly to the point of interest presenting the diagnostic concern of the worker. By doing so the worker may assume unwittingly the role of the censor for the patient and prevent unconscious thought content from reaching the patient's awareness. Thus either because of lack of perception for the meaning of cultural material or because of his own emotional involvement in the cultural material touched upon by the patient, the worker may forge tools for the resistance of the patient.

Repression, observance of cultural taboo regarding the direct expression of negative emotions toward parents, relatives, or the therapist, convention governing what one may or may not discuss with another person, and simply the need to rely on the symbols of expression provided by one's own culture suggest that workers should permit the patient to express his feelings in terms of conscious concerns. This idea has been expressed by Abram Kardiner in the discussion of his method of studying basic personality patterns in various cultures.

> The dynamics to be used are essentially those described by Freud. The point of departure is that the focal ideas are expressed in the language of experience in which they consciously occur.[1]

To exclude from diagnostic inquiry material which appears "merely" cultural may prolong the process of diagnostic dis-

[1] Kardiner, Abram, *The Individual and His Society*. Columbia University Press, New York, 1939, p. 90.

covery and block the lines of communication between the worker, on the one hand, and the patient and his family, on the other. Permitting, however, the patient to develop cultural material may frequently shorten the diagnostic task.

Both attitudes toward cultural material produced by a patient with their various implications for diagnostic understanding are exemplified in the case of Miriam.

> Miriam, age five, was referred to the clinic by a nursery school teacher because she disliked to play with other children and—if she played at all—insisted on playing the mother part. Additional symptoms elicited in intake were clinging to the mother, fears of the dark, of dogs and cats, of policemen, of a bogeyman, and of Hitler. She also wanted continuously to be assured of her mother's love and of being preferred to her younger sister.
>
> Her parents were orthodox Jews, with the orthodoxy being more strongly expressed by her mother. The father, however, yielded to the demands of the mother to the degree of taking, against his professional ambition, a job as night clerk in order to avoid work on Saturdays rather than using his engineering training.

The diagnostic efforts in this case began and continued along the lines of gathering developmental data and looking for direct expressions of the emotional relationships and personality patterns in the family without, however, leading to much psychodynamic information. A few quotations from the record may serve to illustrate the fruitlessness of this abstract and direct pursuit of psychodynamic information. The intake worker's recording contained the following statement:

> The mother and Miriam were seen by . . . at intake and it was felt that the dynamics in the symptom picture were not clear, though there was some suggestion that the child was developing a neurosis. Even had the symptoms been more definite, it would have been difficult to understand them in view of the family situation and the developmental data as presented by the mother. There was some feeling that all the material pertinent to the case had not been uncovered and, therefore, that further exploration was necessary before a full understanding of the situation could be reached and a definitive diagnosis made.

An opening which might have made the gaining of such understanding possible occurred fairly soon in the course of the therapeutic process. Five months after treatment had started, the child
produced material in play, which to a culturally sensitized worker
might have been a valuable clue. At that time we find the recording as follows:

> When we played mother and child she continued to play the role
> of the mother. . . . From the beginning she was very much con-
> cerned whether . . . I would play the bad child who would insist on
> drinking milk during the meal. Every time I played this role she gave
> in and gave me the milk to drink.
>
> In one of the last interviews I attempted to introduce a new toy
> and suggested that we play with blocks. She rejected this idea imme-
> diately but permitted me to play with the blocks when we played
> mother and child. She herself would not touch the blocks. Once in an
> angry tone she said that I could "play blocks" with the boys who
> came after her but with her I should play with the dishes. It seems to
> me that the blocks threatened her. The fact that they were pieces of
> hard wood which made noise when they fell over made her feel
> uncomfortable.

In other words, the child in this play tried to talk about her
problem in the language of the orthodox concerns of her mother.
To a worker sensitized to cultural material in the nexus of Jewish
orthodoxy the symbolic meaning of "badness" in terms of drink-
ing milk during meals (a violation of the food ritual of Jewish law
regarding the separation of "Milchiks and Fleischiks") would
have been obvious. To this worker it meant so little that she not
only failed to pick up a valuable lead but actually interfered with
the child's attempt to communicate with her by attempting to
introduce a new toy—blocks. Even the psychoanalytically un-
trained person will find it difficult not to be impressed by the
dramatic symbolism of the interplay between the worker's unconscious psychological use of her own culture and the psychological use of cultural symbolism by the child. Indeed the blocks
did threaten the child, because the worker "blocked" unconsciously Miriam's attempts to work out her problem.

It is not surprising, therefore, that an evaluation summary prepared a month after this recording showed that very little in-

formation had been gained, as can be seen from the following
tentative and speculative diagnostic statements:

> Various symptoms seem to indicate that a psychoneurosis is
> developing. Her various fears, her overidentification with the mother,
> and her inability to play with other children, seem to be the result
> of guilt feelings both on Miriam's and her mother's part.
> The mother, in spite of her interest, patience, and sensitivity
> toward Miriam's emotional development, lacks security. She has
> always been afraid to limit Miriam in anything lest her development
> be hampered. The mother's insecurity seems to be due to guilty
> feelings, which might originate from an unconscious rejection of
> Miriam. . . . Miriam's various fears might also be an expression
> of conflict between her superego and her impulses.

Another evaluation summary about two years later showed
the same frustration of the diagnostic search. After the sterility of
this approach finally became apparent and a new worker had
been assigned to Miriam, during the fourth year of treatment,
problems of Jewishness were picked up in the therapeutic process.
When the question came up as to whether the child should be
sent to camp, the new worker showed her perception for the
family's orthodox concerns by mentioning to Miriam's mother
that ritualistic observance in this camp might not be adequate
from her point of view. Since the mother seemed unable to make
a decision regarding this matter, the worker arranged to see
Miriam's father. Her readiness to begin the discussion with him
in terms of his religious—that is, cultural—concerns, apparently
helped her gain an immediate flow of emotional associations
which in one interview produced more psychodynamic information than the culture-avoiding interviews with the child's mother
had produced over a period of years. This appears with dramatic
force from the following recording:

> Miriam's father showed considerable resentment toward his wife
> because he had been kept to his job working for ten years at night, in
> an effort to avoid working on the Sabbath. Recently he had been
> changed to the day shift but still deplored the fact that he had been
> unable to use his engineering training. He indicated his feelings of
> helplessness out of consideration for his wife's demands, commenting
> that he knew how deeply it would hurt her if he were to take any

steps, by way of getting a better job, which might require his working on the Sabbath. He admitted that, although he himself did not believe in this, he was interested in Jewish culture, would remain a member of an orthodox synagogue, and would not go into a reform or conservative Judaism. Nevertheless, he felt that there was such a thing as an orthodoxy which was more modern than the orthodoxy which his family was prone to practice. As a means of showing how his wife used the strictest interpretation possible, he referred to the Bible's prohibition of cohabitation between wife and husband before and following the menstrual period. His wife interpreted this in the strictest sense and insisted upon their not cohabiting for a period of two weeks, although the ritual prohibition of intercourse was required for only one week according to Jewish law. This led to a discussion of their sexual problems, in the course of which the father admitted his recognition that his wife was not too happy or satisfied, saying that she never actually seemed to enjoy their relationship.

Thus taking up a religious concern of the family with the parents produced information which showed that the mother neurotically used her culture as part of her defense mechanisms regarding her incompatibility with her husband.

Another incident in this case also illustrates the value of therapeutic readiness to pay attention to the religious concerns of the patients. Three months after the new worker had taken over she arranged a little celebration on the occasion of Miriam's birthday. The incident was connected with cultural material in the child's concern about the kosher quality of the ice cream which the worker had intended to buy for her, and its use for gathering psychodynamic information may be judged from the following passage:

I had planned a party for Miriam. She had asked to be permitted to purchase the cake and candy when she came in. Consequently we made arrangements to go down together to make these purchases. As we went downstairs, Miriam questioned whether the ice cream sold at the candy store was kosher, stating that she would very much like to have the ice cream for her birthday party but wanted to make sure that it was the right kind. I suggested that we ask about this and Miriam started to hem and haw. She then said that she would like the ice cream and why didn't she get it anyway. I commented here that Miriam seemed to be somewhat in conflict in regard to the ice cream, on the one hand, wanting it whether it was kosher or not and, on the other hand, seeming to have some question about it. She looked at me somewhat fearfully and asked if I had ever eaten non-kosher food. She then stated, without waiting for an answer, that she knew that Anna (her previous worker) had not always eaten food that was kosher, and I asked her how she felt about that. Her comment here was that people who did that would not be "good Jews," although it did not mean that they could not go to Palestine. When I wondered what Miriam meant by a "good Jew," she stated that it was necessary for a good Jew to adhere to all of the Ten Commandments, although she did not believe in adhering to one of them— "Thou Must [sic] Honor Thy Father and Mother." Seeming to gain more emphasis here, she indicated that she did not feel it fair for parents to expect children to honor them when they, in turn, did not honor their children. When I asked what she meant by "not honoring," she said, "Yelling and hitting them." When I questioned her as to whether or not her parents yelled at her and hit her she seemed to shut up like a clam and suggested that we go to buy the ice cream, which we did; and in addition to the ice cream she chose marshmallow cookies which I later learned were not kosher, although I had not been aware of this at the time.

From that point on the child was able to communicate to the worker her feelings about her parents.

In one of the next interviews . . . Miriam suddenly asked the worker whether she would ever hit a child, and indicated in the conversation that ensued that she would like the worker to tell her mother not to hit her any more. She said she thought that mothers should be very good friends with their children and although her mother wanted to be friends with her, actually her mother was mean. Her mother hit her, she commented, so she hit her back. It was not that her mother hit her so frequently, but she wanted to be reasoned with. She then leaned over to the worker and said that she wanted her to know that her greatest fear was that of adults. This was the reason, she said, she yelled so much, because only if she yelled at them would adults not yell at her and tell her what to do all the time. Thus the worker was enabled to interpret to Miriam the meaning of one of her original symptoms, namely, her tendency to assume the adult role and more specifically, the mother role in her play with other children. Although Miriam became extremely defensive when given this interpretation, she began to change her negative attitude toward going to camp, which until then had been very strong. In spite of retaining some fears about it, she decided to go through with the camp experience as a means of making new friends, and adjusted in the camp fairly well.

In the further development of the case, it was possible to help the child more and more to assume the behavior corresponding to her chronological age, to play with children, and to overcome her fears. She began to express an interest in boys and in getting married and bearing children.

To be sure, the psychological mechanisms which became clearer when the conscious concern of the child and the parents' problems of Jewish orthodoxy had been picked up and utilized were much more complex than can be indicated here. The point of this presentation is only to show how a worker, who permits a patient to develop psychodynamic material in the language of his cultural concerns, will gain deeper understanding of the underlying unconscious or consciously hidden problems than a worker who insists on getting direct emotional expressions from him.

CHAPTER SIX

Culture and Culture Conflict
in Psychotherapy (continued)

IN ADDITION to being of value as an aid in understanding patients' attitudes and emotions, the concept of *culture* and its derivatives is of potential usefulness in therapeutic planning. Again this is an area of therapeutic concern where the social science concept of *culture conflict* could be integrated with psychiatric theory in order to furnish methodological tools for practice. Its value in diagnostic inquiry has been discussed in Chapters 4 and 5.

Culture conflict can come about in various ways, such as through migration, conquest of one population group by another, the influence of modern mass communication extended to areas with a culture pattern different from that in which the communication originated. Of particular importance for child guidance work and psychotherapy in general, however, are those culture conflicts which arise from social change within one society.

> . . . Culture conflicts are the natural outgrowth of processes of social differentiation, which produce an infinity of social groupings, each with its own definitions of life situations, its own interpretations of social relationships, its own ignorance or misunderstanding of the social values of other groups. The transformation of a culture from a homogeneous and well-integrated type to a heterogeneous and disintegrated type is therefore accompanied by an increase of conflict situations. Conversely, the operation of integrating processes will reduce the number of conflict situations. Such conflicts within a changing culture may be distinguished from those created when different cultural systems come in contact with one another, regardless of the character or stage of development of these systems. In either case, the conduct of members of a group involved in

By OTTO POLLAK IN CONSULTATION WITH YONATA FELDMAN

the conflict of codes will in some respects be judged abnormal by the other group.[1]

Such social differentiations are frequently the result of inventions, discoveries, and experiences which diversely influence various population groups within one larger society. More theoretical attention might be paid by therapists of the clinic and by therapists generally to the degree to which the Freudian discoveries and the therapeutic experience of their impact on human life set the profession apart from other population groups. According to anthropological theory, a person may be not only a *creature*, but also a *creator* and *manipulator* of culture. Cultural environment is an important influence in the formation of personality, but once the personality has been formed the individual may bring about cultural development in turn.[2] There can be little doubt that most child therapists have been exposed to a type of cultural experience which is different from that of the parents of their patients. This differential experience may be due (1) to their own personality structure and motivations for choosing their vocation; (2) to being influenced by the various discoveries of psychoanalysis; and (3) to close contact with cases in which certain types of child rearing have led to disorders in the patient's development. It is understandable indeed that some or even many child therapists should disapprove at times of the culture from which the parents of their patients have come and as a result should pursue treatment goals that reflect values opposed to those of the parents. Such goal setting may present an important source of therapeutic failure because of the familial and societal reactions to which it exposes the patient who is experiencing personality change in the course of therapy, unless the worker is aware of this possibility.[3] It is important, therefore, to find out how culture conflict between the therapist and the key people in the child's family and wider environment may express

[1] Sellin, Thorsten, *Culture Conflict and Crime:* A Report of the Subcommittee on Delinquency of the Committee on Personality and Culture. Bulletin 41. Social Science Research Council, New York, 1938, pp. 66–67.

[2] See, for instance, Simmons, Leo W., editor, *Sun Chief:* The Autobiography of a Hopi Indian. Yale University Press, New Haven, 1942, p. 388.

[3] See Chapter 3.

itself. Perhaps one of the most important expressions may be found in the diverse attitudes which workers and parents may show toward certain aspects of symptomatic behavior. In cases of rebellion against the culturally determined demands of his parents, the child's behavior manifestation may encounter a culturally determined sympathy on the part of the worker. Culture conflict which expresses itself in sympathy with the child's rebellion may lead the worker to pay insufficient attention to the psychodynamic meaning of the child's reaction to his culture. Consequently the therapeutic effort may be directed against this culture rather than to relieving the child's psychological disturbances.

In cases of exaggerated submission to cultural demands the parents may fail to see the seriousness of the condition and even resent the disappearance of the symptom, although from the point of view of psychodynamics this may represent improvement. As a result they may oppose certain therapeutic measures, or even withdraw the child from treatment, when culturally supported symptoms begin to subside. Both these situations have important implications for therapeutic planning.

Special complications can arise when improvement can be brought about only by the therapist's acceptance of periods of regressive infantile behavior on the part of the child. Such periods of regression to earlier levels of development are necessary to make possible the reenactment of previously intolerable situations. Through their acceptance in the therapeutic situation, in contrast to the former parental reactions, the child is helped to overcome the original traumatic experiences and to develop a strong attachment to the therapist. This relationship can then be used to help the child develop self-restricting behavior if this is indicated.[1] Thus treatment may imply a phase of experience in which the child shows even less conformity to cultural expectations than before the therapeutic process started. The child's parents, however, may not understand the therapeutic nature of this temporary regression because they, as well as other persons

[1] See Chapter 8.

in the community, expect from treatment immediate improvement of the child in accordance with the cultural norms for his age-group. Thus a conflict arises between therapeutic values and environmental values, which must be taken into consideration by the therapist if he is to be of assistance to the parents and the community during this temporary stage of the therapeutic process. This will make it necessary for the therapist to know the environmental expectations which the culture of the child implies.

Once it is understood how strongly the customs and value judgments of a culture are rooted in most individuals, workers will be better equipped to adjust their therapeutic effort to that framework. They will be able to distinguish meaningfully between symptoms that are culturally supported and symptoms that make for cultural concern. On that basis they will be able to predict the emotional reactions that parents and the community will have to therapeutic changes and to interpret the necessary therapeutic measures. Because of culture conflict between the worker and the parent, the worker may fail to see the need for such interpretation and to recognize the prognostic impact which the parental attitudes toward symptoms and specific therapeutic measures may exert.

The worker's interpretive task will be facilitated if he realizes that culture conflict between therapists and the key persons in the patient's family and wider environment will be related *more often* to temporary than to permanent treatment goals. It is usually a part of the therapeutic plan to help the patient express his feelings of aggression and hostility as a temporary phase of the therapeutic experience. Administrative requirements of scheduling interviews may interfere with school attendance. Camp experiences may require the child to eat food which is not prepared according to the orthodox food ritual practiced in his home. Such temporary treatment goals or therapeutic measures, which in the overall picture may only be steps toward the ultimate treatment goal of curing the patient, may be in conflict with important values in the culture pattern of the parents.

In actual practice the culture conflict between therapists and patients usually finds more than one expression, as is illustrated below in the case of Kenneth. As will be seen, the parents of this boy failed to realize the seriousness of his condition because some aspects of his personality tied in with their sense of values. The worker failed to help the parents understand the meaning of the therapeutic measures indicated because he was antagonistic to the cultural concerns which these measures violated.

Eight-year-old Kenneth was referred by a teacher of a Workmen's Circle School because he was disruptive in class. The intake worker recorded this as a referral from a Hebrew school, apparently not being aware of or not appreciating the difference in ideology between a socialistically oriented Yiddish school and the orthodoxy and conservatism of a traditional Hebrew school (Cheder). It was with difficulty that the teacher had persuaded Kenneth's mother to seek help from the clinic because she did not feel that such a step was justified.

In intake the following symptom picture was established. Kenneth made excessive demands for attention and material things and had severe temper outbursts when his wishes were denied, throwing dishes and breaking furniture. He quarreled constantly with his sister, of whom he was very jealous, stole on occasions, and suffered from frequent nosebleeds. It appeared to his mother that sometimes he made his nose bleed deliberately when he did not have his own way.

The developmental history revealed that he had soiled and wet himself until he was four years old and had been a thumb sucker until six months before his referral. Also there had been periods of stammering. At the time of referral he suffered from sleep disturbances. In spite of all these past and present difficulties and her wish that Kenneth show her more obedience, the mother did not see any particular reason for considering her son sick, because he was "a bright child" and did well scholastically in school. She said that sometimes when she tutored him she was "thrilled at his rapid learning ability." She had enrolled both Kenneth and his sister early in nursery school and reported with satisfaction that the teacher had "raved" about how bright and well-behaved Kenneth was. She had insisted on having both children take piano lessons even though paying for these lessons entailed sacrifice on the part of her husband and herself. She had personally supervised their practicing. When Kenneth objected to practicing, she made him study theory of music instead.

She admitted always having acceded to Kenneth's wishes as she had to her father's, saying that in spite of the latter's being very strict, she had greatly admired him and enjoyed working for him because she "liked to work with smart people." She had married her husband—who proved to be an inadequate earner and inadequate father—"because he was so smart."

Thus the mother of this boy expressed from the very beginning the keynote of her traditional Jewish value system, which centered around learning, intellectual achievement, and school success.

Kenneth's father was an unsuccessful businessman and spent most of his time poring over his books. He was withdrawn from his children, would never correct them himself, and when they touched his books, he would ask his wife to protect him against such interference with his scholarly pursuits.

Diagnostically Kenneth appeared to suffer from a behavior disorder, having never been able to develop internal controls because of an indulgent and overprotective mother and an uninterested, weak, and withdrawn father. Because of this family constellation and his mother's failure to see any need for individual treatment either for herself or the child, Kenneth was referred to exclusive group therapy. However, no real attempt was made to relate to this mother the nature of her son's difficulties in terms of her conscious and culturally supported concern, which centered around his success in school.

Because of the value put on education by her group and her son's scholastic success, Kenneth's mother was ready to overlook his serious behavior difficulties. The worker, however, realized that his ability to succeed in school might be threatened. In addition to his aggression there was nose picking to the point of bleeding, indicating that Kenneth was unable to deny self-gratification. Therefore it would have been possible for the worker to interpret to this mother that her son's infantile behavior might endanger at some time also his learning process at school. Since it was the school that had made the referral and school success was the mother's concern, it might have been easy, or at least worth trying, to connect these two phenomena in the interpretation of the need for and purpose of therapy.

One might have been able to strengthen this line of communication between the mother and the clinic by making direct contact with the school. That this was not considered important is apparent from the fact that instead of the therapist's making the contact himself a volunteer was sent to the school. When that volunteer failed to find the Workmen's Circle School from which the referral had been made and where Kenneth received his Jewish education, the worker did not follow up this matter. His disregard for the emotional meaning which that aspect of transmitting Jewish culture to their children had for the parents comes out clearly in the following recording:

> "The volunteer was unable to find the Workmen's Circle School.
> . . . Further attempt is not to be made at the present time since it is
> not considered essential to diagnosis or decision about treatment."
>
> No consideration was given to the fact that the schedule of the
> group therapy sessions interfered with Kenneth's attendance at
> the Workmen's Circle School. Therefore the mother became reluctant to have Kenneth attend the group meetings. Since his
> parents preferred to have him pursue his studies and receive a
> Jewish education rather than have him go through with treatment,
> Kenneth attended only irregularly. Although he showed some improvement, they finally withdrew him from therapy.

The worker, steeped in therapeutic culture, regarded the emotional involvement of the mother in the values of her group as an obstacle to treatment, which it was, but failed to see his therapeutic obligation to work this out with her in terms of her own values and cultural understanding. This came out dramatically in his statement:

> In view of the mother's dullness and complete lack of insight as to
> Kenneth's needs and role of his behavior problems, little could be
> accomplished, in this worker's opinion, through work with her. However, the best thing possible would be to continue Kenneth in group
> treatment . . . while the mother is guided on a superficial basis.

It would seem that the mother's "lack of insight" was determined by the worker's lack of understanding of the cultural background of this family and his consequent failure to interpret the nature and aim of the therapeutic process to her in terms of her conscious concerns rather than in those of his specific training and own professional culture.

How differently such cultural concerns of the parents which may interfere with treatment can be handled by a worker is suggested by the case of Eli, which was mentioned in Chapter 5 and is analyzed below. In this case the worker showed cultural understanding of the parents and ability to discuss their concern in terms of the culture from which they originated rather than his own. This was possible for him because, free from culture conflict and possessed of a deep insight regarding the meaning of each culture—i.e., believing it to be life maintaining rather than life inhibiting—he found ways of relating treatment purpose and treatment procedure to the cultural framework of the family.

Eli, thirteen years and six months old, was referred to the clinic because he had been stealing from his parents and from children, was disrespectful to his teacher, was uninterested at school, and had had a period of truancy. At home he displayed a violent temper, was easily provoked, and was destructive. He was abusive to his mother, calling her names and throwing things at her. He had difficulty in making friends and preferred younger children, whom he tried to dominate. He also had several neurotic symptoms of a compulsive nature.

The child of an unmarried mother, he had been placed in an institution shortly after birth. When not quite four years old, he was adopted by an orthodox Jewish couple. The father was a coffee salesman and a fairly good provider. He was suffering from ulcers and played a subordinate role in the child's upbringing. The mother, like the father, of Chassidic Jewish background, suffered from a psychoneurosis and showed an extremely rigid and critical attitude toward Eli. She made excessive demands on him for cleanliness, for adherence to restrained behavior, and constantly nagged him, urging him to read, or occupy himself with some pursuit of which she approved. She would not permit him to play or associate with friends of whom she disapproved. She was still feeding, dressing, and bathing this thirteen and one-half-year-old boy. She controlled his every move and checked his every step. Both parents, in their orthodoxy, were eager to rear Eli as a religious Jew and for this reason were sending him to a Yeshiva, but he constantly thwarted them by his delinquencies.

When in the course of treatment it became apparent that he would have to be placed in an institution, the worker showed his cultural understanding by preparing the mother for the difference in living conditions which this placement would mean for Eli. Actually the worker took the initiative in the matter. He could do so, however, because, having a full knowledge of Jewish ritual law, he was able to use it as an aid rather than fear it as an obstacle to therapy. This appears from the following recording:

> "She discussed with me the possibility of sending Eli to camp or placing him in an institution. Though I told her that the camp did not observe Kashruth, she did not listen to me but built up a fantasy that since the camp was supported by the Federation of Jewish Philanthropies, famous rabbis must be running it. I constantly had to remind her that this was her wish but that the reality was different. However, I did point out to her that both camp and institution were places to help Eli improve and that for this reason just as in cases of curing physical illness, the Jewish law permitted transgression and even eating un-kosher food."
>
> When, two months later, the question of institutional placement reached a decisive stage, the worker again brought up the problem of religious observance. The mother told the worker that she had a surprise for him: regardless of all this, she was still willing to place Eli. And she quoted the worker as having said to her before that it was permissible for a sick person to transgress the law.

It is essential for a therapist to be aware that treatment goals which oppose cultural values in the patient's environment may prove to be unattainable or even harmful to the patient. This does not necessarily imply, however, that the therapist has to accept these values without scrutiny. He will also have to consider the possibility that some aspects of the culture pattern in the patient's environment may be disturbance promoting. First of all, it should be remembered that he is not only a therapist of individual patients but is also the member of a profession, interested in the prevention of such mental disturbances on a general basis, that is, in the promotion of mental health principles in which he has come to believe as a result of his training and experience. As such, he certainly has the right, and perhaps the obligation, to help in bringing about the appropriate changes in child rearing. The question arises, however, whether he may do so in setting individual treatment goals or only in efforts to promote the necessary changes on a broader societal basis.

There seem to exist different schools of thought among psychoanalysts in this respect. Some seem inclined to confine their professional concern to the function of the social reformer only and are generally skeptical of any immediate usefulness of cultural concern in individual therapy. Others, such as Erich Fromm, take the opposite point of view and advocate consideration of cultural change in the individual case if it appears desirable from the point of view of mental hygiene.[1]

From the social science angle the phenomenon of social change may well be worthy of consideration also in the individual case. The point should be made, however, that the therapist would have to combine insight into principles of mental hygiene with anthropological and sociological understanding. In combining the anthropological with the psychodynamic point of view, he would have to understand that cultures other than his own may be also compatible with principles of mental hygiene. Of importance also is the fact that in many cultures there may be elements that are incompatible with such principles, not because they were so originally but have become so as a result of changes in the conditions for which the cultural solution was originally designed. A quotation from Kluckhohn may serve to clarify this point:

> Most groups elaborate certain aspects of their culture far beyond maximum utility or survival value. . . . Aspects of culture which once were adaptive may persist long after they have ceased to be useful. . . . Any cultural practice must be functional or it will disappear before long.[2]

Thus the individual patient may be helped to free himself from such aspects of his culture as have become obsolete and this may be made part of the treatment goal. However, the situational

[1] Fromm, Erich, "Individual and Social Origins of Neurosis" in *Personality in Nature, Society, and Culture*, edited by Clyde Kluckhohn and Henry A. Murray. Alfred A. Knopf, Inc., New York, 1948, pp. 412–413.

[2] Kluckhohn, Clyde, *Mirror for Man.* Whittlesey House, New York, 1949, p. 27.

approach of sociology would suggest that the power position of an individual in his life environment will determine how much of such therapeutic gain he will be able to utilize or to retain. In this respect, the child is less fortunate than the adult. This would suggest that a child will have little chance to develop along the lines of social change much beyond the point permitted by the conscious and unconscious desires of his parents, his agemates, and his schoolteachers. Therapists, therefore, may have to determine treatment goals in accordance with the views these key people hold or may be expected to acquire with the help of the therapist.

This interplay between psychological, anthropological, and sociological insight would suggest moderation in setting the treatment goal for children in relation to the recognition of social obsolescence and vistas of social change. That this opinion is beginning to become accepted in child psychiatry is evident in the writings of Erik Homburger Erikson, who has also engaged in anthropological research.

> It would be interesting to speculate in how far a certain determined lack of maternalism in American mothers is historically founded, not only in religious puritanism, but in adaptation to historical conditions which made it dangerous for a son to believe more in the past than in the future; dangerous to base his identity on the adherence to his childhood home rather than on the migration in pursuit of a better chance; dangerous ever to appear to be a "sissy" or a "sucker" instead of one who has learned to tolerate a certain amount of deprivation and loneliness. We should search in every collective vice for outdated virtues; for only he who understands historical ways of securing survival and identity can in his advice to individuals or communities either suggest measures which are based on existing fragments of cultural identity, or hold his peace until history changes.[1]

The following case is presented in order to show how a therapist's lack of such moderation may drive a patient back into pathology. It is presented, however, only from that point of view,

---

[1] Erikson, Erik Homburger, "Childhood and Tradition in Two American Indian Tribes," in *Personality in Nature, Society, and Culture*, p. 202.

without implying that this worker's opinion on cultural obsolescence is necessarily valid as such.

Leah, one of three siblings, was referred at nine years of age
because she had been a bed wetter for three years following an attack
of scarlet fever, during which she developed "bladder catarrh."
That illness occurred at the time of her brother's birth. Leah had
initiated sex play between herself and her sister, age eight, and during
treatment started to do so also with her little brother. Occasionally
she would try to stand up like a boy while urinating. She was a nail
biter and was moody and unhappy, especially during the two years
preceding intake, and had become intensely jealous of her sister
because of the latter's being also in therapy. Shortly before intake she
had developed pains in her stomach. She was afraid to go to the
bathroom in the dark, a fear shared by her sister. Physical examination revealed the somatic symptoms to be without traceable organic
cause.

Leah's father, a successful lawyer, was a very orthodox Jew. Her
mother, in contrast, was almost irreligious, although she complied
with the father's standard for keeping a Jewish household. There
was, however, some overt conflict between the parents over religion.
The father, for instance, was firm in his desire to have the children
attend a religious rather than a public school, whereas the mother
disapproved of this. The father, a man of high intellectual achievement, blamed the children's difficulties on his wife, who was an unhappy, withdrawn, and inhibited person with deep inferiority and
guilt feelings.

The diagnostic considerations in this case indicated that Leah was
reacting to the marked inconsistencies between the parents and was
prevented from a resolution of the oedipal situation. This expressed
itself in her close relationship to the father of whom she was very
proud, although he was very dogmatic with her and on occasions
beat her, as well as the other children, severely. It was not possible
to make a clear-cut differential diagnosis in this case. At any rate it
so happened that the therapist who treated Leah's sister, as well as
Leah's therapist, was culturally antagonistic to Jewish orthodoxy
and therefore to the value system of the father.

As a result both therapists had a resentful and at the same time
defeatist attitude toward the father's religious concerns and were
pessimistic about the possibility of carrying out the therapeutic
measures which seemed diagnostically indicated. At first the suggestion was made that Leah's sister should be placed, but immediately
it was considered extremely difficult to find an orthodox foster home
for her. The father, however, would not let the child be placed where

the foster parents would not strictly observe the rules of Jewish ritual law.

As far as the record shows, no attempt was made to discuss with the father the latitude in rule observance which Jewish law permits in cases of disease. Consequently it apparently was never discovered whether the father misused his religious beliefs for pathological reasons or not.[1]

> Later on the desirability of placement for Leah herself came up. The plan to place her was considered desirable, but no attempt was made to do so because of the therapist's belief in the irremediable rigidity of the father's adherence to the ritual.

Following this line of negative reaction to the father's convictions, the worker started out on a road of therapy which was bound to bring Leah into conflict with her father's religious beliefs. This was done even though the worker herself considered him so rigid as to abandon a placement attempt that was thought desirable from the therapeutic point of view. By doing so the worker transferred the culture conflict between herself and the child's father to the relationship between the patient and the latter. Her unconcern about the possible consequence of such a therapeutic plan in terms of parental reactions comes out in the following recording:

> On the whole Leah has made great strides during this year. One has seen the maturation process develop with such rapidity physically, as well as emotionally, that almost in the space of a few sessions, Leah has become a different girl. She has emerged as quite an independent, *free-thinking* young lady with a much greater ability to verbalize her feelings, to relax in sessions, to make demands upon me without any hesitation or evidences of conflict; indeed the former dependency and passivity have given way to much greater self assertion and aggression.

If the worker had been aware of the phenomena of culture conflict and social interaction, she might have wondered whether, with an orthodox father with whom the child had a deeper emotional tie than with the mother, this would work out well. As a

[1] See the different handling of a similar situation in the case of Eli, on page 126.

matter of fact the worker's next report revealed that the child was frightened by the impact of such a development. Her flight reaction expressed itself in an identification with her father's religious beliefs and in a behavior pattern of submerging herself, in the orthodox pattern of Jewish religion, as can be seen from the following recording:

> Leah began to use religious dogma and rituals in working out the oedipal situation, making a strong identification with the orthodox religious father, who minutely carried out the practice of the Torah, and openly fighting the less orthodox and disbelieving mother on every infraction of the rules. To Leah at this time, her studies in the Torah became less an intellectual pursuit and more of a confirmed way of life with each action accounted for. She showed tremendous intolerance and hostility toward the mother for her lack of conviction and her disregard of the religious laws which Leah herself accepted so wholeheartedly. She spoke at length of the fact that she and her father only would go to Heaven but that mother would be punished and be "banished" to a far less pleasant place after death. She spoke of all the times that she was forced to pick her mother up on little things that the latter was careless about, but which had such meaning according to biblical law. Her mother in turn was having a strongly negative reaction to Leah's criticism. As the girl continued to bring this kind of material in and I attempted to explain the meaning of it to her, she reacted to me as she did to her mother. She accused me of being a disbeliever and not really being a good Jew, saying that I, too, would share her mother's fate. She was sure that I did not want a kosher household, or to go to synagogue regularly, or to Mikvah (ritual bath) after my menstrual period to cleanse myself, as it says in the Torah.

Actually the child was right. The worker was unorthodox and resented orthodoxy, but the child's statements also indicated a negative mother transference to the worker. Rather than help Leah make therapeutic gains only within the limits of the cultural determinants active in her life situation, the worker pursued the therapeutic goal of freeing Leah of her unconsciously incestuous relationship with her father without coming to terms with its dynamics. She kept the content of the therapeutic sessions geared to the religious concern, thus instituting a moral judgment about the child's father and criticism of his behavior which the child could not endure. The father, of course, reacted negatively to such a moral judgment of his own religious views on the realistic level and of his own unconscious incestuous wishes on the emotional level, and the case ended unsuccessfully.

The various aspects of culture conflict discussed in this chapter suggest basically two implications for therapeutic planning. The therapist must relate the therapeutic goal to the conscious concern of the persons who have social power in relation to the child. In order to do this, it is necessary not only to understand the dynamic structure of their personality, but also to understand the culture of these people in its life-maintaining aspects as well as in its obsolete aspects, and to make sure that one's own beliefs about that culture are in accord with reality.

Where obsolete parts of culture in the life environment of the patient interfere with measures conducive to his health, the first therapeutic task would be to include the carriers of that culture in the therapeutic process. Without success in that direction, being healthy and free from the impact of obsolete cultural material will prove, in most instances, a burden which a child will not be able to bear. In cases where it is not possible to involve the carriers of this culture in social change through therapeutic influence, the treatment goal should be limited, because of the essential dependency of children on adults. This subject will be discussed further in Chapter 10.

CHAPTER SEVEN

Age-Sex Roles and Psychotherapy of Adolescents

PSYCHOTHERAPY of children and adolescents is still largely under the influence of principles established in the treatment of adult patients. Treatment procedures which are successful with adults, however, may result in failure, if they are applied to individuals of other age categories.

That childhood and adolescence represent specific stages of psychodynamic development is recognized by the therapists of the clinic. It is not sufficiently recognized by them, however, that the various stages of the growth process have significance in terms of societal structure, as well as in terms of psychodynamics. Membership in a specific age-sex category determines to a large degree the criteria of appropriateness of behavior which society demands from an individual. It determines his *social roles* at that stage of his development, that is, "the internally consistent series of responses which constitute the culturally expected behavior of an individual in a certain situation."[1] Appropriateness of behavior in terms of role performance, however, does not mean only conformity with patterns of overt behavior. It means also acceptance of restraints. Assignment of certain roles means interdiction of others.

Assumption of a role not befitting the age-sex category to which one belongs may be an expression of internal conflict. It also may produce external conflict. In our society an adolescent girl of middle-class background who engages in promiscuous sexual contacts because of inner conflict is likely to bring upon herself consequences of social disapproval which will tend to increase her

By OTTO POLLAK IN COLLABORATION WITH DOROTHY DUNAEFF

[1] Cottrell, Leonard S., Jr., "The Adjustment of the Individual to His Age and Sex Roles," *American Sociological Review*, vol. 7, October, 1942, p. 617.

difficulties. Correspondingly, refusal to assume a social role which, on the basis of his age and sex, an individual is supposed to perform may be both an expression of internal conflict and a causative factor in producing external conflict. A boy who, in view of his chronological age and his physiological maturation may be expected to go out with girls but for psychological reasons is not ready to do so, will encounter pressure by his peers to start "dating." This in turn may increase his difficulties.

Furthermore it is important to consider that an individual's membership in a specific age-sex category not only indicates what he may or may not do in terms of appropriate behavior, but also defines his position of social importance in the eyes of his associates. It gives him *status*. "Since differences in social importance mean differences in social rewards and thereby in the amount of available and socially permissible need satisfactions, the study of status is germane to that of all adjustment problems of the members of a population group."[1] Belonging to a specific age-sex category therefore implies also an element of relative power as compared with the members of other age-sex categories. This element of power expresses itself both in the quality and quantity of need satisfactions which society grants the individual on the basis of his age-sex category and in the leeway which it grants him with regard to deviations from the patterns of behavior considered appropriate.

No psychotherapy is likely to be free from social repercussions to the development of the patient in and after treatment. The social role and status aspects of the age-sex group to which the patient belongs therefore deserve consideration by the therapist in formulating treatment methods and setting treatment goals. This is an area where disregard of societal structure can be very harmful, particularly to adolescent patients, and a source of grievous disappointment to the therapist. Acting out conflicts in relation to persons other than the therapist seems to be more frequently incompatible with the social roles and the status of adolescents than of either children or adults.

[1] Pollak, Otto, *Social Adjustment in Old Age.* Bulletin 59. Social Science Research Council, New York, 1948, p. 37.

The preadolescent child who, in the course of therapy, carries his acting out beyond the treatment situation is protected for the most part by the special license which society grants to that age group. Furthermore the child is less likely to commit acts of real harm either to himself or to society, and any attempt to do so can be more easily detected. The adult, on the other hand, has relatively more freedom from the wider society and the family in terms of behavior patterns and behavior changes than the adolescent, particularly as far as sexual expression is concerned.

The social role and status differentials between childhood, adolescence, and adulthood therefore affect the repercussions of family and wider society to implications of psychotherapy. They affect them, first of all, in relation to the period of emotional and behavioral experimentation outside of the therapeutic situation, which frequently accompanies effective treatment for a certain period of time before it is completed. They also determine the permission to utilize and retain the therapeutic gains of completed treatment which family and society grant the patient.

To perceive the impact of these differentials, even without underlying social science theory, is relatively easy in the case of child patients because of their physiological immaturity and the degree of their social dependency on other persons in their environment. With adolescents the situation is different. They have physiological maturity and their social dependency is quantitatively less pronounced. Also, as far as the latter still exists, it is relatively hidden under the cover of quasi-adult behavior in the minutiae of daily life.

Another factor which makes it difficult for child guidance workers to perceive the significance of these differentials may lie in their own age. At the beginning of their careers many are chronologically close to the adolescent group. Sometimes they are also emotionally so. As a consequence they are in danger of identification with adolescent patients and negative countertransference toward the adults who form the living environment of these adolescent patients. Such psychological involvements may interfere with the treatment given in terms of the realities with which the patients have to live during and, in all probability, for a period of time after treatment.

It would seem desirable, therefore, to equip the therapists of a child guidance clinic with a concept that would make it easier for them to perceive adolescent patients as persons belonging to a specific population group with an attitude and behavior pattern, as well as a status of their own, which must be considered in the treatment plan. Recognition of the dependency status of these patients is particularly necessary because their physiological maturity makes acting out for them potentially more harmful than in the case of child patients. Nonjudgmental therapy of adolescents may therefore require stronger environmental controls than a permissive therapy of child patients. Also the therapists of adolescents must sometimes bring into the awareness of their patients the existence of limitations with greater clarity than would appear necessary in child therapy.

In this respect a social science concept formulated by Talcott Parsons may be usefully incorporated into the theory underlying psychotherapy of adolescents, namely, the concept of *youth culture*.

> Starting at about high school age young Americans, especially in the urban middle classes, embark on patterns of behavior and attitudes which do not constitute a stage in a continuous transition from childhood to adulthood but deviate from such a line of continuity. . . .
>
> This pattern of attitudes and behavior is sufficiently general and pronounced to be singled out as a distinctively structured complex conveniently called the youth culture. Its principal characteristics may be summarized.
>
> 1. Compulsive independence of and antagonism to adult expectations and authority. This involves recalcitrance to adult standards of responsibility and, in extreme instances, treating the conformist— who, for instance, takes school work seriously—as a "sissy" who should be excluded from peer group participation.
>
> 2. Compulsive conformity within the peer group of agemates. It is intolerable to be "different"; not, for example, to use lipstick as soon as the other girls do. Related to this is an intense fear of being excluded, a corresponding competitiveness for acceptance by the "right" groups, and a ruthless rejection of those who don't make the grade.

3. Romanticism: an unrealistic idealization of emotionally significant objects. There is a general tendency to see the world in sharply
black and white terms; identification with one's gang, or team, or
school tend to be very intense and involve highly immature dis-
paragements of other groups.

There is thus a well-defined sociological problem. In the socialization of the younger generation in the American social system, there is
a specifically structured deviation (a mass phenomenon) from the
path of asymptotic approach to "maturity."[1]

* * * * *

. . . It is notable that the youth culture has a strong tendency to
develop in directions which are either on the borderline of parental
approval or beyond the pale, in such matters as sex behavior, drink-
ing and various forms of frivolous and irresponsible behavior.[2]

Later on the adolescent will be confronted by more complex
problems of choice among contradictory value systems which
characterize different segments of our society. The area in which
behavioral expressions of adolescent recalcitrance to adult
standards is particularly dangerous to the rebel himself is reproductive control. It appears to be the outstanding characteristic
of adolescence that the members of that age category have
attained physiological maturity without necessarily having attained social maturity. Physiologically they are at par with, if not
better than, adults; socially they are still kept in a state of dependency which is akin to, although not identical with, childhood. Kingsley Davis has presented the societal consequences of
this transitional phenomenon as follows:

In its determination of the adolescent status, every society must
somehow recognize the fact that the reproductive capacity first
appears at the inception of adolescence. One crucial question is
whether the adolescent shall be permitted to gratify his sexual desires through normal heterosexual intercourse or whether such gratification must be postponed. A second is whether the gratification, if

---

[1] Parsons, Talcott, "Psychoanalysis and the Social Structure," *The Psychoanalytic
Quarterly*, vol. 19, July, 1950, pp. 378–379.
[2] *Idem*, "Age and Sex in the Social Structure of the United States," *American
Sociological Review*, vol. 7, October, 1942, p. 608.

permitted, shall be in marriage or in premarital relations; and if the latter, whether the illegitimate children shall be killed, disposed of to relatives, or kept by the girl. Finally, there is the question of whether marital choice is free or is controlled by others, and whether marriage establishes a separate household or merely an extension of the parental menage.

. . . American society is unusual, though not entirely unique, in the following ways: It maintains the ideal of premarital chastity in the face of a long period of postponement of marriage after puberty. In connection with this, it upholds the freedom of marital choice and fosters competition and the doctrine of *caveat emptor* in courtship. Finally, it emphasizes the independence and separateness of the wedded couple. As a consequence, the adolescent period becomes one of considerable strain.[1]

Thus the period of adolescence in our society is one of unresolved contradiction between biological maturity and social dependency. The conflict is aggravated by emotional ambivalence of the adolescent's parents, as well as of the adolescent himself toward the implications of his growing up.

. . . With the onset of puberty, the child gradually withdraws from this role and refuses to accept the hitherto established forms of family behavior. Parents react to this situation either by accepting the change and adjusting to the new development, or they resist the change and are unable to renounce their accustomed ways of gratification. Between these extremes there lie all possible gradations. But much more frequent than any consistent and static response is the fluctuating attitude of parents. Warm acceptance of the child at one moment and angry rejection of him at another is perhaps the most common form of parental response, and it indicates the highly conflicted reaction of parents in the face of the changed family situation. . . .

The ambivalent attitude of parents during the adolescent period of their child has a profound influence upon the adolescent himself. As part of his maturation he undergoes a change in his feeling life. The family ceases to be the legitimate place where he can display his feelings. While he often wishes to return to the safety of his childhood state, the investment of his feeling life with sexual components makes of the family a prohibitive retreat for the full satisfaction of his emotional needs. The stronger the family ties have been and the greater

[1] Davis, Kingsley, "Adolescence and the Social Structure," *The Annals of the American Academy of Political and Social Science*, vol. 236, November, 1944, pp. 11–12.

the self-sufficiency of the family group during the period of his childhood, the more difficult becomes the process of weaning during
adolescence both for him and for his parents. . . .

. . . The adolescent is highly sensitive to the reactions of his
parents, despite his carefully concealed and camouflaged feelings
toward them. Though he may meet their reprisals with aggression
or an apparent lack of responsiveness, he is nevertheless painfully
aware of the effect his behavior has upon them. He cannot suddenly
nullify his childhood loyalties to his mother and father. When he
provokes their anger, he is apt to feel guilty; and in an effort to
atone he may overwhelm them with a rush of affection. Particular
situations, of course, evoke the subtle interplay of personalities that
is unique for each family. But in general an unstable family relationship is created, in which the adolescent is as inconsistent in his attitude toward his parents as his parents are toward him.[1]

More than any other age period adolescence is a time of dangerous transition socially as well as emotionally. The experience
of growth in therapy reflects these dangers. The reactivation of
id drives which occurs so frequently in psychotherapeutic situations makes it particularly necessary to examine the risks involved
in treating an adolescent in our present social milieu.

Therapy of the adolescent is thus fraught with dangers which
require careful evaluation of the conditions under which it may
take place. Specifically it is necessary to find out whether the key
persons in the home environment of the adolescent are flexible
enough to contract or extend restraints, as the occasion may demand, during treatment. Unless there are such persons in the
adolescent's home environment, there are only three alternatives: (1) placement of the adolescent, (2) bringing about change
in the parents or parent substitutes through their undergoing
treatment concomitantly with the adolescent, or (3) postponing
therapy until the adolescent has achieved the status of adulthood.
Another point requiring particular attention is consideration of
the ego-strengthening function of the therapist in the treatment
of adolescents because of the risks which our youth culture, the
position of adolescents in our society, and their tenuous emotional balance present in the course of psychotherapy. The three

[1] Blos, Peter, *The Adolescent Personality*. D. Appleton-Century Co., New York,
1941, pp. 236–238. Used by permission of Appleton-Century-Crofts, Inc.

cases presented below illustrate the importance of these considerations. The first demonstrates the risks involved in attempting
outpatient treatment of an adolescent girl, from whose home
environment the necessary safeguards against acting out could
not be expected.

> Margaret, a sixteen-year-old girl, was referred to the clinic because
> of depression following a series of sexual experiences with men, which
> had occurred during the preceding summer and fall. She had a feel-
> ing of complete worthlessness, was moody and irritable, was subject
> to sudden weeping spells, had sleeping difficulties, and could not con-
> centrate on school work. She picked up boys at dances and came
> home very late at night.
>
> The important factors in the pathogenesis of this adolescent were
> overt homosexual tendencies on the part of her mother which were
> directed toward Margaret, the latter's confusion about her sexual
> identification as a result of the resentment and hostility she felt
> toward her mother, and a very strong positive relationship for her
> father. Margaret's own homosexual trends seemed to be neurotic in
> nature and an outgrowth of the oedipal conflict.
>
> The treatment plan decided upon in this case was directed at
> alleviation and relaxation of Margaret's strong unconscious need for
> punishment, pointing out inconsistencies in her behavior, bringing
> out her anxieties and fantasies, and interpreting them.
>
> Sixteen months after the formulation of this plan, Margaret, who
> had developed an intimate relationship with a boy while in therapy,
> became pregnant. Upon learning of her condition she became so
> disturbed that she presented a grave suicidal risk, indicating the
> necessity of a therapeutic abortion.

It should be noted that preoccupation in the treatment was
with the inner dynamics of Margaret's personality and the
therapist's ability to bring about a personality change in her
without due recognition of the existing social implications of her
behavior in relation to men. There were two important criteria
for evaluating the risks in the outpatient treatment of this
adolescent. One was the severe pathology of the mother, particularly centering around her need to direct her homosexual tendencies toward her daughter. It is true that the therapist never
expressed any hope of treating the basic pathology of the mother
successfully. One might have been pessimistic, however, about

the effectiveness of any therapeutic plan which aimed at bringing about a positive change in the relationship of this woman toward her daughter.

Consequently treatment had to be concentrated on the girl. Before deciding on a treatment plan it would have been necessary, however, for the therapist to evaluate not only the clinical syndrome and diagnosis in the case but also the girl's ego strength and defenses. Such an evaluation is necessary in planning the outpatient treatment of any adolescent because of the social risk that accompanies acting out on the part of members of this age group. It would have been particularly so in Margaret's case because of her mother's own deep-seated pathology, which made it highly doubtful whether sufficient restraints in the home atmosphere would be forthcoming during the course of treatment. Actually Margaret's ego strength and defenses were questionable from the beginning. It was doubtful how much anxiety she would be able to tolerate. Certainly her sexual behavior preceding the referral indicated that her capacity for control of impulses was greatly lacking. It might have been predicted, therefore, that even more acting out would occur during the treatment process. That prediction in turn might have led to a visualization of the probability of two further consequences: (1) intensification of the girl's feelings of unworthiness; (2) stimulation of her need for punishment. It might have been clear that such a stimulation would involve the risk of driving her into further violations of the social norms governing sexual conduct.

With all these negative factors militating against successful treatment, the initial diagnostic evaluation should have led to the recognition that a controlled environment was needed as the first step in attempting therapy in this case. This would have been necessary at least in order to test the possibility of establishing a constructive relationship with Margaret. The term "test" is used intentionally here since the question of the integrative forces of Margaret's personality was probably the most important in evaluating treatability. Because of the tenuous behavior pattern represented by our youth culture and the threat of emotional oscillation underlying it, before deciding on a treatment plan for adolescent patients it is of paramount importance to evaluate the adaptive pattern and the integrative forces in the personality—the ego strengths and weaknesses.

The second case presents a somewhat similar situation, namely, existence of a home environment from which the necessary restraints upon the patient's acting out could not be expected. This case is different from the preceding one, however, in the type of risk, owing to the sex of the adolescent, and in the treatment decision reached.

Louis, fifteen years old, was referred to the clinic because of severely rebellious behavior at home and at school, inability to concentrate, free-floating anxiety as well as acute anxiety attacks, periods of depression, a feeling of unworthiness, and a feeling of being deserted and all alone in the world. His parents belonged to the upper middle class; as a matter of fact, his mother was a community leader. In school his adjustment had been so poor that only pressure exerted by the clinic saved him from suspension for what appeared to be provocative disregard of school limitations and authority. Actually he experienced severe anxiety states. He had attempted to join a delinquent gang in the neighborhood as a group that would accept him, but he had quickly left it because of fear. On the other hand, he fantasied about being a big gang leader. He related extremely well to the therapist, could articulate his inner problems, could discuss his inner fears and anxieties, and wanted to overcome them. Of primary importance was his own concern about being unable to inhibit his impulses in relation to his behavior in school and his fear of getting into trouble also outside of school.

In evaluating the alternatives of theoretically possible procedures one could have thought that this case presented a situation which would lend itself very well to treatment on an outpatient basis. The boy's concern about his acting out and its possible consequences definitely seemed to point in that direction. Because of the boy's adolescence, however, the degree and flexibility of restraints upon his acting out that could be expected from forces in his home and school environment had to be evaluated before a decision in favor of outpatient treatment could be reached. On the basis of such evaluation it was decided that outpatient treatment would not be feasible in this case.

The environmental factors which determined this decision were the following. The boy's father was a rather weak and passive person from whom effective restraints could not be expected. The boy's presenting symptoms were a severe threat to the whole ego structure of his mother, who used as her defense against a recognition of her inadequacies in the performance of the maternal role all the community programs she participated in for the betterment of children. The boy was attending high school, and thus was in a school environment which did not permit the same flexibility of handling as an elementary school.

Therefore, after only six weeks of treatment, during which he became even more involved in both school and home difficulties, the decision was reached that he should be placed in a controlled environment. The advantages of such an environment were that he would not have the same opportunities to act out and that his anxieties would be accessible to treatment at the time they occurred. Interesting to note is the fact that both the mother and the boy were greatly relieved by the authoritative stand of the agency, taken when the mother was wavering as to placement. She was told that placement was the clinic's recommendation, that there was no in-between solution, and that the case would have to be closed unless she and her husband could reach a decision to place the boy. It was only because this mother realized that the clinic was truly sharing responsibility for the placement of her son that she was able to go through with the plan.

The third case shows a family environment which was flexible enough to relax controls when from the therapeutic point of view this seemed indicated. It also shows a therapist who was sensitive to the potentially negative consequences for the patient and the treatment process which the reactions of the parents to acting out might have produced, and therefore helped the patient to control her hostile impulses when not in the therapeutic setting.

Barbara, age sixteen, was referred to the clinic because she was practically unable to eat. Her eating difficulties had started when she was thirteen years old in connection with a reducing diet, during which she developed a strong aversion to food. At that time she was taken into treatment in a mental hospital and her case was diagnosed as conversion hysteria—anorexia nervosa. When hospitalized her weight had fallen to 75 pounds. After some gain in weight she was discharged and for a while continued to improve steadily. At the time of referral, however, she had again lost a great deal of weight and both she and her family were very much concerned about her condition. Through contact with the hospital the agency learned that while her case was severe, it was regarded as not requiring hospitalization and as treatable on an outpatient basis. Besides the eating problem there were other symptoms, such as inability to mix with people, clinging to her mother, feelings of anxiety and depression, and cessation of the menses.

In an intensive intake interview with Barbara one of the consulting psychiatrists helped her bring out fellatio fantasies which seemed to account for her eating difficulties, and found in her statements and nonverbal behavior confirmation of the diagnosis made at the hospital. In view of the acute threat of self-starvation he undertook cathartic treatment in this very interview; he ordered lunch for Barbara and himself and, in the presence of a woman therapist, began to explain to the girl the nature of reproduction and the unreality of the sexual connotation which eating had assumed for her. While thus breaking through her defenses, in order to prevent withdrawal from treatment which a slower approach might have brought about, he ate lunch with her; she ate well, enjoying her food without anxiety or spasms.

It appeared questionable from the beginning whether any type of psychotherapy other than psychoanalysis could be fully effective in this case. This seemed impossible because of the financial situation of the family, however, and also because the consulting psychiatrist felt that Barbara was not ready at that stage to accept orthodox psychoanalytic procedure. He recommended, therefore, as an intermediary step, treatment by an experienced woman worker. That treatment was designed to deal only with the superstructure of the neurosis in order to alleviate some of the girl's anxieties and so keep her from starving herself to death.

To carry out this treatment plan, the worker spent a great deal of time with Barbara, showing interest in the most minute details of her living situation. Whenever positive transference expressions were strong, Barbara was told that she must eat for the worker's sake. At the same time it was constantly emphasized to the girl that her symptoms were not organic but emotional in origin, in order to create in her readiness for psychoanalytic treatment. Although there was some elaboration of conscious, and later also of unconscious fantasies, little attempt was made by the worker at insight or reconstruction work. Instead she tried to make Barbara aware of the existence of her internal conflicts and of the way in which she made use of them for the control of her environment, chiefly her parents. In other words, alert to the therapeutic risks which the adolescent girl's abuse of the pattern of youth culture through acting out of her neurotic conflicts in the home environment would present, the worker tried to stave them off as treatment proceeded. At the same time, she gave Barbara a great deal of support in the development of her ability to face and accept her desire to be overtly self-assertive and at times even aggressive and hostile to her parents. However, she never failed to explain that although it was healthy *per se* to express such feelings, to do so would cause a vicious circle in treatment by provoking further hostile acts on the part of her parents.

Thus while controls through the therapeutic relationship were strengthened, contact with Barbara's mother was maintained by another worker, largely in order to give her some support during the trials and tribulations her daughter's treatment caused her. It was also attempted to secure her cooperation so that she would not put any pressure on the girl in relation to eating. The main point around which most of the discussions with the mother centered was her attitude toward Barbara's feeling about food. Even though intellectually she could understand that she would not help the situation by conveying her own concern to Barbara, it was extremely difficult for her to accept this emotionally. She tried very hard, however, and succeeded in changing at least her overt behavior in this respect. In fact, Barbara reported to her worker a short time later that her mother did not press her any more regarding food or eating habits. The mother even persuaded the whole family, from her old orthodox father-in-law down to her youngest child, not to discuss food in Barbara's presence.

The content of dreams which Barbara had during the later stages of the treatment, and was able to report to the worker, finally indicated that she was ready for psychoanalytic treatment, and the agency, with the cooperation of the family, made the necessary financial arrangements.

The outcome of the clinic contact with Barbara showed considerable change in the symptom picture. Improvement of eating habits had set in almost immediately, and at the end of treatment the girl was able to eat with some degree of regularity. Other improvements were a lift of depression, much less fearfulness, and a desire to have friends. Furthermore there was recognition on the girl's part of the existing internalization of her difficulties and awareness that her symptoms were of a psychosomatic nature. In addition to such recognition and awareness, there was now also a strong desire for coping with these difficulties by undergoing psychoanalysis.

From the point of view of clinical psychiatry, it would be possible to question whether the diagnosis and assumed connection between treatment and improvement were really as presented. In this case, as in most cases of anorexia nervosa, suspicion of a psychotic process might have been justified and the improvement shown here might have been a manifestation of remission rather than a cure. However, in the handling of the case several points important to the treatment of adolescents stand out. The home environment was basically flexible enough to carry out the changes in behavior on the part of the family members which seemed indicated. Barbara's mother, although a highly neurotic woman and filled with concern over the girl's eating difficulties, was able to desist from pressing food on her when she understood the vicious circle this created. And even the orthodox grandfather of the girl did not insist on her observance of the dietary laws after the mother had explained to him the disease character of Barbara's difficulties. Thus the family was able to relax controls which would have interfered with the treatment of this adolescent.

Both the girl's therapist and the mother's were not only aware of the temporary increase in rebellion and show of aggression which psychotherapy tends to produce but also were mature enough to incorporate the expectation of such behavior on Barbara's part into the treatment plan. The girl's worker was courageous enough to insert into the permissive pattern of therapy an element of control in order to prevent the aggravation of adolescent rebellion which, if unchecked, would have been a dangerous concomitant of the therapeutic process. The mother's worker, on the other hand, enabled her to endure the "spillover" of acting out from the therapeutic situation into the home environment.

These three cases have been selected in order to show the importance of recognizing the special risks which the *age* and *sex roles* of adolescents, their *status*, and the pattern of *youth culture* present in the psychotherapy of patients belonging to this age group. They have been also selected, however, with the idea of counteracting the impression that the recognition of those risks permits making any broad generalizations regarding the desirability of treating adolescents in a controlled environment. Actually the intention has been to stress the point that preference for any type of treatment is more dangerous in the cases of adolescents than of either children or adults.

It is hoped that the introduction of the concepts presented here will be found helpful in two respects: (1) in broadening the perception of the therapists for the different procedures which different case constellations may require for the protection of adolescent patients; (2) in also protecting the therapists themselves against the danger of overidentification with such patients in their strivings for emotional and behavioral liberation which our society both provokes in, and denies to, the members of this age group.

CHAPTER EIGHT

The Therapeutic Management of Anxiety in Children

ONE OF THE OUTSTANDING characteristics of therapeutic practice in the agency's Child Guidance Institute is a high degree of permissiveness and passivity on the part of the therapist. There is a tendency, especially on the part of inexperienced therapists, to apply these principles without discretion and to disregard the limitations of such an approach, limitations which were pointed out by Anna Freud. In a pungent formulation she stated:

> The child analyst . . . combines in his own person two difficult and diametrically contradictory tasks; that is, he must analyze and he must educate, must in one breath permit and forbid, loosen and hold in check again. If he does not succeed in this, the analysis will be a charter for all of the bad habits banned by society.[1]

This warning, although it is equally applicable to other psychoanalytically oriented types of therapy with children, seems still to be sufficiently disregarded in the practice of the clinic to require attention. Apparently it is much easier for therapists to accept and practice the "loosening" part of their task than the one which demands a holding in check. Where such an attitude exists, treatment failure may result for the following reason. In primary behavior disorders as well as neuroses acting out may continue and actually increase in spite of prolonged therapeutic effort unless it is restricted by the therapist. Without such restric-

BY OTTO POLLAK IN CONSULTATION WITH LIA KNOEPFMACHER

The valuable assistance of Dr. William Seeman, of the Mayo Clinic, Rochester, Minnesota, in the preparation of this chapter is gratefully acknowledged.

[1] Freud, Anna, *Introduction to the Technic of Child Analysis.* Nervous and Mental Disease Publishing Co., New York, 1928, p. 52.

tion sufficient tension which leads the patient to express the ideational content underlying his conflict in communication rather than in overt behavior may never come about. Furthermore some individuals need a higher degree of assistance than others in forming new patterns of behavior. Failure by the therapist to provide such assistance may also lead to treatment failure.

In this chapter an attempt will be made to suggest two safeguards against such treatment failures. One of the safeguards is greater recognition of the socially adaptive effects of nonmorbid anxiety. The other is utilization of concepts taken from learning psychology for an articulation of therapeutic behavior in certain phases of the treatment process. The latter proposition will present special difficulties which must be faced if misunderstandings are to be avoided. Learning psychology is an area of experimental psychology in which there is as yet no agreement upon concepts and emphasis on key phenomena. A number of learning theories have been developed under the leadership of such persons as Edward L. Thorndike, Edwin R. Guthrie, Clark L. Hull, B. F. Skinner, and Edward C. Tolman, to mention only a few.[1] Adaptation of concepts from learning theory to practice presents, therefore, a problem of selection.

Quite apart from this initial difficulty, the formulations of the various learning theories are based on laboratory experimentations with animals and are, therefore, of necessity further removed from the phenomena of concern to psychotherapists than the theories and concepts of sociology and anthropology which deal with human beings. In consequence the findings of the learning psychologists may impress psychotherapists as mechanistic and unrelated to phenomena of behavior which clinicians encounter daily in their work with patients. Finally, the genetic approach in psychoanalysis is also concerned with phenomena of learning. However, it is so at a level of complexity which may make it appear fruitless, if not unnecessary, to attempt a syn-

[1] For a review of the major theories in this area, see Hilgard, Ernest R., *Theories of Learning*, Appleton-Century-Crofts, Inc., New York, 1948.

thesis of the learning theories of experimental psychology and the theories of psychoanalysis.[1]

Still, these difficulties do not seem to be unsurmountable. First of all, there is a group of learning theories, the so-called association theories, which in order to account for the present look to the past.[2] This orientation is basically similar to that followed by psychoanalysis. One of these theories, Hull's systematic behavior theory,[3] has led to an interesting and promising attempt by John Dollard and Neal E. Miller to apply its principles to psychotherapy.[4] There is thus some guidance in the problem of selection.

Even though the phenomena of learning by the child in his natural life situations are highly complex and not so amenable to experimental research techniques as is the case with animal learning, the findings of research on the latter phenomena may still be helpful in identifying some aspects of the learning processes in human beings that are significant. However, present findings and formulations of research on learning phenomena represent only partial explanations and in no way minimize the necessity for the understandings and insights achieved through psychoanalytic procedures.

Actually the genetic approach already developed in psychoanalysis permits a utilization of learning concepts developed in animal psychology without taking over the findings on their interrelationships, which for the human level undoubtedly represent oversimplifications.

It seems desirable, therefore, that the two approaches should be integrated, with full consideration given, however, to their basic differences. Some efforts in this regard have been made. These efforts have followed three distinctive directions. They

[1] For an exposition of the genetic approach in psychoanalysis, see: Hartmann, Heinz, and Ernst Kris, "The Genetic Approach in Psychoanalysis," *The Psychoanalytic Study of the Child*, International Universities Press, New York, vol. 1, 1945, pp. 11–30; Hartmann, Heinz, Ernst Kris, and Rudolph M. Loewenstein, "Comments on the Formation of Psychic Structure," *The Psychoanalytic Study of the Child*, vol. 2, 1946, pp. 11–38; Hartmann, Heinz, "Psychoanalysis and Developmental Psychology," *The Psychoanalytic Study of the Child*, vol. 5, 1950, pp. 7–17.

[2] Hilgard, Ernest R., *op. cit.*, p. 16.

[3] Hull, Clark L., *Principles of Behavior*. Appleton-Century Co., New York, 1943.

[4] Dollard, John, and Neal E. Miller, *Personality and Psychotherapy: An Analysis in Terms of Learning, Thinking and Culture*. McGraw-Hill Book Co., New York, 1950.

have in common the realization of the promise that seems to lie in a combination of the clarity and experimental verification potential of learning psychology with the depth of understanding and appreciation of the complexity of phenomena which students of personality and human behavior can derive from psychoanalysis. The first direction taken by these efforts is toward:

> . . . the development of objective techniques for studying the kinds of behavior to which Freud applied himself. This, together with the practical desirability of dealing with such problems, has led to a healthy growth of interest in Freud's writings on the part of students trained in the experimental tradition. They have sought to resystematize psychoanalytic concepts and principles in terms of current academic psychologies, and have, in a good number of cases, tried to subject these notions to investigation by other than psychoanalytic methods. In some instances, Freud's views have been supported and his principles importantly extended. In others, the new techniques have failed to cast much useful light on the behavior in question. All the work, however, serves to emphasize the increasing significance attached to psychoanalysis by non-analysts, as a guide to the planning of research on personality.[1]

The second direction taken by these efforts aims at a contribution to the existing knowledge of personality formation in general, and pathogenesis in particular, by a reformulation of psychoanalytic findings and an introduction of principles developed in learning theory.[2] The third line of effort represents an attempt to formulate in terms of learning theory what is done by the therapist and the patient in the therapeutic process. A recommendation to this effect was made by Joseph McV. Hunt in discussing Lucille Austin's paper read at the Thirty-Seventh Annual Meeting of the American Psychopathological Association in 1947.

It is true that nearly all the laboratory work on learning has concerned the acquisition and extinction of relatively simple instru-

---

[1] Sears, Robert R., *Survey of Objective Studies of Psychoanalytic Concepts.* Bulletin 51. Social Science Research Council, New York, 1943, pp. ix–x.

[2] See, for instance, Mowrer, O. H., and Clyde Kluckhohn, "Dynamic Theory of Personality," in *Personality and the Behavior Disorders,* edited by Joseph McV. Hunt, The Ronald Press, New York, 1944, vol. 1, pp. 69–135; Mowrer, O. H., "Learning Theory and the Neurotic Paradox," *American Journal of Orthopsychiatry,* vol. 18, October, 1948, pp. 571–610.

mental acts rather than object cathexes and complex modes of satisfaction. Any parallels, therefore, must be accepted as analogies with
the consequent limitations. Nevertheless, an examination of the ways
of getting laboratory animals to try new responses, and of the ways
of reinforcing and sustaining these responses once they have been
tried should be a source of suggestion for behavior therapists. . . .
I cannot refrain from stating the proposition that therapy for a
patient is learning and for a psychotherapist teaching.[1]

As indicated above, John Dollard and Neal E. Miller have
demonstrated how such a formulation of the therapeutic experience may be made. They did so with reference to the treatment of
symptom neuroses in adults.[2] In the pages that follow a much
more modest attempt is made to show how this may be done
in the treatment of children and adolescents. It is not confined,
however, to the treatment of neurotic conditions; it includes
also primary behavior disorders. The interest here is not to
promote scientific advancement but to clarify important considerations in therapeutic practice. There is no intent to imply
that the points developed are fully supported by either psychoanalytic or learning theory. The adaptations proposed are of a
pragmatic and tentative nature, rather than being simple applications of these theories at their present stage of development.
Before presenting them, it seems desirable first to state a basic
proposition of Hull's systematic behavior theory and to introduce
some of the concepts utilized in that theory.

All living organisms show a tendency to react to discomfort by
changes in behavior. As long as the discomfort continues, variation of behavior continues. We speak of *trial and error behavior*. If in
the course of such behavior variations the discomfort is brought
to an end, the behavior variation comes to an end. As the result
of repeated experience of the cessation of discomfort after a
specific type of behavior has occurred, the organism tends to reduce the range of varied behavioral reactions to the experience of
discomfort. The type of behavior which in the past has proved to

---

[1] Hunt, Joseph McV., Discussion of "Failures in Social Casework" by Lucille N.
Austin, in *Failures in Psychiatric Treatment*, edited by Paul H. Hoch. Grune and
Stratton, New York, 1948, p. 222.

[2] *Personality and Psychotherapy: An Analysis in Terms of Learning, Thinking and
Culture.*

be followed by the removal of the discomfort is resorted to more quickly and more consistently. We speak of *learned* behavior. Thus learned behavior is behavior which tends to be repeated because in the past it has been found to be rewarding through the experience of disappearance of discomfort. Readers of Sigmund Freud will recognize this simply as a restatement of his pleasure principle.

In systematic behavior theory the experience of a discomfort is conceptualized as a *drive*[1]; the perception of something which in the past has been experienced as being connected with the discomfort or the beginning of relief of the discomfort as a *cue;* the behavior change leading to the relief of the discomfort as a *response;* and the experience of relief as a *reward.*

> Learning takes place according to definite psychological principles. Practice does not always make perfect. The connection between a cue and a response can be strengthened only under certain conditions. The learner must be driven to make the response and rewarded for having responded in the presence of the cue. This may be expressed in a homely way by saying that in order to learn one must want something, notice something, do something, and get something.[2]

Thus the strengthening of the connection between a cue and a response through the experience of reward appears to the adherents of that theory as the crux of learning.[3] The concept of *reinforcement* is used in systematic behavior theory to designate the phenomenon that the tendency to repeat a response is strengthened by the experience of reward following this particular type of response.[4]

Discomforts may be of an anticipatory nature as well as immediately present in terms of an existing reality. The perception of the probability of discomfort in the future may become discom-

---

[1] It should be understood, however, that this usage of the term should be distinguished from its usage in psychoanalysis, where it has the same connotation as the German word "Trieb" or the psychological concept of "need" in learning theory.

[2] Miller, Neal E., and John Dollard, *Social Learning and Imitation.* Published for the Institute of Human Relations by Yale University Press, New Haven, 1941, p. 2.

[3] *Ibid.*, pp. 17, 28.

[4] *Ibid.*, p. 39.

fort in the present and tend to produce behavior which stops only after the occurrence of the anticipated discomfort has become unlikely. We speak of *anxiety*. According to Freud,

> What this means is: I anticipate that a situation of helplessness will come about, or the present situation reminds me of one of the traumatic experiences which I have previously undergone. Hence I will anticipate this trauma; I will act as if it were already present as long as there is still time to avert it. Anxiety, therefore, is the expectation of the trauma on the one hand, and on the other, an attenuated repetition of it.[1]

It is important to note in this connection that Freud laid stress on the basically self-protective function of anxiety in producing danger-averting mechanisms, be the danger external or internal.[2] Ever since the publication of his work, *The Problem of Anxiety*, it has become increasingly, though not fully, accepted in the psychiatric and psychological literature that anxiety represents one of the central phenomena in the conceptual explanation of psychoneurotic behavior.

Animal experiments conducted by I. E. Farber, Neal E. Miller, and O. H. Mowrer have suggested that anxiety is an acquired *"drive."* Whether one accepts this conceptualization or prefers to call anxiety an emotional state, there is no disagreement concerning its motivating power for learning as well as for resistance to learning. From the same group of scientists the suggestion has come that the persistence of psychoneurotic symptoms can be explained by the anxiety-reducing, that is, *reinforcing* effects which they produce.[3] This corresponds to the psychoanalytic proposition that symptomatic behavior like all behavior is need relevant and

[1] Freud, Sigmund, *The Problem of Anxiety*. W. W. Norton and Co., New York, 1936, pp. 149–150.

[2] *Ibid.*, pp. 146–153.

[3] Farber, I. E., "Response Fixation Under Anxiety and Non-Anxiety Conditions," *Journal of Experimental Psychology*, vol. 38, April, 1948, pp. 111–131; Miller, Neal E., "Studies of Fear as an Acquirable Drive: Fear as Motivation and Fear-Reduction as Reinforcement in the Learning of New Responses," *Journal of Experimental Psychology*, vol. 38, February, 1948, pp. 89–101; Mowrer, O. H., "Anxiety Reduction and Learning," *Journal of Experimental Psychology*, vol. 27, November, 1940, pp. 497–516; and "A Stimulus-Response Analysis of Anxiety and Its Role as a Reinforcing Agent," *Psychological Review*, vol. 46, November, 1939, pp. 553–565.

wish relevant. There exists, however, a difference in emphasis between these two approaches. While experimental psychologists
stress the success of the neurotic symptom in reducing anxiety,
psychoanalysts stress the fact that it commands too high a price
for this "success." Interested in relieving the suffering which the
neurotic symptom implies, psychoanalysts and psychoanalytically
oriented therapists cannot be satisfied with the recognition of its
anxiety-reducing function. They must attempt, therefore, to cure
the patient of his morbid anxiety, or to help him acquire anxiety-
reducing mechanisms of behavior which happen to be socially
more acceptable and personally less painful than his original
symptoms.[1] Presumably the permissiveness of the therapeutic
situation is designed, at least in part, to help the patient free
himself from his morbid anxiety, to "unlearn" it, as it were, and
thus make unnecessary the symptomatic behavior which formerly
served to reduce this anxiety. When such unlearning is achieved,
the therapist may help the patient utilize psychic energy formerly
bound by his anxiety for the mobilization of other drives which
may elicit personally more satisfying and socially more acceptable responses.

Some therapists may be inclined to consider the existence of
all anxiety as necessarily undesirable. In so doing they may disregard the question whether it is not the *morbid nature of anxiety* in
the individual instance or the learning of *undesirable anxiety-
reducing mechanisms*, i.e., of symptoms, that is undesirable, rather
than the existence of *anxiety* as such.

It would be a mistake, however, to regard anxiety as invariably
undesirable. Careful reading of *The Problem of Anxiety* will leave
no doubt in this respect. Suffice it to quote here only the following
lines:

> Two possibilities with regard to the appearance of anxiety, there-
> fore, may at once be distinguished: the one, inappropriate and in-
> expedient, in response to a new situation of danger; the other, a use-
> ful one, as a means of giving warning of and averting such a situa-
> tion.[2]

[1] See Chapter 10.
[2] Freud, Sigmund, *op. cit.*, pp. 95–96.

Psychiatrists have identified and described a type of individual who seems peculiarly unable to profit from experience primarily in consequence of a deficiency in conscious anxiety. If he is an adult, he is designated as suffering from a character neurosis; if a child, as suffering from a primary behavior disorder. Since this latter term is not so generally used as the term "character neurosis," it may be appropriate to quote in this context the description of the syndrome by the late Dr. Johan H. W. van Ophuijsen, who did much to point out and clarify its specificity.

> The conduct disturbances, along with the habit disturbances and neurotic traits, form the large group of primary behavior disorders. The name, primary, is given because these disorders are not secondary to any other pathological condition. They develop in reaction to environmental influences in the form of persisting behavior patterns. . . .
>
> In the mind of the expert the constant conflict with the environment and the absence of guilt, which characterize every single typical case, very soon begin to appear as two sides of one abnormality. This abnormality seems to lie in what has happened to the child's aggressiveness: he shows much more aggressiveness than the average child in his contact with his environment, i.e. much more external aggressiveness, and he shows much less aggressiveness than the average child in his attitude towards himself, i.e. much less self-criticism and reproach, which are the expressions of internalized aggressiveness. Correlated with this and related to it, the examiner finds a narcissistic self-evaluation. The child appears to think of himself as something exceptional, great, strong, a "big shot," etc., always with the expectation of being able to accomplish his aims regardless of the impediments formed by laws, customs, and moral code.[1]

Children who show such behavior may be individuals with weak superego development, or individuals whose impulses are exceptionally strong. Either one of these personality characteristics may lead to empathic deficiencies, which prevent these individuals from incorporating the responses of others in their own reactive system.[2]

[1] Van Ophuijsen, Johan H. W., "Primary Conduct Disturbances," in *Modern Trends in Child Psychiatry*, edited by Nolan D. C. Lewis and Bernard L. Pacella. International Universities Press, New York, 1945, pp. 35–36.

[2] Cottrell, Leonard S., Jr., and Rosalind F. Dymond, "The Empathic Responses: A Neglected Field for Research," *Psychiatry*, vol. 12, November, 1949, pp. 355–359.

With patients of this type the therapeutic method must differ, at least in part, from that employed with patients who do not show such narcissism. Apparently it must be the task of the therapist to induce in such a patient the modicum of conscious anxiety that is indispensable for learning patterns of behavior and to help the patient learn such anxiety-reducing responses as are socially desirable. In such situations we have two phases of the therapeutic process: (1) induction of conscious anxiety and (2) its utilization for the patient's learning of socially desirable patterns of behavior.

In the typical symptom neuroses, however, the therapeutic task—albeit also twofold—would be: (1) to cure the patient of his morbid anxiety, and (2) to utilize his psychological energy which is freed through such anxiety reduction for new, personally less burdensome, and socially more acceptable, behavioral responses. This would seem to imply that the treatment of children in both primary behavior disorders and neuroses requires permissiveness and passivity but for different reasons, and *only up to a certain point in the treatment process.*

The desirability of distinguishing two phases in treating expressions of pathology in narcissistic children and adults has been emphasized by Dr. Maurice R. Friend. When discussing Gordon Hamilton's paper on "Psychoanalytically Oriented Casework," he made the following statement:

> With narcissistic personalities in both adults and in children, it may be necessary for a long time to be warm and giving, and our support may actually take place by our attitude rather than through verbal insight. It seems that this is actually a seduction of the patient to depend on us in such a way that he will forego leaving and will be able to make some efforts at self-sacrifice of which he has not been previously capable. This, however, should be but one phase of treatment and not last forever.[1]

Thus in the primary behavior disorders the purpose of permissiveness and passivity would apparently be to permit the patient a period of satisfactory expression of regressive tendencies so as to

[1] Friend, Maurice R., Discussion of "Psychoanalytically Oriented Casework and Its Relation to Psychotherapy" by Gordon Hamilton, *American Journal of Orthopsychiatry*, vol. 19, April, 1949, p. 222.

make him ready to respond more positively to the environment's demands for social adaptation.

The satisfactory experience of regression is supposed to create in the child a state of emotional well-being in relation at least to the therapist. Once this relationship is established, the child is expected to give up regressive behavior and to postpone satisfactions in order to retain the approval of the therapist. Anxiety to preserve this state of relationship thus is assumed to motivate the child into displaying a modicum of compliance with the social demands. After he has helped the child develop such beneficial anxiety, the therapist may have to give up some of his permissiveness and passivity. This may be necessary in order to provide the child with *cues* for what he can do and what he cannot do, as well as with *rewards* in terms of approval for behavior experimentation within the limits of the socially acceptable. The timing of such a change in behavior on the part of the therapist would depend on the child's having shown signs of ability to undergo some frustration for the positive values of the therapeutic relationship.

In the case of the neuroses, the permissiveness and passivity of the therapist would seem to have the purpose of helping the child free himself from his morbid anxiety. When this is achieved, the therapist may again have to give up his permissiveness in order to avoid leading the child to undesirable release of id impulses. He also may have to abandon his passivity in order to help the child learn the use of his now liberated libidinal energies in personally satisfying and socially acceptable forms.

The conclusions regarding the role of the therapist in producing some useful anxiety in the child and in utilizing it for purposes of helping him learn could actually be inferred by way of analogy from the following psychoanalytic discussion of the learning process in the home.

> There can be little doubt that the better assured the child is that indulgence will follow the postponement of demands, the more easily will the deprivation be tolerated. . . . Any attempt to study the child's reactions to deprivation should therefore take at least three aspects into account: the nature of deprivation, its timing, and the modes of its administration.

The situation seems clearest where the third point is concerned. The mother's role is a double one. She sets the premium on learning: in order to retain her love, the child has to comply. Secondly, once the ego organization is established, by the consistency of her requests the mother supports the child's ego in his struggle against his impulses.[1]

Utilization of this insight in the treatment process requires only recognition of the fact that a learning process also takes place in the therapeutic situation. Substitute "reward" for "indulgence" and "therapist" for "mother" and the essence of the conclusions presented above appears to follow from the genetic approach of psychoanalysis as well as from the approach of systematic behavior theory. Anxiety about loss of the mother's love as a result of noncompliance with her demands or fear of her punishment then appears to be functionally similar to anxiety about losing the therapist's affection or to anxiety about incurring punishment from him as a result of not following his leads for constructive behavior change.

It is easy to understand why some therapists should find it very difficult to accept the proposition that some patients need to acquire anxiety for reasons other than becoming desirous of therapeutic help. Their own personality background is almost of necessity neurotic. Rare indeed is the person who can become an analytically oriented therapist without having received therapy himself. Many inexperienced therapists become threatened by all manifestations of anxiety because they remember their own suffering under its impact. To such workers all anxiety is pathological. For this reason it is particularly necessary to provide them with a theoretical safeguard against this bias. It is proposed here to do so by a stronger emphasis on the social effectiveness of anxiety that is not morbid, or anxiety that is channelized into socially acceptable mechanisms of defense. This is particularly important for patients who come from a middle-class background, because middle-class culture requires social adaptations which are more repressive of direct expressions of sexuality

[1] Hartmann, Heinz, Ernst Kris, and Rudolph M. Loewenstein, "Comments on the Formation of Psychic Structure," *The Psychoanalytic Study of the Child*, vol. 2, 1946, p. 24.

and hostility than the social adaptations commonly required in other strata of society. This has been highlighted by Allison Davis as follows:

> Equally important to effective socialization in our society is the maintenance by the individual of a certain level of anxiety with regard to the attainment of the required behavior for his status. This socialized anxiety plays a major role in propelling him along that cultural route prescribed by his family, school, and later by adult society at his cultural level. The development of adaptive, socialized anxiety in middle-status life is all the more essential because the social and prestige rewards of this status must necessarily be postponed during the prolonged training of the child and adolescent for high skills and complex responsibilities. In the meantime, anxiety which threatens the individual with the loss of both present status and of future gains must serve as the basic instigation in his socialization.[1]

Once recognition of the usefulness of nonmorbid anxiety as a motivating force in learning socially adaptive patterns of behavior is incorporated into the theory underlying child guidance practice, workers may be better able to understand the effects of permissiveness in therapy as well as its limitations. On the basis of such understanding they will find it easier to reward the child— through the expression of approval—for new responses which are socially adaptive, and thus to reinforce them. Also they will find it easier to help the child utilize this newly acquired anxiety by expressions of positive guidance and even by expressions of disapproval.

It is, of course, to be realized that emotionally, as well as culturally, many workers will be very reluctant to accept the psychodynamic interpretation that their permissiveness might be visualized as anxiety-producing and then should be changed to a more directive attitude in the *later* phases of the treatment. They may forget Freud's statements about the positive functions of anxiety, quoted in this chapter, and be tempted to regard such an interpretation as an invidious attack of animal psychology on psycho-

[1] Davis, Allison, "Socialization and Adolescent Personality" in *Adolescence*, pp. 204–205, Forty-third Yearbook of the National Society for the Study of Education, Part 1. Distributed by the University of Chicago Press, 1944. Quoted by permission of the Society.

analytically oriented treatment of children. Actually, however, the workers of the Jewish Board of Guardians were warned by the very person who initiated the psychoanalytic orientation in the agency, Dr. Johan H. W. van Ophuijsen, against their emotional bias in realizing this aspect of their therapeutic influence.

> We lead this child virtually into a trap; as long as it is love's trap, we need not feel guilty about it. To love is to be vulnerable, but without love no permanent and deep happiness or contentment is possible. Our clients have had the painful experience of being disappointed over and over again. They do not want to repeat this experience and that constitutes the core of their abnormalities. It is the task of the worker to bring the client to the point at which he is willing to give love another chance and to find out that, although there may be hurt, there is also very valuable and desirable gain. . . .
>
> . . . In the treatment of primary behavior disorders it is our objective to *curb* as much of the aggressiveness present in the ego as is necessary to establish a peaceful relationship with the environment. . . .[1]

Obviously one cannot "curb" only by permissiveness. Actually one might extend Dr. van Ophuijsen's warning also to continued permissiveness and passivity in the case of symptom neuroses, as has been suggested in the foregoing discussion.

The cases and therapeutic steps analyzed below are presented in order to illustrate the potential usefulness of the effort to bring together psychodynamics and systematic behavior theory in that respect. Bringing these together, however, must be distinguished sharply from displacing one by the other even in part. A special warning seems to be in order against an overemphasis on reinforcement of new behavior patterns without accompanying changes in the personality structure of the patient. Except in cases where limitation of the treatment goal is indicated, only those socially adaptive behavior ventures which are the expressions of personality changes should be reinforced by reward and guided by cues given by the therapist. Otherwise one may get a change in symptoms rather than a cure. The role which gain of insight plays in behavioral change must not be forgotten. On the other hand, emphasis on insight should not lead workers to

---

[1] Jewish Board of Guardians, *Primary Behavior Disorders in Children: Two Case Studies*. Family Welfare Association of America, New York, 1945, pp. 23, 28.

continue interpretations after significant personality change has occurred. The unconscious is inexhaustible. From that angle there is no end to interpretation. Actually continued search into unconscious motivation may prevent the patient from risking ventures in new behavior. Encouraged by the therapist beyond the point of furnishing a new basis for adaptation, it may defeat the purpose of therapy.

The case of Edward shows how opportunities to reinforce anxiety-stimulated behavior experimentation of desirable character were not fully utilized. This case also shows how the worker missed the chance of utilizing the child's desire for her approval (his newly acquired anxiety) to strengthen his willingness to make new behavior adventures, which had been considered desirable by the consulting psychiatrist. It shows, finally, how sublimatory spurts of behavior were not encouraged.

Edward, a nine-year-old boy, was referred to the clinic on the suggestion of the school because of poor academic work, annoying behavior in the classroom, and inability to sit still for any length of time. Further information elicited at intake revealed that he felt mistreated at home, that he threatened to run away, and had temper tantrums. He was careless about his personal appearance and had offensive manners, such as scratching his head and picking his nose while sitting at the table for meals with the family. He was destructive with toys and liked to play with fire. He was a restless sleeper, had been enuretic until he was eight years old, and still had occasional relapses in that respect.

Edward had been unwanted by his mother, who considered his coming an interruption of her mode of life. He was born prematurely and had to be kept in an incubator for two months. During his upbringing the mother had exhibited much hostility toward him and had made frequent attempts to rid herself of the responsibility which his birth had put on her. Her behavior toward him showed oscillation between neglect and occasional attempts to make up for that by being overindulgent. She felt irritated by Edward's demands for her attention and could not respond to his reaching out for her love. Edward's father was only superficially interested in the boy and preferred having a "pal" relationship with him to assuming the role of father.

The consulting psychiatrist diagnosed Edward as suffering from a primary behavior disorder, preoedipal type, with neurotic tendency. In the course of therapy the boy showed the typical behavior expressions of the syndrome for primary behavior disorder. He was demanding of gifts and resentful of reality limitations. The worker was giving and allowed the child sufficient regression to establish a very strong relationship. Under the influence of this treatment the boy began apparently to form some anxiety regarding his ability to gain and hold the worker's affection, but failed to strive for this by conforming to the reality limitation which she had to set up in the treatment relationship. Instead he felt a need to test her affection by provocative and demanding behavior. At the same time, however, there apparently began some superego formation, as can be seen from the following incident.

During one session Edward asked the worker to buy him material for an airplane model which he could put together and paint himself. The worker explained to him, as she had done before on similar occasions, that she could buy him such things only if he worked on them in the office and took them home only after they had been finished. Edward agreed to this condition; he got his airplane material and worked on it during the session without, however, completing his task. At the end of the session he demanded permission to take the unfinished airplane home. When the worker pointed out to him that he knew about the limitations of using her gifts and that he had agreed to leave the plane in the office until it was completed, Edward had a temper tantrum, grabbed the plane, and ran out of the office. Upon arriving home with it and telling his mother that he had taken it from the office, his mother scolded him and told him to take it back the following week. Although Edward had scarcely ever obeyed his mother, this time he complied. Significantly also, while previously he used to be late for his appointments, he appeared exactly on time and stood at first by the open door of the worker's office with a sheepish expression on his face. He held the plane in his hand and when asked why he hesitated to enter, said to the worker, "Gee, I thought you were going to be mad." When the worker asked him why he expected her to be angry at him, he told her that he thought she would be angry because of his behavior last week.

At this point the worker failed to see the opportunity of utilizing the child's newly developed anxiety about his nonconformity with the demands of the therapeutic situation for a reinforcement of his attempts to develop more adaptive behavior. Instead of giving him praise for bringing back the plane, that is, *reward* for this spurt of improvement, she assured him that she was not angry at him, because she understood that he had taken the plane in order to see if she would let him do what he wanted. In doing so, she counteracted the very purpose of therapy in a case of behavior disorder, misunderstanding that the child had been suffering from a deficit of anxiety rather than from an excess of it, and that his concern about her disapproval indicated beginning success of the first treatment phase. She tried to relieve the psychological tension of the child without binding such relief to the adaptive mechanisms which the boy had shown a sign of developing. She did so because of her opinion that the child was still in a phase in which he would take limitations as a sign of being unloved. Thus she made a mistake in timing, by continuing what originally would have been a correct reaction into a treatment phase in which the child had already shown improvement in the incorporation of outside demands.

This failure to see that the development of the patient in therapy had made it possible to change therapeutic reaction to his behavior because of his acquisition of a certain amount of anxiety, led to a disregard of another opportunity of helping Edward.

Upon recommendation of the consulting psychiatrist, an attempt was made to give Edward, in addition to his individual psychotherapy, some experience in group therapy. Arrangements were made accordingly, but Edward attended only one session and refused to return because he felt that the children in the group were too young. Since there was some reality to this reaction, he was reassigned to an older group but refused to go.

The worker discussed this refusal with him only in an attempt to make him understand its psychodynamic meaning. Apparently she could not even conceive it possible that, because of her established relationship with him, she could make him try group therapy once more. Again an opportunity was lost to mobilize in his own interest the boy's anxiety about losing the worker's affection.[1]

[1] This might well be compared with the handling of Barbara's case, in which the worker told the girl, who suffered from anorexia nervosa, that she must eat for the worker's sake. See Chapter 7.

Two more incidents may illustrate the advantage of bringing within the theoretical framework underlying child guidance practice the concepts of reinforcement and reward.

Roughly two years after treatment had started, Edward, at that time eleven years old, brought up the subject of smoking. Under the worker's questioning he was able to see that his wanting to smoke was based on a desire to show off. The worker also helped him see the reality of social disapproval for boys who smoked at his age. In the course of this discussion, Edward said that he guessed there were other and more acceptable ways of showing off, such as being good in sports, and that he could gain recognition in that way. Although the worker in her recording showed pleasure about this, she did not reinforce this trend of social adaptation in the boy by any sign of approval.

In another session Edward, who for a while had expressed great interest in the worker's personal life, suddenly showed her the picture of a girl who appeared to be his own age. The worker thought that, by showing her this picture, Edward might have wanted to convey to her his desire to end therapy. In the ensuing discussion she tried to interpret to the boy this possible meaning of the incident.

The worker's conception of the meaning of this incident might have been correct. On the other hand, it might have represented an attempt on Edward's part to make the worker jealous, and more willing to tell him about herself. There was still another possible meaning. The incident might have been a sign of the boy's developing an ability to form a socially more appropriate object cathexis. At any rate the worker failed to see in this a possibility of helping Edward begin the resolution of his attachment to her by showing interest in the girl and thus giving him encouragement to start looking for other attachments of his object libido. By bringing up the topic of Edward's possible desire to end therapy, she abused his anxiety in relation to herself rather than using it to help him grow out of the treatment relationship.

The case of Edward has illustrated how in the instance of a primary behavior disorder anxiety has to be created and then utilized as a base line for the child's growth in effective social adaptation. In contrast to such a situation, the case of Mortimer suggests how in an anxiety neurosis the excessive anxiety of the patient may be decreased under the permissiveness and passivity of the worker, thus giving the worker a chance to become directive in order to enable the child to test this decrease of anxiety against reality experience and to reinforce responses to other drives.

Mortimer, eleven years old, was referred to the Child Guidance Institute by a social welfare organization because he was shy and withdrawn; he was afraid of noises, of the dark, of strangers, of death, of losing his parents; and he suffered from an idea of reference, that a masked man was following him.

He had a neurotic mother, who projected on him her feelings of unworthiness. Because of guilt over her hostile feelings toward her own mother, she had always feared she might have an abnormal or crazy child. She had adopted an attitude of extreme submissiveness which she tried to force upon her son, thus restraining him to an unusual degree. She had never shown affection for this child and had neglected him. In contrast to this, she showed extreme interest in community activities, which implied welfare interest and social concern on her part. The father lived for no one but his own old and widowed mother, whose only son he was. His concern for her health and his complete lack of consideration for his immediate family bordered on a psychotic detachment from the realities of his home life. Both parents were recent immigrants and felt especially insecure because of having to master a new language and adjust to work in a new country.

The diagnosis of the child was psychoneurosis (anxiety hysteria), with the reservation that his being very much undersized for his age might be due to a glandular disturbance. This consideration, however, could later be ruled out because of the child's spurt in physical growth during the course of treatment.

Mortimer had been treated for over a year by a worker who maintained great passivity and was mostly silent, although friendly, during the interviews. In the course of this treatment phase, Mortimer slowly let down his guard of neurotic indifference and began to unfold one layer of anxiety after another. Finally, he produced such extreme fantasies about being injured or destroyed, and produced them with such realistic details, insisting that the people whom he feared were real people, that the question of psychosis was brought up for psychiatric consultation. The psychiatrist, however, confirmed his previous diagnosis of anxiety hysteria and indicated that the child's acting out of his anxiety was leading to an abreaction, that is, to a decrease of his anxiety. In view of that, he advised the worker to become more directive with regard to certain reality measures, as, for instance, camp placement.

Accordingly the worker changed her attitude of permissiveness and passivity and became more directive. In one session Mortimer put his hand to his cheek and complained about a toothache, but declared in the same breath that he would not go to the dentist because he was afraid of the "machine," of having needles stuck into him, and having part of his body cut off. The worker, by asking him what he was afraid doctors would do to him rather than what they had done to him in the past, helped the boy verbalize and abreact his anxiety to such a degree that she was able to risk encouraging him to see the probable pain which the dentist might inflict upon him in its realistic implication. With that encouragement the boy was able to go to the dentist and to experience the disparity between his anxious expectation and the actual experience of moderate pain. Later on the problem of the boy's continuous attacks of tonsillitis was discussed. After a long struggle with his anxiety, he consented to be examined by a doctor, who insisted that the tonsils were dangerously infected and should be removed. The worker confronted the boy with this necessity and practiced with him in a playful way how to endure anxiety.

In order to do so, she began with the boy's anxiety in regard to using the telephone. She arranged for him to make telephone calls from one room to the other, first between herself and him. Later she enlarged the task by including other people. The first time an outside call came for Mortimer, as prearranged by the worker, he jumped away from the phone and stammered, "I can't, I can't! *You* do it for me!" The worker forcefully put the receiver into Mortimer's hands, told him to talk, and listened with him. After the conversation there were beads of perspiration on Mortimer's forehead, but he sighed with contentment and said, "Now I have made my first American telephone call."

The concept of timing enters, of course, into the decision to change from passivity to a more directional and educative approach. It does so under the same conditions that determine the timing of an interpretation, that is, a constant diagnostic evaluation which accompanies the therapeutic effort. The worker must ask himself: Is the child ready to do what he would like to do without becoming overwhelmed by anxiety and thus forced to regress instead of continuing growth. As soon as the child shows a measure of readiness in that respect, his hesitant anticipation of victory has to be reinforced by the worker. This can be done only, however, if the worker has enough evidence to justify his expectation of a positive outcome of the new behavior adventure.

Mortimer tested the worker to a high degree when he insisted that he would consent to the tonsillectomy only if the worker went with him to the hospital in order to make sure the doctor was informed about giving him an anesthetic. He did not trust his mother to arrange for that because the latter actually accused him of being a sissy for not being "able to take pain." The worker waited for Mortimer three consecutive mornings at the hospital; Mortimer did not appear but each time telephoned later to say that he had not been able to overcome his fears. The worker did not pamper or pity him, but asked him to try again. On the fourth morning Mortimer appeared and did not make any fuss, submitting to the tonsillectomy.

A similar situation occurred one year later when Mortimer returned from camp to spend a few days before returning for another month, as was the procedure at that particular camp. Once home, he refused to go back, influenced by the neurotic needs of his family to have him sick. In that situation the worker went to the home and abandoned the therapeutic stereotype of "office passivity" to the degree of engaging the whole family, including the boy, in a discussion of the arguments for and against his going back to camp. By her particular use of the arguments which the boy brought forth under the protection of the neurotic atmosphere of the home, she reminded him of the gains in insight he had already made in therapy. Of particular significance was the ability of the worker in that situation to counteract the mother's misuse of the boy's anxiety about his throat. In the therapy it had come to be understood by the boy and worker— especially around the time when the tonsillectomy was a problem— that throat pains were a manifestation of the boy's generalized anxiety about physical injury and damage to his body image. It was true that the boy had for some time infected tonsils, but his neurotic mother, instead of helping him keep the impact of this discomfort within the limitation of reality, had supported the boy's tendency to use this condition for secondary gains, thus reinforcing one of his symptoms. In this particular home visit the mother again tried neurotic strategy by pointing out to the boy that he had complained again about his throat aching and that consequently he should see a doctor rather than go back to camp. At that moment the worker winked at the boy. The boy grinned and said to his mother, "Leave my throat alone. I'm okay." After this removal of the neurotic anxiety expression, the boy was able to come out with a measure of justifiable apprehension. He said that he had become accustomed to his counselor during the first camp period and could not face an adjustment to a new counselor now. The worker was able to assure him that he would have the same counselor, and the boy decided to go to camp for a second period. Significantly enough, not only the boy but also the mother gained strength from the initiative taken by the worker. As soon as the boy had decided to go, she helped him with preparations, and he had his full camp experience, which helped him in the course of the therapy.

It would be unfair to give the impression that the incidents related in these two histories were the only determinants for the course of treatment. The whole approach of this book, which is situational and concerned with the interplay between many factors in pathogenesis and treatment, would be vitiated by such an implication. All this chapter aimed to do was to show how a theoretical recognition of the fact that anxiety need not be something that must be removed through treatment, but rather can be utilized to help the patient to better social adaptation, may change stereotypes of therapeutic behavior. In order to do so effectively, however, it has been suggested that a differentiation must be made between syndromes characterized by excessive anxiety and those characterized by an absence of anxiety, and between anxiety created by pathogenic influences and anxiety created by a positive relationship of patient with worker. A differentiation must also be made between anxiety-reducing mechanisms that are maladaptive and those that are adaptive. Finally, it seems important that workers in trying to help patients free themselves from maladaptive mechanisms should be familiar with the concepts of cue, reward, and reinforcement in order to gain a clearer picture of the learning-promoting aspects of their own behavior in the therapeutic situation.

CHAPTER NINE

The Utilization of Volunteers in Sociodynamic Psychotherapy

IN CONSIDERING pertinent factors related to the treatment of children, the social situation of the patient is frequently viewed by the worker as though it were static and something apart from the psychodynamic processes which occur in the treatment situation. Therapeutic procedure based on such an attitude disregards the phenomenon of *social interaction*, which implies, as already indicated in Chapter 3, that every person who is in meaningful contact with others reacts to changes in their behavior with behavior changes of his own. Actually one cannot separate the psychic processes set in motion in the patient during therapy from what happens in his social situation. This implies scrutiny and understanding by the worker throughout treatment of the significant people in the child's environment and should include family members, teachers, friends, and the worker, and their impact upon each other and the child. The importance of the worker's understanding of his own role in the processes of social interaction between himself, the patient in change, and the patient's simultaneously reacting environment deserves particular attention.

Some practical applications of this theory will be demonstrated here by discussing the possibilities of using volunteers as part of the therapeutic process in order to heighten the perceptive power and skill of the workers. In this respect it is necessary to identify several basic phenomena and to conceptualize them so that sociodynamic relationships may not be overlooked in therapy. For example, Big Sisters, Big Brothers, and escorts can be used to fill a gap in family functions and to provide the child with another link to his environment. They can also be used to increase the range of the functions of the worker. In order to under-

BY BERNICE WOLF FRECHTMAN

stand how the volunteers can be of help, one must clarify in advance what may be missing in these relationships.

The normal growth process of a child provides him with a father and a mother who will nurture him, motivate him, and transmit to him patterns of emotional and social behavior suitable to the performance of his roles in society. Thus father and mother are usually the primary factors in this process of socialization.[1] The circumstances of a child's life, however, may result in situations in which one or both parents fail to perform their roles because they are actually or emotionally missing from the family scene. If this lack is severe in intensity and of long duration, it may be one of the causes which send a child into therapy. In addition to the emotional strengthening and insight which individual psychotherapy provides, the child may require the extension of the growth-producing influence of therapy into his everyday life through the introduction of a volunteer. Thus a Big Brother and/ or a Big Sister may be introduced to fill the gap which the ineffective functioning or absence of the parents has created in the growth conditions of the child.

> Rose, an adolescent, whose mother had been in a state mental hospital during the entire period of the girl's growth into beginning womanhood, had to assume prematurely the functions of the mother in a household consisting of father, grandfather, and a younger brother. Many of Rose's feelings of loss because of her mother's absence, of guilt in replacing her in the family constellation, and of confusion as to her own role in the home were resolved in interviews with the worker. But she also needed a mother substitute in her everyday life, from whom she could learn the homemaking functions and the other activities of a woman in our society. Therefore a Big Sister was assigned to shop with her, to assist her in minor tasks such as any daughter is expected to perform, and to provide her with an opportunity of making visits to a household where she could learn by observation and imitation.

> In the course of treatment Rose had been brought to the point of reaching out for some object of identification other than her own mother. With the thoughtful assignment of a Big Sister at this proper psychological moment, Rose was given an opportunity to live out the experience of feminine identification of which she was deprived

[1] For a discussion of this concept, see Chapter 10.

in her own family, and for which she had become ready through the therapeutic process.

Parenthetically, it is interesting to note that, although this principle might be expected to apply equally to cases where either fathers or mothers are missing, experience indicates that this is not so. The physical absence of the father may not destroy the existence of the home, because he has not been the home-maker. Physical absence of the mother, however—especially in the case of younger children—frequently removes the framework of the home and leads to placement of children in institutions or to foster home arrangements. In our culture mothers seem to be able to manage better without husbands than fathers seem to be able to manage without wives. If a mother dies or leaves the home, the father in many instances will either provide a mother substitute through remarriage, asking a female relative to join the household, and so on, or place the children. Therefore as long as the home is maintained for children, it is likely to contain a mother or a mother substitute. This explains why there are fewer children receiving outpatient treatment from the agency who need the services of a Big Sister as a mother substitute than children who need a Big Brother as a father substitute. It also explains why more Big Sisters, proportionately, are utilized in relation to the institutional treatment plan for girls at the Hawthorne-Cedar Knolls School.

There are family situations in which both parents may be physically present but are so disorganized that they cannot pro-vide the child with any emotional atmosphere or environmental structure which he can use as a basis for his own development as a potential mate or parent. Here arises the need to give the child an experience, through demonstration, of types of family struc-ture which can help him form an optimistic attitude toward future family experience. The device which we term "Big Brother-Big Sister Couple" has been evolved for such situations. A volunteer who is married, and whose spouse will also partici-pate in the relationship with the child, is assigned. Sometimes the initial contact and early visits are between child and the wife, sometimes child and husband. Gradually the other spouse is introduced and the child sees them as a couple. Through their own family life the Big Brother-Big Sister Couple offer the child the opportunity of participating in a setting where a family lives happily together, with each member cherished for himself. Thus the child learns that there are other ways of living than those he has thus far experienced and that his adult way of life can be different from that of his parents.

Milly, age nine, came from a family in which father and mother were so involved in mutual conflict that the children were practically ignored. Meals were not prepared for them, and they had to provide their own food with what little money their mother gave them. The parents quarreled incessantly, sometimes to the point of physical violence. With Milly the mother followed the pattern she had pursued with her other children—that of refusing to take responsibility for her behavior—and brought her to the clinic in an attempt to shift to it the burden of responsibility. It was clear that Milly would eventually have to be removed from her home in order to provide her with a living situation more conducive to normal growth. However, Milly herself refused to accept placement because she had had no experience which would lead her to think that life could offer her anything better than her present home, and she preferred to cling to the known, unsatisfying as it was.

Milly consented, however, to meet a Big Sister, with whom she quickly developed a strong but inarticulate relationship. This volunteer was married and had two young children. After some time the Big Sister introduced Milly into her home and allowed her to share in the family life as though she were a third child. The Big Sister's husband participated actively in this plan by treating Milly like an older daughter. Thus Milly not only saw that parents could love each other and their children, but shared in this experience. She, in turn, cared for the younger children and mothered them as she had now learned she herself should have been mothered. With this new insight into what life might hold for her, and with the backing of a meaningful relationship with these "substitute parents," Milly could gradually accept the idea of living away from her home. She entered an institution for children, where the physical conditions and the calmness of the emotional atmosphere provided her with a better foundation for maturity.

When a family fails in its culture-transmitting function, a Big Brother or a Big Sister may be used to make up for this lack.

There may be a family pattern of living that is so different from the predominant pattern of society in which the child will have to live that some mediation between the home culture and the prevailing culture of the community appears necessary. A volunteer who represents the wider culture may then be used to provide such mediation. This can be accomplished only by contact with a person with whom the child can identify, and who is also acceptable to the family. Careful selection of the volunteer, therefore, is necessary to implement some of the goals of treatment, which may include widening of the child's social milieu.

> Stanley was the youngest of six children in a home of marginal income. His father and mother continued to live the secluded Ghetto existence that they had known in their home in Europe. Rigid interpretation of the dietary laws and a fear of experimentation had limited family nutrition. Growing up in this environment, Stanley carried with him a fear of foods and of situations which might be different from those which his home provided. In the course of therapy he showed his first interest in learning about the wider world of which he was not yet a part. A Big Brother, who himself had come from a cultural background similar to Stanley's but was now socially and emotionally well adjusted to the culture of this country, was introduced to the boy. Slowly and patiently he helped Stanley make the transition from the confines of the rigid home to the world outside. As they took trips together and the boy watched the Big Brother eat new foods, he himself was gradually encouraged to experiment. Backed by the feeling of security gained in this strengthening relationship, Stanley was able to try out his readiness for growth into a wider environment.
>
> The parents, on their part, had been prepared by the worker for some of the effects of the relationship of the volunteer with Stanley. They, too, found the volunteer less threatening than they had imagined. This could be achieved only with a Big Brother whose personality was suitable not only for the child but also for the parents. This "matching" of personalities was not fortuitous, but was the result of careful selection of the volunteer and assistance to him as problems arose, through supervision by the child's worker.

Frequently a problem associated with emotional disturbance in children is their feeling of not belonging.[1] This may be con-

---

[1] See Chapter 4.

nected with a lack of status within the child's own family, specifically with his parents, with his siblings, or with other meaningful relatives. It may also be connected with the lack of a significant or strong adult figure with whom the child can identify. A volunteer may then be used to change the position of a child within the family constellation, through the gain in status which he might derive from the interest taken in him by an adult of stature who will be acceptable to his family as well as to himself.

Michael, age eleven, lived by sufferance in the household of his maternal grandparents. His mother, who was employed, also shared the home, and her brother, a successful but unfortunately very neurotic young lawyer, completed the family circle. Michael's father, defeated in his long efforts to get his wife to establish a home of their own and to detach herself psychologically from her parents, had obtained a divorce some years previously. In the eyes of the grandparents, Michael's father was a profligate who had deserted his wife and child. This opinion was freely expressed in front of Michael, and predictions were made that he would follow the same path. There were constant comparisons made between Michael's inability to perform well at school and the brilliant scholastic achievement of his uncle. Michael's mother, too, used her son as an outlet for her hostility toward her former husband. However, she had sufficient tenderness for her son to try to protect him by changing the situation. This was one of her motivations for seeking therapeutic help for her son and herself. In addition to such help, it was apparent that Michael, who had so little status in his family, stood to gain in his self-image by identification with an adult *accepted* in his household.

If Michael's uncle had been more understanding, the boy might have received from him such a relationship. Under the existing circumstances, however, this had to be provided by a Big Brother. A young man was selected who had achieved some success in advertising and was interested in writing, which proved to be an outlet for Michael as well. The boy's family was impressed by the fact that a man of achievement would find Michael worthy of attention, and the child immediately rose in their estimation. This provided an atmosphere for Michael which was no longer constantly thwarting therapeutic endeavor through its ego-deflating effects. It gave him the security to want to grow up and become a man like his Big Brother.

Michael's situation illustrates a principle that is important for the worker to keep in mind. When the introduction of a volun-

teer seems indicated—as in the situations described in this chapter
—the worker should give first consideration to the possibility of
using a member of the child's family of orientation and even the
child's wider environment for this function. For example, frequently an uncle, a brother-in-law, an older cousin, or a teacher
has been found available and drawn into Big Brother service by
workers at the suggestion of the Volunteer Department, instead
of introducing a stranger to the child. Ideally such surveillance
of environmental resources for expanding the child's relationships
should be routine case procedure.

The therapist who understands and accepts the situational
approach will be aware that a volunteer's entrance into a family
as a friend or sponsor of the child will arouse reactions, conscious
and unconscious, on the part of all members of the family of
orientation, such as mother, father, siblings, grandparents. The
volunteer's reports can keep the worker abreast of these shifts in
interfamilial emotional currents. These shifts can then be discussed with pertinent members of the family who are in contact
with the child's worker, or have a worker of their own. This is
necessary, first of all, in order to prevent obstacles to the progress
of the child's interpersonal relations with the volunteer and others.
Furthermore these observations may provide the starting point
for fruitful discussion in treatment interviews because they will
touch on areas in the previous relationships of the child, or important persons in his present environment, which have been re-
activated by emotional experiences precipitated by the introduction of a volunteer.

The very nature of the request for a volunteer from a parent
may have meaning in the therapeutic process: Does a mother
request a Big Brother for her son because she wishes to show her
husband once more that he is a poor father, by comparison with
the volunteer? Is another mother asking for an escort for her
child's trip to the clinic office in order to remove herself further
from any concern with his problems? Complaints about a volunteer from a boy's mother may reveal her unconscious expectations
that the Big Brother will replace the husband she has lost, as well

as befriend her child. Inevitably she has been disappointed. Taken at its face value, the worker might handle the situation matter of factly, perhaps even deciding to end the child-volunteer relationship, if an impasse is reached with the mother. Understood dynamically, however, this situation can be utilized to explore further with the mother her unconscious attitudes toward her past and present life, and the people in it.

The observational range of the worker is necessarily limited by three factors: (1) His contacts with the child usually take place in an office which automatically limits the range of behavior of the patient or elicits types of expression different from those called forth by the home, the school, and the neighborhood. (2) The very fact that he enters the situation with the prestige of a worker and builds up in it a specifically professional relationship may prevent the patient from showing him certain expressions of overt behavior which he might not hesitate to exhibit to a person in another setting. (3) The contacts of the worker, even if he is attempting to gear his diagnostic perception and therapeutic focus to the situational approach, may not reach persons in the environment of the child who influence his development. Volunteers can be used to extend the observational range of the worker beyond the boundaries set by these limitations.

By introducing a planned and controlled relationship through the volunteer, who reports back and is supervised by the therapist, the latter can get a more objective picture of how the child is able to utilize psychotherapy in his actual life situation and of the influences to which he is exposed therein. The worker then can use the information gained from the volunteer for the more purposeful direction of the content of the therapeutic interviews and the understanding of the meaning of the material produced in those interviews. To demonstrate this, the volunteer escort can be used. His initial assignment may have been made to help solve the problem of transportation between the child's home and the clinic. But he also serves as the extended eyes and ears of the worker, since he is able to observe the patient in an atmosphere different from that of the interview. Thereby an opportunity is provided to observe the reactions of the child to a knowledge-able adult in another setting closer to the child's everyday living situation.

Jonathan, a seven-year-old boy, chose to concentrate the content of his therapeutic interviews on the negative aspects of his life situation: his difficulties with other boys, his inability to engage in sports, and his seemingly unhappy and withdrawn response to the adults around him. For unconscious purposes Jonathan's mother, resisting awareness of the growing health of her child, also gave a somewhat similar picture of his seemingly unchanging attitudes. The therapist felt that there had been positive change of which neither mother nor son could be objectively aware. This therapeutic assumption was verified by the reports of the boy's escort which, when viewed in totality over a period of months, gave a startling picture of a shift in response to the volunteer. Jonathan had changed from a withdrawn, uncommunicative boy to a responsive child who ran to greet the escort when he arrived. He showed growing mastery of physical activities, such as running and playing ball. The increase in ease of by-play with other children en route to treatment interviews and returning was also described.

Finally, the therapist must be aware that the volunteer is not an impassive element in the treatment process, but rather will have reactions and counter-reactions that can be helpful or harmful, depending upon how they are anticipated and worked through in the process of supervision by the worker.

Assignment of a Big Brother to Daniel, a schizophrenic boy of fourteen, whose father was completely uninterested in him, seemed indicated. From previous information the worker knew that Daniel had experienced a series of rejections from adults in his environment to whom he was attracted, because of his inability to demonstrate his feelings and to make overtures of friendship. Even with the most mature volunteer there would be the danger of repetition of the rejection experience if the Big Brother were not prepared in advance for the lack of responsiveness that might be expected from Daniel. The worker therefore prepared the Big Brother for the emotional letdown which inevitably was to follow on his first contact with Daniel. She was also ready to see the Big Brother after his first visit with Daniel, so that the volunteer had an opportunity to ventilate his feelings about the boy. Through the helpful atmosphere of a conference with the worker, there was a release of accumulated tensions and resentments which might otherwise have resulted in unconscious hostility toward Daniel and eventual breaking off of the relationship on the part of the volunteer—an unfortunate experience for the Big Brother and a destructive one for Daniel.

Recognition of the interaction of child and human environment in psychotherapy, and planned conditioning of that environment, is especially pertinent in dealing with the chronically schizophrenic child. In the case of Daniel, the volunteer became an additional tie between the child and the object world, thus counteracting the impulse to withdraw, which is so powerful in that disease. The volunteer in such situations can truly become an extension of the worker in treatment and another force in the direction of mental health. Some schizophrenic children, whose capacity to establish relationships is not markedly defective, can use volunteers early in the treatment relationship. Others will need a Big Brother or Big Sister later on, when their interest in other people as libido objects has been developed through therapy. In chronic cases, especially in adolescence, the volunteer through long and consistent interest can help the child maintain, on an even keel, the limited gains made in treatment.

It is important to caution workers that there are children who are too narcissistic, withdrawn, mentally retarded, or organically impaired to form a satisfactory relationship with a volunteer. Such cases, however, would not be accepted for treatment in the clinic of the Jewish Board of Guardians because they are considered inaccessible to the type of psychotherapy offered. Thus they do not come within the province of this chapter, since the Volunteer Department is available only to agency clientele. In this connection another word of caution may be in order.

There is no arbitrary or immutable rule as to what a Big Brother or a Big Sister should accomplish in a case. The illustrations in this chapter indicate that there can be great flexibility. The experience of the Volunteer Department has shown that if a worker is familiar with the dynamic principles involved in the use of this therapeutic aid, almost any child accessible to psychotherapy can make gains by utilization of this treatment method, provided the situation indicates its basic feasibility according to the criteria herein elaborated.

The application of the situational approach presented in this book and of the phenomena discussed in this chapter can be illustrated at some length by the situation of Billy Sanders, his mother, and his Big Brother, Stanley Sandman.[1] In the interest of clarity, the material will be divided by phases into which most cases that involve volunteers seem to fall: the *preparatory phase, introductory phase, continuing relationship phase*, and *tapering-off phase*. An attempt will be made throughout to show the interrelationship of intramural and extramural factors in therapy, and to delineate the effect of occurrences upon the principal persons involved (child, mother, volunteer, and worker).

When Billy came to the clinic at the age of eight, he was a thin, pale, blond boy, somewhat tall for his age. His large horn-rimmed glasses and odd clothing accentuated the difference in his appearance from other little boys his age. He walked in a stooped manner, somewhat like an old man, and his physical coordination seemed poor. Billy had been referred by the family doctor because of having vomiting spells when he became upset, particularly when he feared separation from his mother. He cried easily and turned to his mother when difficulties arose with other children, at the same time resenting her overprotection. He had many fears, including fear of other children, and avoided situations which might involve him in fights. He was also otherwise fearful of physical injury. Particularly, he was apprehensive that he might be cut and see blood flow. At night he had sleeping difficulties and perspired excessively while asleep. He was overconcerned, both about his own health and that of his mother. It was later learned that Billy scavenged in garbage cans, and collected odd items, like a little magpie. In spite of his personal difficulties, he did well in school and was obviously extremely bright. Occasionally, however, his vomiting spells interfered with his school attendance.

Billy's overt difficulties began at the age of four, when his father was hospitalized because of a psychotic episode. Before that time Billy and his father had been rather close to each other, although— as was later learned—the father had been chronically ill for some time before his hospitalization. Billy's vomiting began when his mother left him in a local movie theater in order to visit her hus-

---

[1] These names, as in all cases presented in this book, are fictitious. A similarity between the names of the family and the Big Brother, however, also existed in reality.

band in the hospital. Over a period of six months, each time these separations occurred, he would vomit, and this behavior persisted even after the mother discontinued the practice of leaving him. Billy had never been told that his father was mentally ill and in a hospital. When he asked questions about his father, his mother was either secretive or deliberately untruthful. In addition, the mother kept Billy from contact with the neighbors for fear that they would question him about his father's absence, or might let drop information which would lead Billy to the truth. He seemed eternally to be searching for something (witness the scavenging) and indirectly seemed to express his confusion and his concern about his father's absence through this behavior.

Implicit in Billy's problems were his mother's difficulties, which were reflected in her attitude and manner toward him. Mrs. Sanders gave the impression of being a bitter, hostile, rigid woman, suspicious of everybody around her and fearful that she would be hurt by other people. She had married young and had been aware that her husband had had a psychotic breakdown at the age of nineteen, previous to their marriage, for which he had been hospitalized for a brief period. Mrs. Sanders felt that her sister had been interested in Mr. Sanders during the courtship and had actually tried to take him away from her. Perhaps Mrs. Sanders' interest in marrying arose from the desire to best her sister in this rivalry. Billy's father had been a successful merchant engaged in business with his brothers and father before his breakdown. Against the advice of her husband's physician Mrs. Sanders had attempted to become pregnant, but had had difficulty in conceiving. It was not until she had been married ten years and had undergone intensive medical treatment for a gynecological difficulty that she became pregnant.

Prior to Billy's birth the father had had a second brief psychotic episode and another when Billy was four. The prognosis in this case was extremely doubtful and it appeared that the father would be institutionalized for the rest of his life. At first the mother had paid for private institutionalization. However, after her funds had been exhausted she had sent her husband to a state hospital, and was continually engaged in extensive court litigation in order to gain support from his family. At the time of referral to the clinic, the mother was living on an income of $70 monthly, refusing to seek supplementation from any outside source.

For the first year of treatment the mother and child were treated by different workers. Billy was under the care of a male and the mother of a female therapist. From observation of Billy during the interviews the impression was gained that he related well and potentially closely to his therapist. He was constantly searching around the office and in the desk drawers. Content of interviews was mostly nonverbal and he avoided discussion about his father or his mother. His play indicated that in his relationship to his mother he felt dependent but also rebelled against his infantilization by her.

The parallel contact with the mother revealed her secretiveness about her husband's condition and her inability to tell Billy the truth about the family situation. This resulted in the virtual isolation of herself and her son from any social contacts with relatives or neighbors, as previously mentioned. She visited her husband weekly, although she became extremely upset each time. Her attitude toward money was similarly pathological. She existed on the most meager diet herself, but fed Billy fairly well, all the while, however, unconsciously begrudging him the food she gave him. Her attitude toward him was very inconsistent. At one time she would give in to his whims because she feared he would have a breakdown like his father. At another she was overly strict with him, demanding accomplishment beyond the expectations for an eight-year-old. She bathed him, carried hot lunches to school, shared a bedroom with him, but at times she would leave him for a whole day without giving any explanation or making any provision for his care in order to visit her husband.

At the end of the first year the case was evaluated in treatment conference. It was felt that Billy's ability to establish some relationship with a male worker provided a good base for therapy. When Billy's therapist was no longer available, however, the case had to be assigned to a woman therapist. This was not counterindicated because it was felt that Billy could also profit from an experience with a woman who would be more motherly and consistent than Mrs. Sanders. To compensate partly for the loss of a male worker, the suggestion was made that a Big Brother might be introduced in the future. It was also thought that a Big Brother would provide an object for masculine identification of much importance to this fatherless boy. Billy's mother seemed to be keeping Billy as weak and inadequate as possible in order to prove that he was like his father and unable to change basically. Although mother and child had difficulty at that time in separating from each other, it seemed doubtful that Billy could be permanently helped to a more satisfactory emotional adjustment in the pathological environment of his home. Placement of the child was therefore considered a possibility as an eventual goal.

PREPARATORY PHASE

Shortly following this conference Billy and his mother were reassigned to the same woman therapist. From this point on, treatment became accelerated. The thinking behind assigning one therapist to both was that neither mother nor boy was yet ready for separation even for their treatment hours. This problem had created great hostility with Mrs. Sanders and had been an obstacle in treatment so far. With the new therapist Billy continued to be uncommunicative in his interviews, resisting any attempt to get him to discuss his ideas and his fantasies about his father. However, four months after the inception of treatment with his second therapist, when the idea of a Big Brother was introduced for the first time, Billy began to talk about his father, and the therapist recorded:

"I introduced the possibility of a Big Brother, and as soon as I said this, Billy said, 'Oh, as a substitute for my father.' He sat down in the chair near the desk. I asked him to tell me why he thought I wanted to substitute somebody for his father. In a very sad voice he told me that his father was in the hospital and had been there for six years. He is almost ten and hasn't had a man around for six long years. This makes him feel very sad. He wasn't really sure why his father was in the hospital. He had asked his mother many questions which she tried to answer as best she could, but he wasn't satisfied with the answers that he got and he had a few questions left. His father's condition was not any better and it would not get any better until a new drug was discovered. His father was sick from overwork. Then, after a moment of deep thought, he said he thought he knew what his father had, but he hated to say. He then blurted out in a very frightened tone, 'What is Bronchitis?' Billy couldn't tell me what he really thought his father's illness was, and I told him that I knew it was something very hard to talk about and we would discuss it more next week. Although I thought Billy had left me, he ran back to say that his mother had told him what was wrong with his father. His father had a nervous attack. He wanted to know whether this was right and I said his father had a nervous disorder but that I knew these words didn't mean much to him, and we would have to discuss it further. He said he couldn't talk about it now but he would next week."

In the weeks that ensued between the initial discussion of a Big Brother and the actual introduction of one, Billy talked about the idea with all the play of imagery that gives breadth to treatment. His fears, fantasies, and wishes were thus elaborated and discussed with him as far as possible before he met the man who would be his own adult friend. Billy's ambivalence toward the suggestion came to the surface when one day he said that he did not know whether he would have time to see a Big Brother. Later, in regard to imminent camp placement, Billy expressed his fear about not being able to defend himself, which the therapist recorded as follows:

"The other boys he saw at the same examination were bigger and stronger than he—they were taught by their fathers or by Big Brothers, but he never had a chance to learn how to defend himself because he did not have a father or a Big Brother. He wished he could learn how. He wanted a Big Brother, a man, who would help him learn to be strong."

With the discussion in treatment made richer in content by the introduction of the idea of a Big Brother, Billy became freer toward both his therapist and his mother. His play seemed less secretive, more childlike, and spontaneous. In other relationships, too, especially with other children, he acted like a child from whom some burden had been lifted.

The change in Billy's behavior toward his mother and the outside world partly determined and partly paralleled similar changes in his mother. As she became more deeply involved in treatment, she was gradually able to express her own needs and feelings and to become more dependent upon the therapist, as the first step toward more independent functioning. Gradually, in her mind and feelings she was able to separate Billy from his father and to be less pessimistic in her outlook for her son. Her overprotectiveness toward Billy began to diminish. Her need to keep secret from him the nature of his father's illness then became the focus of treatment. This resulted in her becoming able to discuss her husband's illness with Billy.

With Mrs. Sanders, as with Billy, introduction of the idea of a Big Brother helped to crystallize many of her problems and bring them to the surface in therapeutic interviews. One of her fantasies, elicited in relation to the Big Brother, was that he was really being supplied as a husband for her, rather than as a friend for her child. This wish had to be understood and worked out in treatment as much as possible before a Big Brother was actually introduced in order to ensure that the relationship between Big Brother and Billy would not be wrecked on the shoals of the mother's unrealistic expectations. In anticipation the mother had also to work through the further step of separation from Billy that the introduction of a Big Brother would mean. In line with her willingness to relinquish somewhat her inordinate hold on Billy, she gave permission for him to go to camp for the summer and also made plans to set up a separate bedroom for the boy when he returned.

Simultaneously with this preparation of mother and child in treatment, selection of a Big Brother was under way. Stanley Sandman, a man in his middle thirties, was tentatively chosen for Billy. Mr. Sandman was a sensitive, intelligent, quiet man, who was married but childless. He had come through the usual channels of screening by the Volunteer Department professional staff, and had completed the required orientation course. When he was interviewed by the therapist, his ability to identify with the boy was impressive. But at the same time he showed understanding of Mrs. Sanders and her barren life. The resemblance between the Big Brother's name and Billy's father's name was accidental but enhanced Billy's tendency to identify his Big Brother with his father and was a small, but important element in the emotional conflict that ensued.

In preliminary conferences with the therapist, the Big Brother learned about some of Billy's background, of his interests, and his abilities. These talks also provided the therapist with an opportunity to help the volunteer air some questions as to what this new relationship would mean to Mr. Sandman: What did he expect of the child, of himself? Did he see that his friendship with Billy might have some effect upon his marriage? In these talks volunteer and therapist got to know each other better and laid a good foundation for the relationship they were to have in the period ahead. It was agreed that Billy and his Big Brother would meet after the boy's return from camp.

In this preparatory phase, before the actual introduction of a volunteer to a child, it should be noted that the very mention of the idea of a Big Brother in itself has meaning to the treatment situation of child and parent and to the child's relationship with the worker. At the time of transfer Billy had difficulty accepting the loss of his male therapist. Unconsciously this represented for Billy a repetition of the loss of his father. Again, in therapy as in life, he was to be left with the mother-person alone. Now the new therapist, in her mother-surrogate role, was not only giving Billy permission to have meaningful contacts with a man, but was actively obtaining someone for him who would replace his father, for whom he yearned so deeply. To the boy it seemed to mean unconsciously that the therapist, who was substituting here for the mother in fantasy, was not only willing to share him with a father figure, but was actually providing one for him. To the mother it indicated that the "good mother," with whom she was identifying in the therapist, was able to give up some of her claim to the boy to another person who could provide him with a relationship she was unable to supply. Fantasy material, important to the therapeutic process, was elicited from both child and parent in this connection. Billy's ambivalence toward the idea of a Big Brother was connected with his guilt over giving up the image of his father, which he unconsciously felt was a condition of his acceptance of a Big Brother. Through the security of his relationship with the therapist, Billy was able to discuss this problem and to understand that acceptance of a Big Brother did not involve disloyalty to his own father. Had his conflict not been anticipated and worked through in advance, the Big Brother-child relationship might not have proceeded so well.

The element of timing of the introduction of a Big Brother has importance in this situation as well. It was approximately two years after the acceptance of this case for treatment that the idea of a Big Brother was introduced. Although the time period might have been shorter, it is preferable to proceed slowly and cautiously in most instances. Preliminary study and exploration is usually necessary to evaluate the child's ability to relate to an adult. Also a firm therapeutic relationship must be established as a basis for introduction of a volunteer. This will safeguard the continuity of treatment for the child, which is, in the first stages, the foundation of the relationship with the volunteer. It should also be noted that an additional time interval of several months elapsed between the first discussion of a volunteer in treatment interviews and the actual introduction of a Big Brother to the child. This period, as indicated above, can be an exceedingly rich one therapeutically; conflicts can be partially resolved in advance which, if allowed to remain unresolved, may cause difficulties in the volunteer-child relationship.

INTRODUCTORY PHASE

When Billy returned from camp, his mother and he were told that a Big Brother had been found for him, and he became quite tense. Billy expressed some fear that the Big Brother would not like him and wanted help in knowing what to discuss. When his fears were explored with him, he was reassured that the Big Brother would like him if he were just himself. The mother's reaction was strikingly similar. She, too, became very tense. She displayed curiosity about the Big Brother's life and his motivation for wanting to do this work. She immediately associated the Big Brother's name with her husband's and tears filled her eyes. This led to a discussion of her fear of being left out when Billy took trips with the Big Brother. She said she would probably lie to the neighbors if they were curious. She implied that her neighbors might think the Big Brother was her husband or lover. Her wish to have someone for herself, especially with Billy's growing independence of her, was then discussed.

The Big Brother had been similarly prepared for first contact with Billy. His questions about Billy had been answered as fully as possible and some of the things that might arise in their initial contact had been considered. The three people were to meet in the worker's office. When the therapist entered the waiting room, she saw Billy, his mother, and Mr. Sandman, all seated at some distance from each other and studiously reading. She introduced them immediately. Billy came with her toward the Big Brother and shyly acknowledged the introduction and Mr. Sandman's warm greeting. The therapist noticed that Mrs. Sanders was wearing an attractive dress and cosmetics. She seemed quite anxious but smiled approvingly. The therapist suggested that Billy and Mr. Sandman come into the office so they could get acquainted, and afterward the Big Brother could speak further with Mrs. Sanders. There was some awkwardness in the situation, which was handled very aptly by Mr. Sandman, who promptly offered Mrs. Sanders a new magazine he had brought with him. Once in the office, Billy's first response was to sit down and silently stare at Mr. Sandman. The therapist made a comment regarding the length of time since the idea of a Big Brother for Billy had first been discussed. She knew Mr. Sandman had been looking forward to meeting him. The Big Brother picked this up and asked Billy about his cold and about camp. (Mr. Sandman and the therapist had held several telephone conversations during this period about recent events in Billy's life.) After further discussion Mr. Sandman asked Billy whether he would like to go rowing sometime. As response Billy excitedly asked the therapist if they could. She said that he and Mr. Sandman could certainly plan together anything that they were interested in doing. From this point on, Billy concentrated his attention on his Big Brother and did not include the therapist in the discussion.

Later Billy had a chance to talk with the therapist alone. In his usual taciturn fashion he did not offer any spontaneous comments, but indicated that he liked Mr. Sandman. He dawdled on leaving the worker's office and acknowledged that it was because he was shy about seeing the Big Brother again. He asked the therapist to go out with him, which she did. They found Billy's mother and the Big Brother talking together. Billy had previously indicated he wanted his mother and the Big Brother to have a chance of getting acquainted.

The impact of actually meeting the volunteer brought to a head some of the conflicts and fears of the child and parent, which have been described above. The volunteer, too, needed preparation and some reassurance, both before this initial meeting and afterward, in supervisory conferences. The therapist is the catalyst uniting, through her interest and her therapeutic endeavor, the disparate elements in the situation. Particularly important was her demonstration in this first meeting that she was willing to share Billy with the volunteer and leave their planning to them, while continuing her interest in Billy in the therapeutic interviews. The relationship between the Big Brother and the child was something they were being left free to develop in their own way. This demonstration also had its effect on the mother. Seeing that the therapist could share the child, made it easier for her to do so, too. The volunteer's acceptance of Mrs. Sanders, and his obvious desire not to exclude her, eased her fears that the Big Brother would steal her child's affections from her. In this phase the therapist had enlarged the compass of treatment and acted like a shuttle among mother, child, and volunteer to weave a tight cloth of therapy from the threads of interpersonal relationships which the introduction of the volunteer had created.

CONTINUING RELATIONSHIP PHASE

Billy and his Big Brother saw each other weekly. They played together in the sand at the beach, walked in the park, explored the corners of the city. What they did together was less important to each of them than the growing feeling between them. Billy responded to this new relationship positively. That he was able to do so was largely attributable to the preparatory process of treatment. For all four persons involved, Billy, his mother, the Big Brother, and the worker, the contacts between Billy and Mr. Sandman were a constant source of revelation about the boy. The Big Brother sent weekly reports to the therapist, which revealed new aspects of Billy's problems, behavior, and potentialities. These gave her an opportunity to discuss with Billy in interviews the layers of personality to which she now had entree. Some areas of Billy's problems were allocated to the Big Brother to work out in the living relationship with Billy. Together, volunteer and therapist were changing the direction of Billy's growth process.

The second time the Big Brother and Billy went for an outing together, Mr. Sandman recorded that a youngster in the street called after them, "Hey, Billy, is that your father?" Billy did not answer, but brought his reactions to the therapist in his next interview.

He wanted to buy his father who was still hospitalized a birthday present, but was not sure what to get. He weighed the possibility of something to eat against something to wear. When the therapist pointed out to him that perhaps he was not so much concerned over the choice of the present as he was about remembering the occasion, he admitted that he had never given his father a birthday present before; he had always planned to do so but he had forgotten. This year he would not forget. Why was this year different, the therapist asked. Might it have something to do with his having a Big Brother? Billy nodded and then said that he did not want his father to think he had forgotten him or that he was "gyping" him. Since he now had a grownup man as a friend whom he went out with, his father perhaps might feel bad. He knew more about his father now, particularly that he was very sick. He wanted to see his father, although his mother said he still could not visit him. He felt awful about his father being sick and wondered when he would come home. Maybe he would never come home. The therapist said that perhaps it was true that his father did not seem to be getting better. But he could select a present for his father if he felt it was important. She added that she thought it was all right for him to go out with his Big Brother and have a good time. He would not be "gyping" his father. She was sure that his father would approve.

From the volunteer's reports she also learned about other fears that Billy had. He seemed fearful of heights and of open places. Billy did not discuss these fears with the therapist, but she helped him through his Big Brother. Mr. Sandman was encouraged to help Billy slowly, with considerable reassurance, to experiment in new situations that might be fear-producing for him. In the growing ease of their friendship, Billy's questions about the facts of sexual relationships, and sexual differences, emerged for the first time. During a visit to a museum together, Billy's comments about the nude statuary made it clear how confused he was about anatomical differences between the sexes. Since it had been decided that it would be preferable for Billy to discuss sexual questions with a man, the therapist helped the Big Brother handle these implied questions about sex directly with the boy, and did not inject herself into the situation. Although Mr. Sandman had some trepidation about the responsibility, he carried it through calmly and helpfully.

The growing relationship between Billy and his Big Brother accentuated Mrs. Sanders' feeling of deprivation and loneliness. When these were discussed in treatment, she began to obtain some insight into how much she had expected from Billy; in many ways she had wanted the attentions of a husband, father, and son from him, and had unconsciously attempted to force him into these roles. With the advent of a Big Brother, the impossibility of her endeavor became apparent. Mrs. Sanders' unconscious rivalry with Mr. Sandman came to the surface as well. She began to take Billy out more, and to give him toys and other gifts, in an attempt to compete with the Big Brother for the boy's affection. Sometimes she attempted to belittle the boy in front of his Big Brother or to use the Big Brother in order to influence Billy to follow the rigid patterns of behavior that she had laid down.

The other side of the rivalry with the Big Brother was her fantasied interest in becoming more meaningful to Mr. Sandman herself. As though for the first time, she described to the therapist how shocked she had been to hear that the Big Brother was married, although she had been advised of this fact prior to the introduction of the Big Brother. She wondered why a married man would want to do Big Brother work and felt that his wife must resent his leaving her to go out with Billy. She thought it was not right for him to leave his wife, and that the wife might think Mrs. Sanders was responsible for this desertion. Suspicious people in her neighborhood would gossip about her when they saw Billy go off with Mr. Sandman. She thought it would be impossible to explain the Big Brother relationship to her kind of neighbor. She had already told Billy to speak of Mr. Sandman as a friend of the family, even though he was really Billy's friend. The Big Brother could not telephone Billy at the home of a neighbor because she thought that if any word leaked out of men calling her, there would be suspicion that she was divorced, widowed, or having an affair with a married man.

Mrs. Sanders complained that Billy's behavior became provocative and disobedient after he had seen his Big Brother. She wished to use Mr. Sandman as a disciplinarian with her son. She thought he was also overindulgent and fed Billy to excess. These complaints and comments led to discussion of Mrs. Sanders' own feelings of deprivation about money, food, and, basically, affection. As time went on, she was able to accept more positively the growing independence which Billy's relationship with his Big Brother fostered. His identification with the Big Brother, and his evident reaching out toward new masculinity in his own behavior, began to meet with more of her approval, as she herself was helped in treatment toward greater independence. For the first time Mrs. Sanders began to talk about a job for herself. She was subsequently able to carry out this plan without undue concern about herself or her son. As it became clear to her, through experience, that Billy's new relationship would not deprive her of his affection, but rather that it would assume a different aspect; and as she was willing to relinquish her pathological overprotectiveness of Billy, both mother and son developed in the direction of greater independence, which the volunteer was helping to effect.

In the first flush of the new relationship, the Big Brother enjoyed Billy with all the gusto of a man who had been deprived of seeing his own children grow up. "A beautiful thing happened today," he said in the opening paragraph of one of his reports, and went on to describe Billy's introduction to the world of science through the Big Brother. Mr. Sandman discovered that Billy had a natural ear for music that coincided with his own. They played baseball, developed tricks in jujitsu, and engaged in snowball fights. With a critical faculty that did not impede the natural give-and-take in the relationship, Mr. Sandman observed and recorded Billy's behavior, taking seriously his role as the helpmate of the worker: "Did I tell you he insists on holding to the bannister when he walks down the stairs? I asked him if he had ever fallen downstairs and he said he had. This time I said, 'Let's hold on to each other.' So he let go of the bannister."

As the friendship developed, Billy's inhibitions about displaying some aspects of his behavior changed. The "honeymoon" was over and he was beginning to react to his Big Brother as he would to any adult. Although the Big Brother had been prepared for this eventuality by the worker, the impact of his first experience with Billy's negativism was an important one for him and the child. At the end of a day's expedition, Mr. Sandman had difficulty getting Billy back to the car. He began to find himself feeling annoyed and irritable at Billy's loitering. "Then it occurred to me that he couldn't feel he had had a full afternoon unless he had gotten tired!—so I got him to race me as often as possible on our way back to the car. It helped." Another day the Big Brother bought tickets for a baseball game, anticipating that it would be Billy's introduction to Big League baseball. It turned out, however, that Billy had gone before, with the neighborhood boys' club. This initial letdown for the Big Brother was followed by Billy's seeming nonchalance at the game. Later the boy complained because they had not bought a souvenir, as the Big Brother had promised. He also found fault with the seats they had, requesting better ones. Mr. Sandman felt his face set, with the sudden hurt of the complaints, but was able to report: "I kept my mouth shut, while I remembered your warning that I might expect some kind of surprise." In the pressures of the day-to-day relationship with his Little Brother, the volunteer found the worker standing behind him when she was needed. During this time, the Big Brother had difficulties in his professional and personal life, and was unable to see Billy as regularly as previously. With some preparation Billy was able to accept these absences, and they continued a steady contact, sometimes by telephone, sometimes by mail, in the intervals between visits. Billy's ability to accept this temporary separation without trauma was an indication of the degree of improvement he had achieved.

The Big Brother's relationship with Billy's mother went through several stages. At first the mother attempted to interfere with the outings, or to dominate them in absentia. The Big Brother's ambivalence toward the mother was evident. As he reported: "Billy ran to his mother and greeted her with a warm embrace. He stayed close to her, and I had the feeling that he wanted to cheer her up. But she humiliated him before me by complaining of his terrible behavior during the week, that he had not eaten the food she left for him, that she had licked him so hard he couldn't go to school the next day." That Mr. Sandman forgave the mother, however, is indicated by this remark: "Guess she has been much more easily upset recently because of the situation in regard to her husband." Because of his hostility toward the mother, Mr. Sandman leaned over backward not to step on her toes or violate rules set by her in relation to Billy. However, as he became freer, and was supported by the worker's understanding and encouraging attitude in conferences, he accepted more responsibility for planning activities together with Billy, with little reference to the threatening presence of Mrs. Sanders in the background.

Toward the end of this phase the Big Brother mentioned in several of his reports that he had not seen the mother for a long time. The volunteer had been more secure in taking responsibility for the child at the same time that the mother, through her experience in treatment, had been more able to relinquish part of her son's interest to the Big Brother.

As indicated above, contact between volunteer and worker continued on a smooth and mutually enjoyable basis, with ambivalence on the volunteer's part toward supervision held to a minimum. While identifying with the worker in her attitudes toward Billy and his mother, he was able to translate the intellectual concepts and the emotional impact of the experience into his own terms. For Mr. Sandman, who had looked forward so much to his relationship with a Little Brother, identification with

Billy was immediate. Here, however, the worker played the role of the balance wheel, to keep Mr. Sandman from going overboard in his feelings about the boy, and to protect Billy from being pushed faster than he was capable of moving. In the calm atmosphere of the conferences between volunteer and worker, these tendencies and others of Mr. Sandman's were discussed and clarified.

The relationship between the volunteer and Mrs. Sanders was more complex. Here the worker first brought into consciousness Mr. Sandman's ambivalence toward the mother and, with her acceptance of his hostile feelings, made it possible for him to be relaxed about himself. Then she slowly built up a picture of this mother as a deprived child herself, and the Big Brother slowly grew more accepting of Billy's mother. In regard to the mother's attempts to place Mr. Sandman in an authoritative position, the worker advised him to remain as neutral and uninvolved as possible, while maintaining a friendly attitude.

> When the Big Brother encountered a period of difficulty in his own life, he turned to the worker, not for treatment but for discussion of some of his problems as one would turn to a wise friend. It was during this time that the volunteer became aware of his own need for the relationship with Billy and was now more realistic in saying that he obtained something from Billy, as well as giving something to the boy. He commented that he now knew what was meant in his training for Big Brother work—that the relationship could be a mutually gratifying one.

The continuing phase of the relationship between volunteer and child was a period of experimentation in human relationships for everyone concerned. Billy was learning that it was possible for him to accept a partial father substitute without being disloyal to his own father. With the worker's permission he was having the experience, extraordinary for so withdrawn a child, that life need not force one to make choices in relationships, that the more friendships one has, the richer one's life can become. In dynamic terms Billy was being tied closer to life through multiple object relationships. In the warmth of his new-found friendship he was also free to express his fears more openly, and to try to work them out on an overt level by identification with the man he admired so much. Together they engaged in various ego-building activities that demonstrated repeatedly for Billy that one could assert one's masculinity without fear of retaliation from one's mother or other people in one's life. This freedom was also reflected in the naturalness of the discussion of sexual matters that arose between volunteer and child.

During this phase Mrs. Sanders demonstrated her capacity to loosen her grasp upon the Big Brother-boy relationship. While giving up part of Billy was painful, the mother also began to learn that relinquishing total responsibility for her son and acknowledging that he was a personality in his own right brought with it some measure of relief and greater freedom for her. This new-found independence could now be used by her to advantage because of the greater emotional stability she had gained from treatment. The fact that worker and volunteer saw eye to eye on their approach to the mother and integrated their handling of her, in the treatment interview and in friendly contact with her on the outside, made for a consistent approach to which the mother could more easily respond. During this period the volunteer had the experience of recognizing the existence of ambivalence within himself, which made it easier for him to accept ambivalence on the part of his Little Brother. This phase solidified the process of identification between volunteer and worker. Because the worker was able to accept Mrs. Sanders, the volunteer was more accepting of her. Because the worker was able to accept Mr. Sandman's hostility as well as his positive feelings, Mr. Sandman was able to accept them in others. A new insight was achieved by the Big Brother when he recognized that he was receiving his own satisfactions from his friendship with his Little Brother. This recognition of satisfaction of their own unmet needs is a sophisticated one on the part of volunteers, but when it comes, it is usually an indication that the volunteer has overcome the fantasy that he is in a one-way giving position. He is therefore better able to engage in the give-and-take relationship with his Little Brother from that point on.

TAPERING-OFF PHASE

At the end of the second year of the Big Brother-child relationship, Billy entered the tapering-off period in the treatment relationship with his worker. While he continued to see her regularly, the emphasis in the interviews shifted, and the relationship between Billy and Mr. Sandman was brought more directly into interview content. Billy also began to use the worker as a bulwark against his mother and as a sustaining influence to offset the pressures that were still brought to bear upon him. One day he asked the worker to sing, which she did, and finally he joined her. He said that his mother did not think he sang very well, but his Big Brother liked his voice and they often sang while they were driving together. The Big Brother had a very deep voice which Billy admired. The worker encouraged this growing identification between Billy and Mr. Sandman, in preparing termination of direct contact with the boy.

In periodic treatment conferences the gradual ending of treatment contact with Billy had been anticipated. He was now in the latency stage and had obtained maximal benefit from individual interviews, going as far in obtaining insight into his problems and their bases as could be expected in view of his pathological background and difficulties. In this ending period there had been some regression in behavior. Billy had had a long illness and had been at home for six weeks. The mother had stayed with him, and in her disappointment at being once more tied to him, she had returned to her former patterns of behavior toward him. Billy, too, had regressed and displayed some of his previous fears of separation. With return to treatment, however, and a renewal of regular visits with his Big Brother, Billy was able to pull out of this setback and to achieve his former standard of adjustment.

It was during this time that Billy wrote a composition about his Big Brother, which he titled "My Best Friend." Billy's mother spontaneously sent the original to the Big Brother. This incident was typical of Mrs. Sanders' expanding ability to allow the Big Brother to have some part in her son's life. She continued to see the worker weekly and to discuss the problems that arose in her daily life, particularly those centering around the Big Brother and Billy. There were further setbacks in her adjustment that paralleled regressive phases on Billy's part. However, she, too, was able to weather the ups and downs of life during this peroid.

Her attitude toward Billy reflected the new status he had achieved in her eyes. Whereas before, she was sure that he was doomed to a life of mental illness, she now began to view the future for him more hopefully. When volunteer and mother attended a school play together, she openly expressed her pride in Billy. "His mother," reported the volunteer, "began to talk about how smart Billy was and mentioned that she had plans and hopes for him, but realized that he would have to choose his own career. I asked her what she would like him to be and she said, 'a psychiatrist.' " Billy indicated that he had his own ambitions for himself during this time, by questioning his Big Brother whether actors made money. The Big Brother realistically said that very few did, and recommended acting only as a hobby. It was obvious that mother and child were enjoying each other much more fully, and that their relationship had achieved a new depth and meaning which had been highlighted by the introduction of an understanding volunteer.

Mr. Sandman was moving out of his dependence upon the worker into a phase of security and relaxation with his Little Brother. He described this aptly in one of his last reports while there was still contact with the boy: "You know, I am beginning to appreciate the meaning of the somewhat literary expression, 'the ripening of friendship.' Oh, I have always enjoyed being with Billy, most of the time anyway, but I can see now that almost all of the time I was with him, I was watching him, studying him, filing in my mind what I thought was 'significant' to pass along to you. Today, more strongly than ever before, I felt that there was between us that easy, casual relationship, that comradeship, which is such a precious and rare thing." Mr. Sandman was now in the period of knowing that his relationship with Billy was a sound and a good one, and that, although he would make mistakes, just as parents do, he and Billy would survive them because of the strong bond between them. He had now lived through two years of experience with his Little Brother and Mrs. Sanders, and could predict and anticipate without too much anxiety the crises that might arise. Less frequently, but still regularly, he was in contact with the worker to clarify his thinking and to refresh his feelings about Billy. He was prepared to continue carrying the responsibility, which was now a pleasure, of being a Big Brother to Billy in the years ahead. On his own he was preparing his wife for introduction to the Little Brother who had been an important part of his life for the previous two years.

Although therapeutic interviews were to end, the plan was for Billy to continue seeing his Big Brother regularly. It was anticipated that the Big Brother would remain in contact with Billy for many years, seeing him through his adolescence. The worker would continue her interest in Billy by talking with the Big Brother so that she could keep informed as to what was happening in their relationship. The mother would continue to see the worker. She would be helped to accept the fact that Billy could participate in the daily life of the

Big Brother without threatening his relationship with her. As time went on and Billy's mother was able to accept it, Mr. Sandman would be encouraged to introduce Billy into his own home and have him meet his wife. This would provide an important experience in living for Billy in a home where husband and wife had a good marital relationship. If, in adolescence, Billy's problems reappeared to some degree, Mr. Sandman would be there as a close friend to tide him over the disturbed period, or to refer him for treatment, if that seemed necessary.

In this tapering-off period the relationship between Big Brother and child began to change from a somewhat self-conscious extension of the therapeutic process to what one might term "controlled friendship." The emphasis in therapy was now on the volunteer rather than the child. This occurs frequently in cases where volunteers are used. However, the choice of emphases can vary. In some cases, parents are not seen at all intensively throughout the time the volunteer sees a child. In other cases, contact with the parent can be intensified, especially in preparation for the tapering-off phase. The possibilities in the therapeutic approach are as varied here as in any other aspect of the treatment process. The age of the child also is a determinant in the plan for the volunteer's continuation. Sometimes contact between volunteer and child is terminated at the time active treatment by the worker is discontinued. More often, especially in cases of very severe pathology, like Billy's, the volunteer is encouraged to continue his relationship indefinitely.

While the volunteer during the tapering-off period needs a different kind of supervision by the worker, he must continue to have help in whatever areas anxiety may be manifested. Frequently it is found that when the worker plans to end direct contact with the child, the volunteer becomes anxious because of a feeling that he is now being left to carry the total responsibility alone. It is therefore necessary to offer him not only the assistance of periodic conferences and meetings, but the reassuring contact with other Big Brothers in educational meetings and committee functions. During these sessions Big Brothers who are working with youngsters no longer under treatment care of the agency can learn from, and mutually sustain, each other. In Billy's case, for instance, it may be that as he grows older the Big Brother will need help in allowing him more independence, changing his own attitudes and the nature of the contacts as the boy's needs shift.

In this long-term case the contribution that was made by the Big Brother to the therapeutic process and subsequent changes in Billy cannot be completely evaluated. One can only conjecture what might have happened if there had been no Mr. Sandman. When an integrated approach is utilized in successful cases, one cannot separate the result of the therapist's work with the child from the volunteer's influence upon the end result with the child.

An attempt has been made in this chapter to identify some of the elements in the setting within which a child moves that have meaning for him, and thus have meaning for the psychotherapeutic process. The interdependency of a child's inner and outer life has been stressed. When translated into practice in psychotherapy, this concept involves a broader orientation by the therapist toward the child and his environment than is usually practiced. It means that extrapsychic, as well as intrapsychic, factors must be brought within the province of psychotherapy. The worker must first have an understanding of the total life situation of the child in order to understand his total treatment needs. From this understanding should then flow the creative use of selected people or elements in the child's environment to enhance the healthy trends and minimize those that are unhealthy. Sometimes, where constructive influences are absent, a volunteer can be introduced to bring about improved conditions for mental and physical growth.

In addition to satisfying libidinal needs, changes in ego functioning can be furthered by a relationship with a Big Brother or Big Sister. The varying reactions to the introduction of the volunteer by all members of the child's family of orientation can be observed and their effects incorporated into therapeutic sessions. Without this scientific scrutiny, and without realization of the impact of a volunteer as a sociodynamic force upon the child, the family, and the treatment, results obtained by his introduction into the therapeutic process will be at best haphazard, and at worst, harmful.

Such an approach to treatment demands a persistent and far-reaching sense of awareness on the part of the worker. In addition to the traditional understanding of the child as evinced in interviews, he must now have awareness of the ebb and flow of the multitudinous other relationships that center around his patient. Child and family, child and volunteer, therapist and child, and therapist and volunteer are some of the social interaction patterns formed. As in all therapy, the necessity for the therapist to understand his own counter-reactions is paramount. This caution assumes greatest importance in relation to the supervision of the volunteer who participates in the helping process of therapy as a Big Brother or Big Sister.

CHAPTER TEN

Limited Treatment Goals

THE SETTING of treatment goals in a child guidance clinic is a difficult task which seems to require more theoretical consideration than has been given to it so far. The present diagnostic and therapeutic framework of the clinic has no special category under this heading. It foresees only the setting of a treatment plan. In consequence the workers in planning for the future concern themselves mostly with treatment techniques, with methods rather than goals. Because of the amount of experience and insight which has been gained in regard to the dangers of dealing with symptoms rather than with disorders, there is understandable reluctance to formulate a treatment goal in terms of those symptoms which have formed the basis for the agency contact with the child.

Since the treatment goal remains unspecified, the workers consciously or unconsciously visualize the resolution of the personality conflict which is the reason for the child's difficulties as the goal of their therapeutic effort. Desirable as such goal setting ideally may be, it is difficult to achieve in practice. To pursue it in case constellations which make it impossible, may be harmful to the client, to the therapist, and to the utilization of mental health resources by the community as such. This is an area in which the combination of the social science approach with psychodynamic understanding as presented in this volume may help to produce clarification.

Before attempting to develop criteria for situations in which limited goal setting seems to be indicated, it might be desirable to scrutinize the social purpose of child guidance work. The reason a child is brought to an agency in that field is invariably the concern of adults about his development, in terms of either behavior or affect, or both. Difficulties in these respects usually

By OTTO POLLAK IN CONSULTATION WITH FREDERIKA NEUMANN

present a serious problem of day-by-day living for the child and the persons in his environment at the time of the referral. There seems to be a widespread concern, however, that it is not so much, or at least not only, the difficult situation of the present which requires remedial care, but its effect on the future development of the child. In other words, childhood difficulties are considered developmental risks. Even when the referral source does not show awareness of the developmental impact of the child's difficulties, the therapist always does. The question has to be asked, therefore, into which direction the development of the child is to go and in what way his mental disorder may interfere with his development.

From the point of view of society the developmental process is intended to produce an adult who combines functional efficiency with social acceptability and to produce this result in such a way that individual stages of this process do not impose undue hardships on the persons in the child's environment. From this angle the developmental process of the individual has been conceptualized as *socialization*. It has been defined, for instance, as:

> The change by which the individual member of society becomes a functioning part of the group, acting according to its standards, conforming to its mores, subject to its traditions and feeling himself a part of it sufficiently to command the tolerance if not the admiration of his fellows.[1]

This definition reflects the thinking of most parents and teachers who refer children to the agency. With whatever other motive this overtly expressed concern about the social adaptation of the child may be connected, it is a rational concern in terms of the demands of society and of the ultimate adjustment of the patient. It coincides, therefore, with the mandated function of the agency. What parents cannot always know, or emotionally accept, is the therapeutic procedure which seems to be indicated in order to help the child achieve this goal of meeting social demands. To the

[1] Blackmar, Frank W., and John L. Gillin, *Outlines of Sociology*. Macmillan Co., New York, rev. ed., 1923, p. 291. Reprinted with the permission of the publisher.

person trained in psychodynamics, the sociological emphasis in the definition quoted above and the corresponding concern of parents usually encountered may appear questionable. It may be pointed out that socialization so defined seems to disregard the emotional price which the individual has to pay for such a development and which occasionally may be so high as to leave him without sufficient emotional resources to continue paying this price. The comment may be expected that it is exactly this *emotional price* for socialization which, in essence, appears to be the core of functional mental disorders. This is undoubtedly true; the value of the definition lies, however, in its emphasis on the social demands which growing up and living among other human beings makes upon the individual and which must be met with emotional adequacy if the person is to develop successfully as a member of society. This point is important to consider in child guidance work because psychotherapists living with the experiences of emotional overpayment under which their patients suffer are frequently in danger of discounting the value of the social return which stems from conformity. Living in a way acceptable to the standards of one's associates is a condition of living. Even overpaying for essentials does not change the essential nature of what one is paying for.

Once this is clarified, it becomes not only possible but even necessary to incorporate the emotional component in our understanding of the process of *socialization*. This has been done admirably in a paper which significantly was written by a psychologist who received his original training in medicine and a cultural anthropologist.

> Beginning in the nursery, the process of socialization continues throughout life. Among other things, what must be learned is: the power to inhibit, or to moderate, the expression of unacceptable needs; the ability to transfer cathexis from a prohibited goal-object to an acceptable substitute; the habitual and automatic use of a large number of approved action patterns (methods, manners, and emotional attitudes); and the ability to adapt to schedules (to do things at the proper time, keep appointments, etc.). It is assumed that, having acquired these abilities, the average person will be capable of establishing satisfactory interpersonal relations within the legal and

conventional framework of society. When the child begins to behave in a predictable, expectable manner it is well on the road to being socialized. But degree of socialization cannot be estimated solely on the basis of objective evidence. The everlasting practice of suppression, demanded by some societies, may be extremely painful, and the not-infrequent result of these repeated renunciations is a deep-seated cumulative resentment, conscious or unconscious, against cultural restrictions. Held under control, this resentment manifests itself in tensions, dissatisfactions, irritabilities, recurrent complaints, periods of dejection, cynicism, pessimism, and, in more extreme cases, in neurosis and psychosis. A high degree of repressed resentment is indicative of a fundamental emotional maladjustment, and hence, of the partial failure of the socialization process, regardless of how successful the individual may be in "winning friends and influencing people." The goal of the socialization process is an unreluctant emotional identification with the developing ethos of the society, though some conflict is inevitable in all personalities.[1]

In this sense socialization does not have the goal of producing unconflicted, "happy" acceptance of social demands by the individual. Its goal is rather an acceptance that is sufficiently supported by positive affect to make the meeting of cultural demands emotionally possible without withdrawing positive affect from other areas of life also needing an attachment of emotional energy. From the social science point of view this note of realism in the definition quoted above deserves serious attention by the child-rearing professions.

So realistic an approach to the phenomenon of socialization and the role which the child-rearing professions may play in bringing it about is likely to suggest in some cases even more modesty in the setting of the treatment goal than the acceptance of residual conflict in the life of the patient after treatment. Clinical observation shows that there are different degrees of incapacitation which may be the result of a failure in the socialization process. There is certainly a difference in functional effectiveness between the neurotic on the one hand and the psychotic or psychopath on the other. Most people will definitely agree that

[1] Murray, Henry A., and Clyde Kluckhohn, "Outline of a Conception of Personality, in *Personality in Nature, Society, and Culture*, edited by Kluckhohn and Murray. Alfred A. Knopf, Inc., New York, 1948, pp. 25–26.

it is better to be a neurotic than either a psychotic or a psychopath, or—differently expressed—that a neurotic individual is closer to socialization than the psychotic or psychopath.

In child guidance work this means that a child suffering from a primary behavior disorder may be helped to a degree if under the therapeutic influence he can become neurotic, because in doing so he may become more socially acceptable to the persons in his environment. Thus he may be enabled later on to seek help for the neurosis under more favorable circumstances than exist at the moment. In other words, if socialization, even in the realistic sense of leaving some conflicts unresolved, cannot be fully achieved, there still are differences in degree to which people fail to achieve it with the corresponding differences in the degree of incapacitation. Consequently the socialization process to which an individual is exposed may have different degrees of failure. In the individual instance of a mental disorder, child guidance work, assisting the socialization process of the patient, may correspondingly have to aim at different degrees of success. The phenomenon that sometimes an undue emotional price may have to be paid by an individual for socialization has definite implications for the setting of therapeutic goals. Child guidance workers, although interested in helping the patient reduce this price to normal levels, must accept the fact that sometimes a patient has to be helped to socialization even though this demands from him an emotional price which is higher than other children have to pay.

These various considerations may have considerable implications for setting the treatment goal and evaluating treatment success. In the situational approach proposed in this book, this aspect of child guidance work is very important. This approach represents an attempt to guard against the selective consideration of any one specific factor in the determination of a child guidance problem. By identifying and considering an ever-increasing plurality of factors, one will stand a fair chance of increasing one's effectiveness in the attempt to produce change. On the other hand, one will in certain constellations also gain insight into the difficulties of bringing about such change which otherwise may go unnoticed and thus may lead to unrewarded, because unrealistic, effort.

In this chapter an attempt will be made to analyze situations where the limitation of treatment goals seems to be indicated because pursuit of more than limited treatment goals might appear to be unlikely of attainment or even impossible. It will be seen that such an analysis represents to a degree a synthesis of the concepts discussed in the earlier chapters of this book with the concept of *socialization*.

As on other occasions, we must again stress the social dependency of the child as a starting point of our discussion. This social dependency expresses itself, first, in the fact that he cannot live by himself. He must be attached to the household of adults, usually his parents, or take his place in institutional living arrangements. This exposes him of necessity to the influence of other persons from whom he cannot remove himself by his own power in functionally effective and socially acceptable form. When he attempts a separation, he is designated as a runaway and presents a problem requiring protective and remedial action on the part of society. An adult in therapy has much more power to rearrange his housing and living conditions in a form conducive to better mental health than a child. In child guidance cases this dependency of the patient in housing and living conditions may present a serious obstacle to successful therapy. Since many emotional disturbances of children are created by emotional disturbances in the persons surrounding them, the pathology of these persons, if unremedied or unremediable, may present limitations beyond which treatment success cannot be expected.

The primary patient of the child guidance clinic differs further from the adult patient of an outpatient clinic in the crucial fact that he does not come for help on his own initiative. Although he may fairly soon in the contact, or later on, experience a desire for therapeutic help, the fact is that he has been brought to the agency because his parents want him to be in treatment, a teacher has suggested its desirability, or some other person of greater power than he, for instance a consulting physician, has proposed treatment. Similarly a child may be withdrawn from treatment because of opposition on the part of these same powerful persons in his environment to a continuation of the treatment process. Frequently such opposition may not express itself in open withdrawal of the child but simply in counteracting its effectiveness, while on the surface treatment is permitted to continue. The possibility of continuing treatment successfully depends, therefore, to a considerable degree on the attitude of persons other than the patient.

The material presented in this book suggests that situations of counteracted, and therefore ineffective treatment, may occur because pathogenic influences to which the child is exposed are exercised by persons outside the therapeutic orbit. They may also occur because persons in the life environment of the child may engage in negative social interaction with the child as he changes in treatment. They may occur in cases of culture conflict between parents and therapists or simply because of failure of parents and parent substitutes to understand that a disappearance of symptoms frequently does not indicate removal of psychodynamic disturbances. In all these instances it would seem desirable, first, to prevent such a development by extending the therapeutic influence to these persons so as to bring about greater harmony between the therapeutic goal and the life environment of the child. Where that cannot be achieved, however, limitation of treatment goal seems to be indicated in order to avoid wasted therapeutic effort, which in view of the scarcity of therapeutic help is a point of serious social concern.

Limitation of treatment goal frequently encounters serious difficulties because it may interfere with omnipotency strivings of the particular therapist and lack of recognition on his part of the fact that life contains not only pathogenic elements but also elements conducive to health. It is certainly true that a child who becomes a patient of a child guidance clinic has probably been exposed to more pathogenic conditions than to conditions that are health conducive. The question must be raised, however, whether the psychotherapeutic process does not in certain cases enable a child to utilize the positive resources of his environment for development toward health before the disorder is completely cured. In other words, what might have to be counteracted in the interest of an adequate distribution of mental health services is the false belief of many inexperienced workers that psychotherapy has always to do the job completely and that nothing at all can be left to the positive interplay between the individual and his environment. Effective therapy may be slowed up or even be doomed to failure if attention is directed only to the conflict areas in the personality. Attention to conflict-free areas is also important.

A problem of great therapeutic impact is the time at which the limitation of the treatment goal should be determined. Ideally this should be done at the point of diagnosis. Frequently, however, it will not be possible to do so because phenomena of untreatability as well as phenomena of health may become apparent only in the course of attempted therapy. In such situations the decision of treatment extension or treatment limitation should be made as soon as these phenomena can be identified. What should be prevented is, on the one hand, limitation of the treatment goal before the possibility of more intensive therapy has been fully explored, and, on the other, continued pursuit of a treatment goal after its attainability has become highly doubtful.

In the following pages three cases will be presented in order to illustrate some of the situations and the aspects of timing involved in the problem of setting limited treatment goals.

The case of Ben shows how an evaluation of adverse circumstances in a case constellation can be used at the point of diagnosis in intake for the decision to pursue only limited treatment goals.

Ben, a thirteen-year-old boy, was referred to the clinic because he had begun to absent himself more and more frequently from school since he had been transferred to junior high school. He did so ostensibly because of attacks of abdominal and chest pains. In an interview with one of the consultant psychiatrists of the clinic, which was arranged for him early during the intake process, he described his emotional reactions to school as "getting a bellyache and the runs." In that connection he pointed out that he was not like the other boys who cut school and went to the movies; he went home because he was in pain.

Further symptoms elicited in intake were the following: He showed considerable hostility to authority at school and in the summer before contact with the clinic had run away from camp because he felt that the counselor was brutal and unfair. Ben was also defiant and negativistic at home. He lied, particularly concerning his absences from school, and made demands on his mother for money which she was not able to meet. At times he got so angry that he broke furniture in his home. He was also a nailbiter and picked his nose to such an extent that he often hurt it. He was restless and unable to sustain interest in a specific activity for any length of time. In contrast to having been neat when a smaller child, he had become slovenly in his appearance and did not even brush his teeth or wash his face without being nagged to do so. Recently he had developed a dislike of sleeping alone and had expressed fears that he was "crazy."

Ben's family background and developmental history showed an unusual number of pathogenic factors. Before Ben was born his father had become mentally ill and was hospitalized on a permanent basis, so that the child had never had the experience of having a father. The delivery had been difficult and the mother had been sick for a whole year afterward. Because of the father's hospitalization and her own sickness, the mother had gone back to live with her mother and younger sister. After her recovery she had started to work and supported the entire household, leaving Ben's care to his grandmother and aunt. The latter was mentally retarded and thus anything but a satisfactory mother substitute. Little information could be elicited about her handling of Ben, except that she force-fed him and was jealous of any show of affection on his part to his mother.

About five years before intake the grandmother had developed a mental disturbance; she was suspicious of people, refused to leave the home, and was incoherent in her speech. Since the outbreak of the grandmother's illness, Ben's mother had stayed at home, living on public welfare assistance. Because of the grandmother's refusal to sign an application for old age assistance and the aunt's inability to hold regular employment, the whole household had to be maintained on the public assistance support granted to Ben's mother for herself and the boy, plus that given to the aunt.

Thus the child grew up in a household consisting of three women and no man, becoming increasingly aware that his father and maternal grandmother were mentally sick, and that his aunt was mentally defective. The mother herself was an emotionally unstable person who looked to the boy for support and intended to solve her dependency needs by marrying a widower with three grown-up children, although this man disliked Ben and was disliked by him in turn.

In addition to all these unfavorable conditions, Ben, who had been satisfied with his school experience in grade school to the degree of crying when because of illness he was unable to attend, had been transferred to a junior high school which he disliked. The students were all boys and the teaching staff all men, and, he felt, unsympathetic toward him. For a boy with Ben's all-feminine home environment, and in consequence feminine superego development, an all-male school environment was hard to "take." This was apparent from his description of the teachers, whom he designated as crude in their speech though not using "real bad language."

Thus the presenting symptom of his absenting himself from school, which had started upon the transfer to this high school, probably was a reaction to the impact of an environment for which his upbringing had not prepared him. He showed sufficient ego strength to attempt himself to arrange a transfer to another school, but had not succeeded in this effort.

The boy and his mother were seen by one of the agency's consulting psychiatrists for clinical evaluation and therapeutic recommendation. The tentative diagnostic impression was that the boy suffered from a neurotic character disorder with somatic equivalents (not true conversion symptoms in the strict sense of the word), associated with reactions entirely due to environmental stress. In view of the presence of two problem adults in the boy's family who were outside the therapeutic orbit, and the convergence of anxiety-creating school conditions for a boy of his personality structure with the pathogenic factors in his family, no recommendations that were made aimed at any basic change in the personalities of this boy and his mother. Instead limited goals were set for both, with the purpose of producing an improvement in the environmental growth conditions of this child.

With regard to the boy, the recommendation was made that the school situation should be investigated and if stresses should be found as described by him, a prompt transfer should be arranged. In the psychological area it was planned to help the boy understand and accept his own feelings of resentment against his home and family situation and to understand the psychological derivation of his somatic symptoms. With regard to the mother, it was planned to help her make definite plans for institutionalizing the grandmother and for separating her household from that of the aunt with a minimum of guilt feelings.

The treatment goals decided upon in this case show how a realistic evaluation of a specific case constellation can lead to a decision to confine oneself to what one might call a symptomatic cure. The selection of the symptom which was made the focus of the therapeutic effort, however, shows an understanding of the differences in developmental impact which various symptoms may have. It was obvious that the psychosomatic discomforts of this boy and the impact of a school environment which for him was intolerable, presented his most serious areas of incapacitation from the point of view of the socialization process. No matter what his psychological disturbances may be, in our society a child must go to school if he is to develop into a functioning adult. In that sense, the recommendation of the psychiatrist took care of the most immediate need of the child. It was rightly felt that some amelioration of the home environment would be helpful even though the boy's emotional involvement with his mother needed more intensive treatment than it was possible to provide. This was based on the recognition that a home environment such as that to which he had been exposed so far would militate against any utilization of opportunities in his wider environment which might permit him some male identification or feeling of normality. Therefore it was planned to help the mother carry out the necessary separation from the senile grandmother and the mentally defective aunt of the boy in terms of household arrangements. To go further in planning would have been unrealistic because no positive prognosis for intensive psychotherapy could have been made unless the school and home conditions were changed. The possibility of achieving such changes, however, could not be assumed as certain at that stage of the diagnosis.

While this case shows how recognition of the preexisting aspects of a case may lead to a limitation of treatment goals before actually starting treatment, the case of Cora illustrates how such aspects may be recognized only after a considerable period of treatment because they have developed during the course of the latter. Over and beyond this difference in the time at which the decision to pursue only limited treatment goals can be made, this case shows also a different basis for the decision. In the case of Ben the reason was the existence of pathogenic influences in the growth conditions of the child which could not be reached by any therapeutic effort. In the case of Cora the reason for limiting treatment goals was the recognition of the probability that further therapeutic effort would produce negative social interaction between the father and the child which would jeopardize treatment gains already achieved.

Cora was referred to the agency at the age of eight years by her father, who had read about the Child Guidance Institute in a newspaper. The child's symptoms, which had brought the father to the clinic, were frequent vomiting of solid food without traceable organic cause; excessive fears of the dark, doctors, and illness; and anxiety attacks after seeing sad or scary movies, or listening to radio stories of the same character. In intake it was learned that she also had temper tantrums, was hyperactive, and suffered from sensations of ticklishness in her thighs, face, and neck. Two years before intake she had begun to have frequent nosebleeds, which had continued up to the time of contact with the clinic.

Cora's mother was a neurotic woman who suffered from almost daily headaches. She had an unsatisfactory relationship with her husband which had continued since the first year of her marriage and she indicated her own feeling about it by saying, "One can get used to hanging." With regard to the child, she complained that Cora had made her a nervous wreck. She admitted that she became anxious whenever she was separated from Cora unless the child was at school, and considered herself a failure as a mother. Thus she indicated her feelings of guilt over her negative attitudes toward Cora. She easily flared up and screamed at the child who, in turn, screamed back at her. She also tried, albeit unsuccessfully, not to hit Cora when the child angered her.

The father, a very orthodox Jew, was a tailor who had failed to be a good provider to his family, but was concerned about the upbringing of Cora and her sister. The mother described him as being so stubborn that she had to give in to him constantly, indicating the strong power position which the father held in this family. Cora rarely screamed in the presence of her father. His word was law to her. Although overtly affectionate toward him when younger, she had become inhibited in showing affection to him after she entered school, and by the time treatment began she had become very modest with him, refusing to undress in his presence.

The developmental history of the child suggested that her vomiting had started in early infancy on an organic basis but had been perpetuated by inappropriate handling on the part of the mother, who had infantilized her continuously because of her overconcern about her physical well-being. She had permitted Cora to have a bottle until she was four, force-fed her frequently, and still bathed the eight-year-old girl. The child had undergone a number of surgical traumas, such as a tonsillectomy at the age of one and a half, five lancings of ear abscesses at the age of six, and a second tonsillectomy during the same year which, in turn, was followed by the removal of her adenoids. The latter had been accompanied by a severe hemorrhage, which the doctor checked by a suturing operation. This he performed without an anesthetic. The father had to hold the child down during that operation and recalled with horror what an experience it had been for the child as well as for himself. Finally, the nosebleeds which the child had developed in the two years before treatment had necessitated some cauterization, as well as nightly spraying of her nostrils with albolene.

The psychiatrist diagnosed the child's condition as a primary behavior disorder with neurotic traits and habit disorders. He pointed out that many of the child's fears were realistic reactions to her various traumas with surgical operations and to the overconcern of her mother about her physical welfare. In view of Cora's ticklish sensations and recently developed shyness toward her father, some of her fears, however, were considered of oedipal origin. The vomiting symptom finally was seen as having developed on a nutritional basis and having become a habit pattern, which at the time of the contact with the clinic had begun to be utilized in a neurotic manner.

Both child and mother showed quick response to therapy. Cora's main symptom, the consistent vomiting, stopped very early in treatment. Somewhat later her acting out behavior subsided. She ceased having temper tantrums with screaming. She was able to listen to the radio and go to the movies without becoming really frightened and was developing intellectually to a very satisfactory degree. The mother also learned to handle the child better and to gain satisfaction from Cora's response.

About two years after the case had been opened, however, the child began to show the syndrome of a severe obsession neurosis. She suffered from obsessional doubts which forced her constantly to erase and rewrite her homework and interpreted the frequent colds and operations of her earlier years as punishments sent her from God for her badness. She increasingly insisted that God was right in punishing people who did not adhere strictly to His rules and began to fit this idea into the orthodox system of her father's religion.

Thus while the child's behavior disorder had been treated successfully, the development of the neurotic symptoms, already noticed in the original psychiatric examination, into a full-blown neurosis had not been checked. This in all probability was unavoidable because the treatment of a behavior disorder makes it difficult, if not impossible, to prevent superego formation under all circumstances from taking a neurotic turn.

At the same time the mother, with whom therapeutic effort had been centered around the problems in her relationship with the child, began to show signs of increasing readiness to discuss herself and her marital relationship. She mentioned her desire to get a separation from her husband and wanted help in working out her emotional problems in relation to this.

Thus there arose the question whether a cure of the neurosis of which the child was suffering should be attempted and whether the neurosis of the mother should be made the focus of an intensive treatment effort. After some oscillation it was decided, however, not to do so and to terminate treatment on the basis of achievement so far made. This decision was based on the following reasons: The child had stopped vomiting and therefore was better able to develop physically. Her relationship with the mother had improved to the degree of permitting her a satisfactory feminine identification. She had in part transformed the more open expression of her oedipal attachment to her father into a neurotic conformity with his orthodox religious beliefs, which made her more acceptable to him. It was recognized that this latter development was part of the price which she had to pay for her personality gains. To attempt a treatment of that neurosis, however, would have required a positive attitude of her father toward a continuation of treatment, and such an attitude was nonexistent.

The therapeutic considerations which led to treatment termination here show the value of some of the concepts introduced in this volume. There was, first, recognition of the likelihood of negative social interaction on the part of the father. Although he had made the initial contact with the clinic, he had become increasingly antagonistic toward it as the treatment process went on. Part of the reason might have been that he had not been involved in the treatment process to any significant extent. It might have been also due in part to his recognition that his wife, as a result of her contacts with the clinic, showed increasing signs of independence, which frustrated his own need to dominate all the members of his family.

Second, there was recognition of the probability that continued treatment would produce culture conflict between father and child. It is true that the child abused the orthodox Jewish culture of her father by neurotic submissiveness. The father, however, did not see it in that light. Behavior changes which might have been expected on Cora's part, had her neurosis been effectively attacked, would have impressed him as rebellion. Such a therapeutic effect would have led to a culture conflict between Cora and her father.

The case shows also the value of setting therapeutic goals in accordance with the conception of different degrees of socialization. Cora was undoubtedly helped in that respect. The physical and psychological impairments which had interfered with her growth had disappeared to the degree of facilitating her further development along socially acceptable lines. To be sure, the neurosis which Cora had developed during treatment had not been attacked. This imposed on her a heavy emotional price for the gains which she had made. The decision, however, not to attempt a cure of the neurosis was justified because it protected those improvements which already had been achieved.

The limitation of treatment goals suggested here implies, of course, confidence that the child will find significant resources for healthy development also outside the therapeutic influence. It so happens that Cora, some years after termination of treatment, applied to the agency for counseling in the selection of a career. At that time the worker noted that her obsessional adherence to religious orthodoxy had subsided. There were still some indications of the continued existence of a neurosis but a deterioration of the child's condition had not occurred. Actually the incapacitating grip of the neurosis on the child had been lessened.

As has already been pointed out, it is not always the existence of pathogenic factors that from the start suggests limitation of the treatment goal. Nor is it the probability of culture conflict and negative social interaction within the family during treatment that may suggest such limitations. It can also happen that diagnostic information gained at an advanced stage of treatment, or the development of the patient during treatment, reveals the existence of a more severe psychopathology than was originally assumed. This may mean greater treatment difficulties than those foreseen at the time of formulating the treatment plan, or even basic untreatability.

How recognition of the various degrees of success which the concept of *socialization* implies can be helpful in redefining the treatment goal in such a situation is shown by the case of Anne. It illustrates how the need for such a redefinition may be recognized only after a considerable period of treatment. It shows further how such a development can be handled without either continuing apparently hopeless therapeutic effort or without complete acceptance of defeat for the patient as well as for the therapist. Finally, the limitation of treatment decided upon in this case shows how a change in the external situation of the patient was used to bring her to a point where she was enabled to function more effectively in the social sphere, although the psychological disturbance could not be resolved. By achieving this, the incapacitating consequences of the condition with their impact of progressive deterioration were at least arrested.

Anne was referred to the clinic at the age of fifteen by her mother because she was not working up to capacity at school, was moody and depressed at home, and withdrawn from the other members of her family. Other complaints were that she wore conspicuous make-up and dress, flaunted her body and related in questionable fashion to boys, first attracting them by seductive behavior and then staving them off; there was also fear of the dark accompanied by some compulsive traits, such as being able to fall asleep only if the bed and chair in her room were in a certain position against the wall. Furthermore there was a conversion symptom in the form of partially blocked vision in one eye (cloudiness), for which no organic basis could be found.

The girl's parents were greatly disturbed persons, who were suffering from marital difficulties of long duration. These difficulties had expanded to all areas of their marriage and were particularly obvious in their sexual relationship and handling of Anne and her brother, Frederick.

Anne's mother was a controlling and compulsive woman of great rigidity. The father, a bookkeeper by occupation, was a confused and passive person with rather schizoid behavior expressions.

Anne was caught up in the long and bitter struggle of her parents. The father, disappointed in his marriage, at first concentrated his object libido upon the girl, taking her out a lot, and spent all his free time with her to the exclusion of the mother. The child, in turn, idolized the father. The mother was left out, felt that Anne did not want her, and referred to the child as "her father's daughter." She projected a great deal of her negative feelings against her husband onto the girl, and in criticizing and disciplining her pointed out that Anne in her objectionable traits resembled her father.

When Anne reached the age of ten and became interested in boys, the father became indignant and transferred his affections completely from her to the younger child, Frederick. Anne was deeply hurt by this shift of her father's overt affection. She reacted with sarcastic remarks, unruly behavior, a decline in her performance at school, and strong resentment against her brother. At this time she began to reach out toward her mother and accused her of not having any love for her. Mother and daughter became closer, but the child's identification with the mother remained confined to their now common feeling of rejection by the girl's father. Anne continued to mistreat the mother, rebelled against her attempts at control but took the mother's side in family arguments, and on occasion grudgingly accepted her mother's advice. The mother, in turn, felt that Anne continued to prefer her father and resented him only because he had discarded her.

As the girl grew into adolescence, she engaged increasingly in sex play with boys but her sexual relations remained on a masturbatory level, a type of sexual expression which she maintained also during the greater part of the therapy. Thus her acting out expressed itself more in quantitative increases of this behavior than in qualitative change.

On the other hand, the father reacted to his daughter's acting out by occasional outbursts of severity which seemed to be an expression of sexual jealousy. He began to enter her room at night and to beat her severely for her misbehavior in staying out late and playing around with boys. Furthermore he made attempts to block her communication with the boys by having the telephone disconnected.

Under the impact of this pathological situation in the home, the child developed severe ambivalence about growing up. She could not decide whether to engage in a college career or take a job, and whether to leave her home or accommodate to it. She also remained confused in her attitude toward boys, oscillating between being seductive and negatively controlling.

The diagnosis of the consulting psychiatrist was psychoneurosis, anxiety hysteria with compulsive traits, and conversion symptoms accompanied by conduct disturbances. In view of the limitation which the child's unresolved oedipal conflict put on her sexual relationship with boys, keeping her relatively free from pregnancy risks, it was not felt necessary to recommend placement in a more protective environment. It was decided, therefore, to treat the child in individual psychotherapy, although it might have been indicated to consider placement in a more controlled environment as treatment progressed. Prognosis was considered good, particularly in view of the fact that the parents at the same time had made arrangements to receive therapeutic help themselves.

In the course of therapy Anne developed considerable intellectual understanding of the meaning of her negativistic ties with her father and boy friends. She also showed some spurts of improvement in overt behavior which, however, were not maintained. She managed to improve her school performance and to graduate from high school. She gave up her acting out behavior at certain periods only to revert back. After one of these episodes another interview with a psychiatrist was arranged. On that occasion she expressed realistic fear of becoming more disturbed if she continued to stay in her home environment, but on the other hand, spoke with such glibness about remorse and anxiety that it appeared that she did not feel these emotions at all and therefore could not learn from her past experiences. At the same time there was marked expression of a great need for personal gratification and self aggrandizement, indicating that the features of a psychopathic personality were coming into the foreground. In this connection it should be mentioned that the treatment plan of the parents did not work out because very soon the father, and somewhat later, the mother dropped out of therapy without having achieved any significant gains.

In view of this development of the girl's personality and its recognition in psychiatric examination, as well as in view of the lack of improvement on the part of her parents, the treatment goals in this case were revised and limited. The psychiatrist recommended shifting the therapeutic intent to trying to achieve the following changes in personal equipment and environmental opportunities in order to produce a better social functioning of the girl: (1) to help her become self-supporting by learning something useful which would enable her to get and hold a job, and (2) to help her carry out her separation from the continuing pathological influence of her home environment.

Actually these goals were achieved in approximately three months. The mother was helped to see that it would not be harmful to the girl if she lived away from home. Therefore she did not oppose Anne when, after a scene with her father, she left the home and went to live with a family, where she received free room and board in return for taking care of the children a few nights a week. Therapy with Anne was directed at giving her support while she became adjusted to this new mode of living and at helping her get settled in a job, which she had found on a part-time basis. At the same time Anne was advised that treatment would be terminated after she would feel more settled in her job. After a while she was able to accept this time limit and continued her employment as well as her separation from home. In view of the achievement of these two basic conditions in her functioning in a socially acceptable form, the case was closed, although it was realized that Anne remained a deeply disturbed girl.

In this case we see clearly how an understanding of the socialization process and a realistic evaluation of its various possible degrees of success and failure may permit the therapist to be helpful to the client in spite of severe psychopathology and an unfavorable home environment. If the goal of therapy had been seen only in terms of a cure of the underlying mental disorder or of a basic change in the personality structures of Anne's parents, it might have appeared impossible to be of any assistance to the child. The discovery of the pattern of a psychopathic personality in the child and the unsuccessful termination of treatment on the part of the parents would have led in all probability to either a defeatist termination of Anne's treatment or a continuation of psychotherapy against insuperable odds. The realization, however, that even so basically and deeply disturbed a person might be helped to develop some capacities for self-support and be freed from the impact of further deterioration-producing home influences by a separation from that environment made it possible to help the child reach a certain degree of social functioning and social acceptability. In other words, she was more socialized after termination of treatment than she would have been without it, or than she would have become if she had been continued in treatment without redirection toward the limited goals which the consulting psychiatrist recommended. This case suggests the value of asking in the face of severe psychopathology to what degree of socialization the client can be helped in spite of his illness, rather than of engaging in a hopeless battle with the illness as such.

In conclusion, it might be said that the solution of the problem of setting limited treatment goals in child guidance work might be facilitated by basing it on a theory combining the situational approach of social science and the conceptualization of certain phenomena, such as family of orientation, social interaction, and culture conflict, with the principles of psychodynamics and clinical psychiatry. The considerations which such an integrated theory of limited goal setting might suggest are five:

1. Consideration of the degree of modifiability of all persons exercising pathogenic influences among the growth determinants of the child.

2. Necessity of predicting the type of social interaction which personality development of the patient under therapy probably will produce on the part of other members of the family, particularly on the part of those members who hold greater social power than the child. In that respect special attention might be paid to the possibility of creating culture conflict between parent and child which might result in negative social interaction between them.

3. Realization that a particular disturbance may be the result of a constellation problem and thus could at least partially be attacked by only one of the factors operating in the situation, such as, for instance, by change in sleeping arrangements, housing arrangements, or school arrangements.

4. Recognition of the fact that health-conducive forces can be trusted to operate also outside a therapeutic relationship, so that it may be necessary only to help the child overcome his disturbance to a degree that will enable him to use these resources.

5. Recognition of the fact that socialization is a process which might be accomplished with different degrees of success, so that even partial removal of incapacitation or partial emotional relief may be considered a therapeutic gain.

Once these considerations are realized, the setting of limited treatment goals will not be experienced by therapists as a failure in their effort and as a lesser evil, but as the setting of the correct treatment goal which a situational approach combined with clinical evaluation suggests in the individual case. Limitation in the setting of treatment goals has been practiced by experienced therapists in the past. It has been practiced, however, with a heavy heart and with a feeling of frustration rather than with the

conviction that such a limitation when situationally and diagnostically indicated was the only thing that could be done. One
word of warning may be in order in this connection. An understanding of the theory underlying the setting of limited treatment
goals may help workers overcome their strivings of omnipotence
or simply help them approach case situations more realistically
than they may have been able to do without such theoretical
grounding. It should not be abused, however, as a cover for failures in diagnosis or therapeutic practice. Only when the possibilities of more intensive help are at least tentatively explored in
diagnosis, prognosis, and even therapeutic experimentation will
limited goal setting be helpful to the client, the therapist, and the
community.

This may appear surprising because it seems to contradict the
principle of therapeutic effort, which suggests that one should
proceed with guidance and redirection on a less intensive level
before attempting to achieve a basic modification. The apparent
contradiction resolves itself, however, if it is realized that only
cases of severe pathology seem to reach the agency. The very
degree of their pathology suggests frequently, not so much a
limitation of therapeutic effort, but limitation of goal setting.

CHAPTER ELEVEN

An Evaluation from the Psychiatric Point of View

THE FIELD of child psychiatry lends itself particularly well to collaboration with the social sciences. It is now apparent from the latest researches of Spitz, Goldfarb, Ribble, and others that more than physical care is necessary for the complete emotional development of the infant.[1] If at certain times during the first year of life mothering is inadequate, there will be an emotional arrest and even death may result, as in cases of "hospitalism." There is now a growing body of psychoanalytically oriented investigations concerning the early social reactions of the infant. Research on the so-called "smiling reaction" shows that at about three months after birth the infant makes this response to an adult's eyes and facial movements. This is a landmark in the differentiation of the infant's ego. It becomes a specific social response when the child is about six months old.[2] The development of what approximates an anxiety reaction, occurring about eight months after birth, is also an index of ego differentiation, by which is meant that there is objective evidence of differential perception by the infant of the mother and other child-rearing figures. Thus from the earliest phase of child development there is definite recognition of the complexity of the social situation. This view fits well in the social science approach expressed in this book and is part and parcel of the present-day child analyst's concep-

BY MAURICE R. FRIEND, M.D.

[1] Spitz, René A., "Hospitalism," *The Psychoanalytic Study of the Child*, International Universities Press, New York, vol. 1, 1945, pp. 53–74; Goldfarb, W., "Infant Rearing as a Factor in Foster Home Placement," *American Journal of Orthopsychiatry*, vol. 14, January, 1944, pp. 162–166; Ribble, Margaret A., *The Rights of Infants*, Columbia University Press, New York, 1943.

[2] Spitz, René A., with the assistance of K. M. Wolf, "The Smiling Response: A Contribution to the Ontogenesis of Social Relations," *Genetic Psychology Monographs*, vol. 34, 1946, pp. 57–125.

tual picture of such clinical instances as arrested development, childhood schizophrenia, and some of the problems in failures of treatment of these children, whether in their homes, under foster care, or in institutions. In cases of a deficit in the infant's supply of positive feelings from mother or mother substitutes, personality deviation appears to occur despite the achievement of normal levels of intelligence and physical maturation. Observation of infants of the type carried out by K. M. Wolf shows the importance of these social phenomena earlier than the first birthday.[1]

This is in thorough accord with the genetic theories of psychoanalysis, particularly of drive development. There appears very definitely to be a natural sequence of libidinal development with oral, anal, and urethral phases of maturation, followed by an oedipal phase and its resolution into the so-called latency period. In the early days of psychoanalysis, attention was focused upon the infantile sexual aims and objects. There followed increasing emphasis on the maturation of aggressive drives and it is now generally accepted by analysts that there is fusion of the aggressive and sexual, or erotic, components in libidinal development. The genetic approach always takes into consideration frustrations of the individual stemming from other social objects during his maturational processes. They are particularly important in parent handling of the preschool child. Excessive erotic stimulation which cannot be mastered by the child constitutes a traumatic influence and may lead to significant and deviant behavior patterns. No longer is one specific traumatic event thought to be the precipitant of deviant behavior. Current opinion holds that such behavior results from more subtle environmental influences, which are perpetuated, without being understood, by the people rearing a particular child. It is only by persistent observation and detailed knowledge of these facts, whether in therapy or research, that meaningful understanding can be obtained. This in itself would make for a close liaison between the field of psychoanalytically oriented child psychiatry and sociology.

[1] Hetzer, H., and K. M. Wolf, "Babytests," *Zeitschrift für Psychologie*, vol. 107, 1928, pp. 62–104.

Another phenomenon which is familiar to child therapists is that of transference. By transference is meant an unrealistic, repetitious, and illogical feeling toward the therapist, reenacting early relationships to members of the intimate family circle. This problem has many ramifications. Understanding the phenomenon of transference presupposes recognition of other figures in the environment than the therapist and patient. The preschool child, unlike the adult, is in a state of constant development from the standpoint of drives, defenses, and ego adaptations to his family. The child-rearing environment, that is, the family, is much more important to him than other persons in his environment. He is dependent on his parents or parent substitutes for approval and exposed to punishment by them. Consequently he does not develop feelings of similar intensity toward other adults. Patterns have not been so consistently inculcated as in the adult and, therefore, transference manifestations of children are found to differ from the transference manifestations of adults described in the classic psychoanalytic literature. Anna Freud, in her original formulation, stated that absence of transference manifestations in the child presented an important distinction between child and adult therapy.[1] In her more recent statements, however, she has acknowledged the existence of capacities of transference in the very early periods of development, through the first three years of life, based on thought and affect that have succumbed to the infantile repression. Still, the behavior of a child encountered by the therapist may be reactive to current experiences rather than being an expression of transference.

In consequence there is a constant need to distinguish current relationships of the child to present realities from those phenomena which are more definitely transference manifestations. In other words, children's behavior expressions, which may often be thought of as irrational and therefore to be interpreted in terms of theoretical explanations of inner conflict, turn out to be attempts at reality adaptations. It is commonly observed that a child's reactions of provocation to the therapist are a result of

[1] Freud, Anna, *Introduction to the Technic of Child Analysis*. Nervous and Mental Disease Publishing Co., New York, 1928, pp. 37-39.

some unpleasant experience with the mother a short time before the session. One should be wary, therefore, of interpreting this behavior without actual information from the mother as to what occurred. That children up to about nine years of age cannot be treated without the full knowledge and cooperation of the adults in their environment, is axiomatic. The social science concepts proposed by Dr. Pollak for incorporation into the doctrine underlying child guidance practice, such as *family of orientation, socialization, social interaction,* must form the basis of reality discrimination by the therapist.

The pleasure pain and reality principle of psychoanalysis has important bearing upon the phenomena of children's behavior. With increasing growth in all spheres of development, the child learns what is pleasurable, that is, the absence of tension, and to postpone immediate goal gratification in order to avoid other displeasures or to achieve greater satisfaction later. This learning, however, is a process which takes time. It is for this reason that children tend more to act out their impulses, have the capacity for play, and are unable to communicate in a more verbal manner than adolescents and adults. Since there is less frustration tolerance, the child's behavior seems to be more irrational to the adult therapist. Consequently the help of others in the child's environment is necessary to provide him with a background for evaluation. Here again is an opportunity for applied sociology.

It is exactly in the therapy of children that phenomena of peer experiences operate. Berta Bornstein in a recent paper pointed out the unique difference between the world of adults and that of children, and particularly the countertransference problems of the therapist resulting from this difference.[1] If the child therapist has gross unresolved problems stemming from his own childhood, they will certainly be provoked by the child's impulsive behavior. The child therapist cannot split his allegiance between the child and his parents, whom he must consider jointly in therapy. Neither can he adopt an authoritative role so frequently assumed

[1] Bornstein, Berta, "Emotional Barriers in the Understanding and Treatment of Young Children," *American Journal of Orthopsychiatry,* vol. 18, October, 1948, pp. 691–696.

by inexperienced child psychiatrists. If he does, he will only be acting out his own impulses and will precipitate unreliable or inadequate adaptations on the part of the child or parents without arriving at a dynamic understanding.

These therapeutic considerations all necessitate on the part of the child therapist a social science approach both to the child's culture and to his own childhood culture. It can thus be seen that this field is peculiarly adapted for an interdisciplinary approach.

If an attempt were made to summarize Dr. Pollak's findings from the point of view of their usefulness to psychotherapy of children, one might say that what social science at its present stage of development can do for psychotherapeutic processes is to break down the concept of environment into its various components. The individual chapters of this book demonstrate the diversity and plurality of factors which fall under this blanket term.

The concept of *family of orientation* differentiates the actual family environment of a child from the stereotype of the biological unit, which we customarily designate as a family. The concept's level of abstraction is high enough to assure attention to such family members as grandparents, uncles, aunts, and cousins, and those other permanent members of the household who are not relatives of the child. At the same time it is specific enough to single out from the environment the permanent human relationships of the child in the intimate atmosphere of the home. As such, it designates and circumscribes the most significant, but still only a part of, the child's total environment. The psychoanalytical abstraction of "oedipal involvement," as erroneously utilized by the inexperienced therapist, can no longer hold the force that it originally had. Furthermore the psychoanalyst, even though he takes account of all the factors which this concept designates, is sorely tempted by pressures of teaching to omit consideration of family members other than the parents and the child. As long as behavioral manifestations of the child dominate as indices of individual dysfunction, there is usefulness in this total sociological viewpoint. On the other hand, this writer is convinced that the intimate interplay of conscious and unconscious aspects of the child's relationships to all the persons of the family of orientation, as well as the characteristic ego defenses brought out in relation to and involving the members of this constellation, can only be filled out by application of psychoanalytic principles.

Similarly the concept of *social interaction* presents a sociological representation of everyday assessment in the practice of a mature child therapist. Translated into psychoanalytic understanding, personality change effected by therapy often produces disbalance in other members of the family. The unconscious motivation of parents may be touched off by intrapsychic improvement in the child. A decrease in separation anxiety on the part of the child may often involve intensification of it in the parents. Improvement of stealing behavior in the neurotic child often increases unresolved problems of the parents when they become aware of hitherto unknown inconsistencies in their consideration of the child. As already mentioned, it is an axiom that any treatment of a child on a nonmoralistic basis must have the support of the dominant member, and preferably, all members of the family. It is only too common that unless these persons have been prepared, the child therapist is construed by them as a threat to the inner family life. At the earliest modification of the child's behavior, treatment is likely to be interrupted in order to remove the therapeutic threat, which to them is like the voice of conscience.

The concept of the *peer group* again designates only a part of the human environment of the child, but one which at certain stages of development has considerable influence on the child's growth processes. This sociological concept has always been an important part of the child therapist's philosophy, whether it is translated into appropriate behavior for various age levels, phases of personality development, or differentiation of accessibility to different types of treatment at various age levels. It is interesting that the concept has been known and used for a long time in clinic practice, so that it had not to be newly introduced in the course of this project but only to be realigned with the other concepts brought forward for consideration. That the use of play is a means of communication for the younger child, in contrast to verbal communication in the adolescent and adult, is obvious. It is of particular significance that activity group therapy for the preadolescent has an effectiveness dynamically related to capacities of defense and diminution of libidinal drives. Observation of children in a group emphasizes the completely different relationship of the child with peers from his relationship with an adult therapist.

The concept of *culture conflict* between therapist and child, or therapist and the child's parents, the child's teachers, the child's neighbors, elucidates a part of the child's environment frequently overlooked in treatment. Lack of appreciation of details of different cultures tends to prevent a dynamic understanding of actual interplay. This leads to false therapeutic attitudes, rigid generalizations, and such arbitrary concepts as "weak fathers," "punitive fathers," "aggressive mothers," "rigid schoolteachers," and "orthodox Jewish parents whose children must wait for adolescence to break away from their parents' religion," which are frequently found in the phraseology of case recording. What is needed by the child therapist is the capacity for inner freedom, so that alien customs are not transposed into fixed images, as so frequently happens in dealing with anything alien to self. A lack of this capacity plays a great role among the phenomena of countertransference. If the therapist is not sufficiently aware of his personal reactions to different cultural upbringings, he will react as he would nontherapeutically to something alien and threatening—that is, by repression, by fearfulness, by excessive effort to change, or by a flight reaction expressed in such defeatist terms as "one cannot do anything with such parents," or "with such schoolteachers." The child therapist, of all persons, must resolve early narcissistic problems of his own development.

In the case of Miriam, discussed in Chapter 5, lack of cultural understanding on the part of the first therapist deprived the parents of outlets for the expression of conflict and thus prevented the constructive resolution of the child's difficulties. Discrepancies between two isolated cultural value systems will produce lack of positive transference and result in consistent misinterpretation.

The proposition of visualizing the therapeutic process as learning helps in clarifying aspects of therapy which deserve stress.

Probably there is no therapeutic situation, or interrelationship between any two human beings, which would not involve some of the phenomena of learning. It may be achieved through conscious imitation or unconscious identification of the patient with the therapist. The therapist's role of restraint of his own emotional inter-reaction serves to increase the patient's self-understanding. This familiar phenomenon of differentiation of inner feelings and ideas previously projected onto the outside world from the reality of the latter forms one of the important aspects of learning. The therapist's response to the child patient's behavior is in such sharp contrast to the family members' responses in the same type of situation that new patterns of adjustment may result. Release and change of ineffective ego defense mechanisms always produce a capacity for sublimation, which in itself, experienced and worked through, is to be construed as a type of learning. All psychotherapy follows some type of personal reeducation.

Use of volunteers in connection with psychotherapy and supervised by the therapist may be an important element of the total treatment process. It is not necessarily to be construed as a simple environmental replacement, either of a family member or the therapist, but rather as a provision of certain generic functions, which may be performed by a Big Sister or a Big Brother. The use of such volunteers may serve to change, or to supply, necessary ego ideal aspirations. A differential cultural environment brought into emotional experience by close personal relationship may help to stimulate strivings for change which would not otherwise be possible. The interesting phenomenon of status change within the family resulting from the use of such an auxiliary person may strengthen the effectiveness of the therapist.

The use of supervised volunteers as described allows a certain role-playing function which might be considered in more active forms of treatment. This is an expression of the same principle which makes it advisable to help certain borderline psychotic patients by active reality measures rather than by an insight approach. Some individuals need more actual demonstration and active support than others. Mothers in a nursery group, for instance, will gain considerably from a chance to observe teacher handling of children and this may serve to supplement the relatively isolated treatment situation.

Treatment goals in child therapy, more frequently than treatment goals in adult therapy, may need some limitation for the following reasons: Children are more dependent upon other supporting figures than are adults and do not have fully matured intrapsychic organizations; and the key people in their environment have to be assessed. There are instances of arrested emotional development, despite normal intellectual functioning, which seemingly defy the best efforts of families and therapists to help the children relate. In other instances, the familial figures present such obstacles that only the provision of effective social channels for the child's further, if limited, growth may have to constitute the therapeutic goal, that is, specific types of schools for certain children, or institutional placement, until such time as a greater maturation and more self-need for treatment develop. Where impulsive parents are constantly providing a succession of traumatic stimuli to children, treatment goals need limitation. The concept of *socialization*, as a matter of degree rather than an absolute, promises to be helpful in bringing this to the awareness of child therapists.

What this book has attempted to do is to help the therapist in the perception of pathogenic factors other than those considered in routinized diagnostic procedures, and also in the thought process which is geared to the visualization of the effects of therapeutic effort in terms of the living environment of the child. The instrumentality for achieving this purpose is an enrichment of the theoretical basis of child guidance work by concepts taken from various fields of social science.

To the psychoanalyst who recognizes the usefulness of these concepts, the phenomenon still appears decisive that unresolved personality difficulties of the individual therapist may prevent him from utilizing conceptual aids in specific situations. This, however, is not an argument against their incorporation into the doctrine underlying therapeutic work.

Such doctrine incorporated in teaching and practice must be continually worked through in individual and group supervision and psychiatric teaching so that the frame of reference of therapy is not seen in terms of the intrapsychic processes of the individual patients versus their environment. It is always a matter of grave concern that the inexperienced therapist will think only of "uncovering" unconscious thought content without taking note of the external stimuli which activate the particular content. Neither emphasis on social science concepts alone nor emphasis on psychic mechanisms alone can be considered adequate attempts at diagnosis and therapy. Only their integration can make constructive therapy.

One more point merits attention. In Chapter I, Dr. Pollak has scrutinized the attitudinal problems of the social scientist who is called upon to function in a practice setting. He has emphasized that a spirit of replacement is fraught with dangers for a successful outcome of interdisciplinary ventures. It seems proper for a psychoanalyst to do the same thing in reverse and to scrutinize the attitudinal problems of therapists who find a social science consultant in their midst. The introduction of social science into a body of theory which has largely been drawn from psychoanalysis is threatened in its effectiveness by the narcissism natural to every professional discipline. Some social scientists may want to "take over"; some therapists may feel that they do not need information from other fields where clinical questions are concerned. This study represents an attempt to avoid such a danger. The social science propositions here presented are made in the spirit of cooperation rather than of criticism. They are synthesized with psychodynamic understanding. In view of the resistance of many social scientists to the type of material psychoanalysis has unearthed, the attitude expressed in this book by the social science consultant is remarkably free from defenses. It would seem that his attitude should be met by a similar freedom from defenses on the part of therapists. It is a reason for considerable satisfaction to this writer that the staff members of the Child Guidance Institute were able to achieve it to such a degree that the study was possible. The value of such attitudes of cooperation and of broadening the team approach in clinical work is also reflected in the perhaps less visible, but actually more important, accomplishment of giving new impetus to the expression of clinical concerns which had been somewhat dormant. The appearance of an outsider in a practice field often has value in drawing attention to considerations whose importance for the task at hand may not have been fully recognized. It may also emphasize preexisting concerns which may have been perceived but not carried out to the degree deserved. The stimulus a social scientist entering a practice field as a consultant can give in these respects does much to counteract the inertia which is commonly attached to human effort.

One of the most interesting impressions this writer has gained in the course of this project is recognition of the fact that a social scientist and a psychoanalyst can reach agreement on almost all questions arising in diagnosis and therapeutic effort. The concepts of social science are rational and are more easily understood than those of psychoanalysis. The concepts of psychoanalysis emphasize phenomena of a lower degree of accessibility to intellectual perception. The concepts of social science may be more easily taught than the concepts of psychoanalysis. If all collaborators in the interdisciplinary venture have understanding of personality development in terms of its unconscious as well as its conscious aspects, a synthesis and integration of the two approaches can be expected to prove useful to practitioners in ways that have not yet been tried and cannot now be foreseen in their full richness of detail.

Index

Index

ABE, case of, showing pathogenic effects of rejection by neighborhood children, 88–90

Abreaction, instance of, 166–167

Ackerman, Nathan W., 11, 39, 41, 52, 60

"Acting out," 26, 134, 135, 140–143, 146, 148–149

Adelphi College School of Social Work, 16

"Adjustment of the Individual to His Age and Sex Roles" (Cottrell), 133n

Adolescence (Nat'l Society for the Study of Education), 160n

"Adolescence and the Social Structure" (Kingsley Davis), 138n

Adolescent Personality (Blos), 139n

Adolescents: acting out of, 26; age-sex roles and status of, 133–136; formulating treatment methods and setting treatment goals for, 136, 139–147; id drives of, 139; importance of youth culture in psychotherapy of, 136–137, 139, 141, 147; risks in outpatient treatment of, from inflexible home environment, 140–143

"Age and Sex in the Social Structure of the United States" (Parsons), 137n

Age and sex roles, 133–136, 205

Alfred, case of, illustrating behavior difficulties caused by unresponsive parents and rejection of peer group, 85

Alt, Herschel, 8, 11, 26

American Association of Psychiatric Clinics for Children, 12

American Board of Psychiatry and Neurology, 12

American Psychopathological Association, 39, 151

American Sociological Society, 28

Animals, laboratory experimentation with, 149

Anne, case of, illustrating need during treatment to redefine goals, 215–218

Anorexia nervosa, with fellatio fantasies, instance of, 144

Anthropology, cultural, 7, 101–132

Anxiety: as defined by Sigmund Freud, 154; case showing need to create, 162–165; function of symptoms in reducing, 154; illustration of need to decrease, 165–169; reaction of infant, 221; morbid, 155; socially adaptive effects of, 149, 154, 158, 160; therapeutic management of, 148–169

Anxiety hysteria, instances of, 54, 166, 216

"Anxiety Reduction and Learning" (Mowrer), 154n

Association theories of learning process, 150

"Attainment of Concepts, The" (Heibreder), 32n

Attitudinal problems: of a social scientist in a practice setting, 24–25; of a therapist, 230

Aunts, 38; importance of contacts with, 42–43, 56–59; instance of pathogenic influence exercised by, 208

Austin, Lucille N., 151, 152n

"BABYTESTS" (Hetzer and Wolf), 222n

Bales, Robert F., 62n

Bar Mitzvah, illustration of impact of, 96–98

Barbara, case of, showing a family able to relax controls when indicated in the therapy of an adolescent, 143–146

Belongingness, 90–91, 174

Ben, case of, showing timing of decision to pursue limited treatment goals, 207–210

Benedict, Ruth, 102n

Bernard, Jessie, 62n

Bias. *See* Concepts; Social science consultant; Therapist

Big Brother-Big Sister Couple, 172

Big Brother relationship, value of, 170–199, 228

Big Sister relationship, value of, 170–199, 228

Billy, case of, showing phases into which most cases involving volunteers fall, 180–198

Black, Bertram J., 3, 19

Blackmar, Frank W., 201n

Bloch, Herbert A., 62n

Blos, Peter, 139n

Boring, Edwin G., 30n

Bornstein, Berta, 224n